A
SUDDEN
SHOT

A SUDDEN SHOT

The Phoenix Serial Shooter

CAMILLE KIMBALL

BERKLEY BOOKS, NEW YORK

THE BERKLEY PUBLISHING GROUP
Published by the Penguin Group
Penguin Group (USA) Inc.
375 Hudson Street, New York, New York 10014, USA
Penguin Group (Canada), 90 Eglinton Avenue East, Suite 700, Toronto, Ontario M4P 2Y3, Canada
(a division of Pearson Penguin Canada Inc.)
Penguin Books Ltd., 80 Strand, London WC2R 0RL, England
Penguin Group Ireland, 25 St. Stephen's Green, Dublin 2, Ireland (a division of Penguin Books Ltd.)
Penguin Group (Australia), 250 Camberwell Road, Camberwell, Victoria 3124, Australia
(a division of Pearson Australia Group Pty. Ltd.)
Penguin Books India Pvt. Ltd., 11 Community Centre, Panchsheel Park, New Delhi—110 017, India
Penguin Group (NZ), 67 Apollo Drive, Rosedale, North Shore 0632, New Zealand
(a division of Pearson New Zealand Ltd.)
Penguin Books (South Africa) (Pty.) Ltd., 24 Sturdee Avenue, Rosebank, Johannesburg 2196,
South Africa

Penguin Books Ltd., Registered Offices: 80 Strand, London WC2R 0RL, England

This is a true story. However, the names and identifying characteristics of certain people have been changed to protect their privacy.

A SUDDEN SHOT

A Berkley Book / published by arrangement with the author

PRINTING HISTORY
Berkley mass-market edition / September 2009

ISBN: 978-0-425-23019-0

BERKLEY®
Berkley Books are published by The Berkley Publishing Group,
a division of Penguin Group (USA) Inc.,
375 Hudson Street, New York, New York 10014.
BERKLEY® is a registered trademark of The Berkley Publishing Group.
The "B" design is a trademark of The Berkley Publishing Group.

PRINTED IN THE UNITED STATES OF AMERICA

10   9   8   7   6   5   4   3   2   1

Most Berkley Books are available at special quantity discounts for bulk purchases for sales,
promotions, premiums, fund-raising, or educational use. Special books, or book excerpts, can also be
created to fit specific needs.

For details, write: Special Markets, The Berkley Publishing Group, 375 Hudson Street, New York,
New York 10014.

This book is about men who destroyed lives.
I would like to dedicate it to two men who save them.

To Ted and Hrayr,
the world needs more of you.

Men never know where wandering fiends wait in the dark.

BEOWULF

Well, a lot of it is I didn't want to lose my place to stay.
Uh, stupid.

SAM DIETEMAN

Table of Contents

Prologue

No one wants to wake up to headlines that a serial killer is active in one's own community. How much more horrifying, then, to stare at the TV as authorities in angry voices declare there are not one, but two serial killers actively plucking victims off our streets and ending their lives. In 2006 in Phoenix, Arizona, that's exactly what happened. Even after having lived here more than twenty years, I had never heard of even one serial killer operating in this city. Like most other Phoenicians, I was incredulous. The words of the mayor and the police seemed incomprehensible, as if spoken in a foreign language. Our faces collectively scrunched up as if knit brows, narrowed eyes and dropped jaws could help us uncrack their code.

To those of us in the Valley of the Sun, a metroplex with a small downtown surrounded by hundreds of square miles of desert suburbs, a place where swimming pools are more common than public transit, and golf courses far outnumber factories, the words "serial killer" seemed like an import or, better yet, a fantasy. Serial killers could be found on movie screens or far away in the more crowded and established areas of the country, but surely not in sun-baked Phoenix, a place too busy still inventing itself to foster such curdling evil.

And yet, here were familiar and trusted faces, Phoenix Mayor

Phil Gordon and Assistant Chief Kevin Robinson and Sergeant
Andy Hill of the Phoenix Police, earnestly warning us to stay off
the streets after dark. They insisted we had two separate killers
in our midst. One, they said, wanted women. He raped them,
often two together—sisters, coworkers, etc. Sometimes he killed
them. He was operating along the southern edge of the metroplex, generally along a thoroughfare called Baseline Road,
which is the final major dividing line between city life and raw
desert. He would come to be known as the Baseline Rapist. The
word "rapist" was used in his moniker, because the word "killer"
was in high demand at the moment.

The other serial killer, they told us, was a much different
person. He did not care to get as close to his victims as did the
Baseline Rapist. This one remained unseen, blasting a shot in
your back, then speeding off in a car. This one didn't care if you
were a man or a woman, young or old, white or black, red or
brown. He wanted everything in his path—if he didn't take *your*
life, he'd take your pet's.

The occurrence of two separate serial killers operating independently in the same city at the same time is rare. This was a
city that had not seen any serial killers at all in more than a
generation, at least, and the law enforcement community, as fine
and dedicated as it was, was not institutionally experienced in
the phenomenon. The information over the months of 2006
came out in sputters and contradictions. At times, the authorities
even talked about having three serial killers working. It was a
nightmare bounded only by Baseline Road and sundown.

The Baseline Rapist abandoned some of his victims after as-
saulting them but not killing them. These survivors gave police
a consistent description. Police developed a sketch of a man
with a turned-down fishing hat, dreadlocks and a dark complexion.

By contrast, there were no sketches of the other killer. Most
of his victims were unable to describe him because they had
been shot in the back, had died, or were animals. Anyone who
did catch a glimpse and also survived could only describe the
vehicle, and this vehicle seemed variable.

Whether the victim died or managed to survive, lives were
changed. Indeed, the entire community was changed. Phoenicians—at the water cooler, at the bus stop, at the sandwich

shop—struck up conversations comparing notes and trying to understand.

Citizens developed strategies for safety. Habits were changed and plans altered. In this hot desert town, it's not uncommon for people to work, play or exercise after sundown, when the brutal UV rays of daylight retreat. But in 2006 more and more people canceled their night activities. By summertime, the town was in a frenzy of fear, with hundreds showing up at community meetings held in school auditoriums. Police fielded questions from frightened and outraged citizens at these meetings and offered their best advice for safety. They distributed the sketch of the Baseline Rapist and advised women to avoid all strangers, as survivors reported that the Baseline Rapist had tended to engage them in innocent conversation before he attacked, asking directions or the time.

But for the other guy there was no sketch, and the advice amounted to "keep yourself and your pets inside after dark." And the advice wasn't being directed just to women—it was for everyone. As prosecutor Laura Reckart would later say to a judge, "Everyone in this room was a target."

The second killer left no psychological or geographical footprint to incorporate into a moniker. His attacks were random and scattershot. His name became simply "the Serial Shooter." Not all of his attacks were made public. Indeed, as this story will demonstrate, police themselves often did not know which cases to lay at his feet. But the cases that found their way into public consciousness seemed to show the Serial Shooter working on the farthest western edge of the Phoenix metroplex, a side of town characterized by farmland and rodeo. Then he moved to downtown Phoenix, where our high-rises and our urban blight are. But in the spring he started moving farther and farther out of Central Phoenix, until the hideous day when young Robin Blasnek was killed in the stalwart pillar of the East Valley, Mesa.

The shooting of Robin Blasnek shocked the Phoenix area a magnitude of order higher than all the others. Robin was the victim we knew the most about. Her photo appeared everywhere, and the entire community grieved with and for her family. She became everyone's daughter. After she was shot on a Sunday night, everyone in the Phoenix area followed her case daily—

hourly—and before long we all knew that her funeral would be Saturday. It would be a public one, in the way that sudden celebrity takes over such events.

With the shooting of Robin Blasnek, the last vestiges of security left this community. The killing had now swept from the rural Westside more than thirty miles to the yuppie East Valley. It had devastated Central Phoenix and touched down in the northern neighborhoods as well. The Baseline Rapist was also expanding his territory. Law enforcement resources, as every citizen could deduce for himself, were stretched to the breaking point. Publicity went nationwide. Squads of Guardian Angels arrived from out of state to help patrol.

This book is the story of what happened that year. Because the Baseline Rapist was easier to recognize as a single perpetrator soon after he began committing his crimes, his case had already usurped many of the resources of the Homicide units of the Phoenix Police Department. By the time investigators strung together, painfully, the other random cases of murder and mayhem that had languished on many different desks, the Homicide units were so overworked that an assault detective ended up being the lead investigator on the task force for the Serial Shooter. Thankfully, by the end of 2006, law enforcement had performed the amazing feat of taking into custody suspects for both cases.

I do not pretend to the great skills and resources of the Phoenix Police Department, who were required to deal with both cases at once. For me, it is not possible to tell the story of both the Baseline Rapist and the Serial Shooter in the same book. Indeed, the Serial Shooter's story is so vast, it has been a difficult task to decide what will make it into the book and what will have to be left in my files.

This book is about the case where every one of us was a potential target, where not a single person could tell himself or herself that the serial killer would not be interested. This book is about a city under siege, a city being strafed by the Serial Shooter.

Chapter One

Fuzzy Blue Slippers

Petite, naïve twenty-two-year-old Robin Blasnek received a text message from a special friend. It was a hot Sunday night, 10:51 p.m., July 30, 2006:

"*come over*"

"*when,*" she typed back.

"*now*"

Robin's parents were already asleep. She didn't stop to put on shoes—what if they woke up?—just a spaghetti-strap tank top for the baking Arizona night, a pink one, sweatpants and fuzzy blue slippers. It had been many months since she had slipped out like this at night.

Robin was twenty-two, her parents would later say, but she acted more like she was fifteen or even twelve. They had gotten custody of her when she reached her majority. A special needs child, they planned to take care of her all of their lives.

Blue-eyed Robin, one hundred pounds with bracelets on each wrist, toe rings and anklets on each foot, cell phone in hand, slipped out the back door.

Following the outlines of the roughly L-shaped freeway system, Robin was in the farthest east section, the bottom of the L. At the most opposite possible point to the north and west of her by a good thirty miles or more, a middle-aged construction worker, a proud father to three young sons, was struggling with his conscience. Just a day or two before, Ron Horton had phoned his mother, who was visiting with family in Boston. His sister Rennee recalls the family going silent and gathering around to listen in on their mother's side of the conversation: "I don't like the way this sounds, Ronnie. You be careful. Oh, Ronnie. Oh dear. No, Ronnie." Now the whole family was worried and no one knew exactly why.

Ron Horton had a Willie Nelson–type grizzliness, with long, graying hair, a mustache with goatee, and piercing brown eyes. He was known for an "ornery" sense of humor, running with a biker crowd and skyrocketing devotion to his three boys.

On this Sunday night, after he put the three boys to bed in his northwest home, the single father was on the horns of a dilemma. One course of action, he might be jeopardizing all he loved, including the silken faces slumbering down the hall. He might also be betraying a biking "bro" for no good reason. The other course of action, he might become what amounted to a silent partner in an enterprise of murder.

If only things were more clear. If only things were more safe.

————————

Right between Robin and Ron, in the heart of downtown Phoenix, Cliff Jewell, a veteran of a law enforcement career that stretched from California to Thailand, was turning his detailed mind to a huge stack of files. It was high summer on this night, and he'd been working these files, adding to them till they grew fat and unwieldy, since the turn of the New Year. Jewell, a tall blond man with three grown sons of his own, was a man on a mission.

————————

Robin headed out of the pleasant little residential cul-de-sac, so tucked away and protected, and padded down the block to a slightly larger street. She turned south. In that way of young teenagers, her phone never stopped. Her boyfriend Tremain called. Well, ex-boyfriend. They'd been close for two or three years, but recently their paths had been diverging. She told Tremain she was going over to a friend's house, but coyly refused to tell him whose. Next she both took calls from and made calls to a couple of girlfriends, reporting her feminine triumphs.

She turned east onto a bigger street. This one was a major thoroughfare.

Up in the Northwest Valley, Ron Horton fiddled with his cell phone. He was waiting for a call. He'd been waiting for it for days now. He felt a frisson when the device chirped and the number he'd been waiting for lit up the screen. It was a text message. The caller had been in Vegas, the message spelled out. Ron was very anxious to continue the conversation.

"Did you win or lose?" he typed in.

Then he stared at the phone.

And waited.

As she trotted down the hot street in her fuzzy blue slippers, the nighttime temperature easily still over a hundred degrees, Robin would have had somewhere in her thoughts both her deeply religious parents and her fun independent life at the home. Not her parents' home, where her dad took her every Friday night, but the group home where he returned her every Monday morning. She'd made "Employee of the Month" a few weeks ago at a job she'd gotten through the group home. And she had a lot of friends. She'd had dinner with several a couple of hours ago at the Olive Garden. She continued to text back and forth with the boy she was meeting. He lived with his parents also, and they were asleep as well. It was way too early for that; so much better to be young!

Robin's parents clearly adored her. Calls to and from Dad this weekend were scattered throughout her phone history. She was their youngest child, the youngest of four daughters. Her name had been chosen specifically to placate her big sister, Rachel, who was three when Robin was born. Rachel was mad that the two older girls had "T" names, Tara and Tami, and she didn't. So the new baby got an "R" name to make Rachel happy. When Rachel was fifteen, she was killed by a drunk driver. Now Robin was the only "R" name left among the three surviving daughters.

The twenty-two-year-old baby of the family, a special needs girl who loved skiing and ATVs, turned south onto one of the main arteries of the East Valley, Gilbert Road.

Ron Horton's phone chirped. He got the answer he was waiting for:

"*I lost.*"

Ron typed in another comment and waited.

Thirty miles away from Ron, in the East Valley, a silver Camry turned onto Gilbert Road.

Robin's nose was buried in more text messages. She expected to have a good time when she arrived. She would not have noticed the same silver Camry passing her again.

And again.

Ron Horton sent another text, hoping to knock loose a response. He stared at the silent phone. It was around 11 p.m. by now, and he figured he was wasting his time.

"*You're obviously busy,*" he typed. "*Call me when you're free.*"

Robin thought of her friend Robbie. If Tremain was going to be like that, she might as well give Robbie a call, too. She wondered if he'd be up.

Robin was looking for Robbie's number in her contact list— she hadn't used it in a couple of weeks—when homeowner Frank Bonfiglio slowed down on Gilbert Road as he approached his own block. Returning from a quick trip to the store, Frank noticed a female, thin and white, walking down the sidewalk. He wondered what such a young girl was doing out alone at night. He didn't know that less than a mile away her sleeping parents thought she was tucked in her own bed just down the hall.

Frank pulled into his garage.

Robin found Robbie's number.

Frank pulled out a beer and sat down in the backyard.

Robin reached the end of the block.

Frank heard a loud bang.

Robbie was watching a movie. He never heard the phone ring.

In the corner house one block down Gilbert Road from Frank's, the Chase family was also watching a movie. All of them heard the same loud pop and went running outside.

They saw a figure in the darkness, kneeling.

Mr. Chase, the father, approached carefully.

"Are you okay?" he asked. He could see the person was holding a cell phone, attempting to use it.

"I've been shot," he heard a female voice say.

He ran up to the figure and saw blood everywhere. He started shouting instructions to his children. His daughter called 911. The boys and his wife brought towels and blankets. They soaked up blood with the towels and put the blankets underneath her to protect her from the scalding pavement. They applied pressure to what seemed to be the source of the blood that ranged from her chest to her feet. Mr. Chase cradled her. Robin's last moments were spent in the arms of a loving father. It was a place Robin knew well, a place that would have comforted her, a place where she always went before she started her biggest journeys.

On Sunday night, after receiving a series of slow and one-word responses, Ron Horton had given up on his text messages.

He dialed someone else. "He's up to something," he said into the phone. "He always responds right away and writes a whole book." Ron said he wasn't going to text any more tonight, the conversation was too forced. He'd try again another time.

Early Monday morning, before the shooting reached news-rooms, Ron Horton's phone rang: a twenty-two-year-old girl had been shot while walking—at 11 p.m.—from her home to a boyfriend's.

At 11 p.m.

Ron felt the bile rise. Now he had blood on his own hands, he would later say. He vowed he would do whatever was in his power to stop this. He could have saved Robin Blasnek, he felt, if he had just tried harder.

Ron Horton never got over it, not to his own dying day.

Police and rescue arrived in front of the Chase home within minutes. All the neighbors had collected around the now unconscious girl, everyone doing what they could to help. Many people heard the shot and came running out of their houses. Police unrolled yellow tape, paramedics started revival attempts, and sirens and flood lamps pierced the night. Police fanned out, searching the streets, their radios buzzing with constant communiqués; a massive canvassing effort was started.

By the time Robin's ID was established at dawn, one investigative lead had already been stopped, searched, interrogated, GSR'd, released and crossed off from the list. Even the lead himself was very cooperative. "You're just doing your job," he told detectives during his own interrogation. "Anything I can do to help." He was just someone who had driven through the crime scene but had not lingered when he saw so many people already gathered. Spots of potentially suspicious activity in the night—any cigarette butt in a shrub, any moving shadow—were hunted down and evidence researched and bagged, but they were all false leads. Law enforcement was relentless, and the neighbors on the street were eager to help.

As she left this life, Robin was encircled by the best in the human family, people who were willing to comfort her, to attempt to save her, to shower her with the milk of human kindness. Now everyone was searching for the worst in humanity, those who would track us down and kill us all just for sport.

Chapter Two

Love You, Dog, Call Me

A year earlier, at three in the morning on June 29, 2005, in the dark summer heat, Vicente Espinoza-Verdugo of Tolleson loaded up his mom and his sister, and headed out for Jack in the Box. They passed money through the drive-thru window just off McDowell Road and pulled out onto Eighty-third Avenue with the car smelling of Jumbo Jacks and curly fries. As the vehicle's headlights arced into a southerly direction, they lit up the horrifying form of a dead body sprawled across the sidewalk.

Heart pounding, Espinoza-Verdugo turned the car around and went straight back to the Jack in the Box. He ran inside and told the cashier there was a dead body just outside the restaurant. Then he pulled out his cell phone and called Phoenix Police.

The cell phone records the time of this call as 3:19 a.m., June 29, 2005.

All personnel—police and paramedics—who responded to the call could see the devastating trauma to the head of the victim on the sidewalk: the unknown male was pronounced dead at the scene by firefighters at 3:33 a.m.

Inside the victim's pocket, officers found a handwritten note: "Love you, dog, call me, never throw this away."

A hundred feet away from the body lay a guitar.

At the Circle K on the corner, out of the way of investigators, officers from Phoenix and Tolleson pored over jurisdictional maps. Cross-checking one another and defining the crime by the location of the body, not the guitar, or the other miscellaneous items found, such as loose money, a gym bag and some CDs, the officers concluded it would be a case for the tiny Tolleson Police Department.

By eight feet.

A short time into the budding investigation, the Tolleson police officers putting up crime tape were disrupted by a call to the Burger King a short block north of the scene of the homicide. The Burger King was not open for business overnight unlike the Jack in the Box. A security company had called in that an alarm had gone off in the night and a window had been shot. The officers found bullet fragments in the play area, among the children's play sets, behind a large window painted with cartoons. A large hole now punctuated the big blue thumb of the clown character facing the street on the outside of the window.

But soon the Tolleson detectives determined that the restaurant was on the other side of the jurisdictional line, and they handed it off to Phoenix Police. No one had been hurt at the Burger King.

They returned to the homicide across the street.

By one thirty in the afternoon, the fingerprint lab of the Arizona Department of Public Safety, or the state troopers, called with an ID from the victim's fingerprints. The white male with a bullet in his chest and in his head had been twenty-year-old David Roy Anthony Estrada.

Now that they knew who he was, detectives took out the slip of paper found in David's pocket and called the number of the person who had assured David, "Love you, dog, call me, never throw this away."

A man answered. The Tolleson detectives said they needed to speak with him and it needed to be in person. They arranged to meet at a Chevron gas station in Central Phoenix, almost twenty miles from the scene of David's death.

The officers' log states, "A white male approached me [at the

Chevron] and identified himself as James Carlos McCormick, a cousin of David Estrada. He stated he was from California and had come here to help the mother Rebecca Estrada locate her son to get him into a mental institution."

When the detectives called, cousin Carlos must have been anticipating that David had either gotten into a scrape and been ashamed to call his mother, or had been found disoriented and lost.

Instead, Detective Rock informed him of the boy's death.

"McCormick asked me several times if I was sure of the identification of the body," wrote Detective Rock. It took some time before cousin Carlos could accept what Detective Rock had to say. "He didn't believe me," said Detective Rock later. But, after all, not only did they have the fingerprints, they had the note: McCormick had to know there was only one pocket in which that note could be found.

When Carlos McCormick finally seemed ready to believe, Detective Rock asked him for help in giving the sad news to David's mother.

Rebecca Estrada doted on the strikingly handsome boy who was her only son. His five sisters doted on him, too. Two of those girls were just twelve and fifteen on this terrible night. They lived in a large and comfortable home with columns in the front and a custom tile embedded on a post at the curb. It was in a very good neighborhood, even prestigious, located at the foot of Squaw Peak, one of Phoenix's treasured desert mountains. Until four years earlier, the family had been headed by Ralph Estrada, a successful lawyer. Rebecca, a devout Catholic, loved her stay-at-home life taking care of the children.

On the day her nephew came knocking on the door with two Tolleson police officers, however, the family was subsisting on Rebecca's new job as an airline reservations clerk. Mr. Estrada's career as a prosperous attorney had come to an end when he pleaded guilty to fraud, was disbarred, and entered an Arizona prison.

Just sixteen at the time of his father's fall from grace, David had been popular, athletic, and movie-star handsome. He loved music and taught himself to play guitar. But then the family's life changed drastically. They couldn't sell the house because it was encumbered by liens related to Ralph's fraud case. Ralph couldn't contribute at all from prison. So Rebecca got herself a $12,000-a-year job, and extended family chipped in to help her and her minor children get by.*

Extended family also helped Rebecca cope with David's increasing difficulties. By the time the boy was eighteen, a heartbroken Rebecca had successfully petitioned a judge to have her son committed. David completed his inpatient treatment, but a few months after he was released, Rebecca was despondent to see him again slipping away inside an erratic mind. In the summer of 2005, David could have gone home to the big white house with the columns and custom tile at the foot of the mountain, but when officers first found him dead on the sidewalk near a makeshift campsite on a vacant lot in Tolleson, they assumed he was a homeless person.

To Rebecca and those adoring cousins and sisters, David was anything but homeless.

The Tolleson detectives drove to the big white house and informed Rebecca of the boy's death. "We conducted a limited interview with Mrs. Estrada," states the incident report, "because she was obviously upset over the death of her son."

They called a priest to her house and left.

It had been 4 a.m. when Tolleson detective Ron Rock, a goodlooking man with a full head of blond brown hair accented by a tuft of white on the left side of a widow's peak, was roused from sleep and called to the scene of the young man found at the Jack in the Box. He ordered that the body be left where it was until sunrise, because he wanted photos taken in better light. "We never considered robbery as a motive for that crime. It was obviously he wasn't robbed—he had money in his pockets, he hadn't lost any property," the detective said.

While Rock was at that scene, he received a call from an animal control officer with more bad news. Sometime during the night, while David Estrada was strumming his guitar under an open sky, over on the rural Westside, a children's pet, a quarter

----

*From divorce records.

horse named Sara Moon, had been shot dead with a .22-caliber rifle.

No one connected David Estrada, Burger King, and Sarah Moon.

Neither was anyone thinking about Tony Junior Mendez or Reginald Remillard, two names that had been entered into the Phoenix Police blotter the month before. On May 17, Tony's death had gone something like this:

A house without air-conditioning, even as early as May, can be brutal during the overnight hours in the sprawling desert metropolis.

Tony Mendez, thirty-eight, was thinking about a family he knew that had lost their electric service. He knew they would be miserable without air-conditioning through the desert night. He discussed it with his roommate, Ricky Kemp. Together, they planned to visit the family and bring some candles. "We didn't really know 'em," says Ricky. "We just knew they didn't have power and they had kids." Late in the evening of May 17, 2005, found Tony Mendez rummaging through Ricky's house for candles. At least he could bring the family some light, both for their eyes and their hearts. As Tony's sister Paulina said, "He never left the room without throwing a joke at you."

Tony, who was separated from his wife and family, had been rooming with Ricky for about a year. They had grown up in the same neighborhood. Ricky considered him "like my brother." The two often worked together in a repair shop and installing drywall.

On this night, they hooked up a little trailer of Ricky's to Tony's bike.

"I went inside to get some water bottles," Ricky says, tearing up. "He took off without me."

Tony pedaled along, perhaps carefully selecting the right jokes to cheer up what he knew would be sweaty, forlorn children and stressed-out parents. Lost in his reverie, Tony didn't notice he was being followed.

Two blocks behind, someone watched.

Tony cleared a pothole and aimed for the next street lamp.

Someone else was aiming, as well.

Tony had recently taken the first steps toward reconciliation with his wife. He hoped to reunite with his children soon.

Life was definitely on the upswing. Tony began to whistle.

Then someone squeezed a trigger.

———————

Marcos Portillo got home at the same time every night from his job as a custodian. On May 17, 2005, he turned the corner from Encanto on to Forty-eighth Lane at 10:55, saw nothing of interest and no other traffic, and pulled into his own driveway two houses up. He went inside and showered. Fifteen minutes later, he went outside into the warm night to water the lawn and light up a cigarette.

"That's when I saw this person, laying sideways on top of his bicycle, just laying there. I started to run to him because I thought he needed help, but when I got about five feet away from him some other people came into the street and said, 'Don't touch him.' I knew they were right, because at first I thought maybe he was drunk and passed out, but when I got close I could see it looked like he was dead."

Ricky Kemp was standing in his carport figuring out whether to try to catch up with Tony when some other friends from the neighborhood materialized out of the darkness. At first, he couldn't understand their emotional response at seeing him.

"Someone's dead over on Forty-eighth," they said. "We saw that trailer on the bike that we know is yours. We thought the dead man must be you."

Now Ricky felt the impact of their statement. He knew who had been pulling that trailer. He rushed over to the scene. Police were already there. They had at first assumed the man was either a heart attack victim or perhaps had been hit by a car. But when paramedics turned him over, they discovered a small bullet hole in his shirt. It went straight through his heart. When Ricky Kemp walked up to the scene, just blocks from his own house, he told the 911 responders the name of the man they would not be able to revive.

Detectives scoured Tony's life for clues. They rounded up informants and lowlifes and got nowhere. The case went cold, very cold.

———————

A week later, fifty-six-year-old Reginald Remillard, a man beloved by two sisters and a brother, wearily sank down on a bus bench on Camelback and Seventh Avenue, a spot close to the strip of high-rises along Central Avenue as well as to neighborhoods. It was also across the street from a bar called Charlie's, a plain building with just one basic sign.

Reginald had a sweet oval face and sparkling eyes, and he'd served his country in Viet Nam. That was a time when he was still big brother to the other kids. But he was choppered out in 1971, when he developed schizophrenia. "As a child he would take care of me," his sister Becky Lewis later testified, "then our roles reversed."

Reginald's perception of people and things altered. He couldn't think through consequences. And Reggie had developed a fondness for sleeping in the open air. "As we got older, I felt responsible for him," Becky said. All his siblings saw Reginald at least once a week and frequently conferred on his living situation and options. This particular spring, Reggie had complained to all of them that he didn't like the assisted living facility he was currently in. He wanted a change. The devoted three siblings worked through all the paperwork and phone calling and meetings that entailed, and arranged for Reggie to be transferred to a place he would like better.

On May 23, 2005, big brother Reggie, for whom some days were better than others, took his place in a hospital transport to be taken to his new home, something he'd wanted for several weeks and that his brother and sisters had worked hard to achieve for him. Described as "very spiritual," Reggie felt "no one could hurt him." At a stoplight, dressed in hospital clothes, Reggie let himself out of the vehicle and fled.

"We had calls from him," Becky testified. "He told us he was fine. But we told him it wasn't safe."

Late in the evening found Reggie on his favorite open-air bed, a bus bench. This one was at Seventh Avenue and Camelback, just in front of a strip mall with Japanese fast food, a submarine sandwich shop, a beauty products outlet and a Blockbuster Video, and just off a major Central Avenue intersection that saw its fair share of the city's elite in frequent trade. It was a nice cozy spot. The bus bench even had a little roof. Perfect.

Reggie took off his tennis shoes and settled in.

That night thirty-one-year-old James Hernandez, a sharp dresser with dark good looks, went to see the new Star Wars movie, *Revenge of the Sith*, with a friend. After watching Anakin Skywalker evolve into Darth Vader, the two men walked over to Charlie's bar. By 1 a.m., the pair were done shooting pool and stepped out of the building. They stood on the sidewalk, on the south side of Camelback, discussing their next move. They were thinking of walking a few blocks north to another bar. James had his back to Charlie's, while his friend had his back to Camelback Road. Directly in James's line of sight, as he looked at his friend, was a man on a bus bench across the street.

James's conversation was interrupted by a loud blast. He and his friend froze, putting their arms out in a defensive posture, wondering if more shots would ring out and they might be hit. A light-colored vehicle passed them westbound on Camelback Road.

Across the street, James watched the man on the bench crumple.

The two moviegoers ran across the street.

"At first, I wasn't sure just what was going on," James testified. "The first thing I remember when I got across the street was looking around for a sprinkler because I was hearing the sound of a sprinkler, like gurgling. But I couldn't see the sprinkler that was making the noise. Then I smelled blood and I realized the sound was coming from the man on the bench."

James illustrated by moving his hand in an arc. "It was blood coming out of his neck, swoosh, like a fountain."

James called 911, but before his call had been processed through dispatch, Officer Darren Burch was pulling up to the intersection of Seventh and Camelback. He saw a man frantically waving him down and screaming. Burch pulled into the side parkway of the strip mall, not knowing what the trouble was. He had not heard from the dispatcher; he just saw the hysterical man trying to get his attention. Burch left his vehicle and approached the agitated man, whom he could now hear screaming, "Someone's dying, someone's bleeding!" When Burch got close, "I saw someone laying on the bus bench shooting a stream of blood in a fountain effect from his neck." He was faceup, his eyes were open and he was extremely gray. On the ground underneath him was a very large pool of blood, six feet or more in diameter. Soaking in the pool of blood—a pair of tennis shoes.

Officer Burch, in an amazing moment of ingenuity, reached down for one of the shoes. He knew with the rate the blood was coming out, the difference between life and death was a matter of seconds.

"I grabbed the rubberized tip of the tennis shoe and placed it in the nape of his neck to stop the bleeding."

Officer Burch wasn't even a hundred percent sure the victim was alive, he was so gray and still, his eyes unfocused. But at the rate the blood was shooting out, Burch assumed there was life to pump it. After the rubber shoe blocked the fountain of blood, the gray started to subside, the eyes came back into focus and "he started looking up at me. 'Stay with me!' I told him."

At the same time, Officer Burch had no way of knowing what had happened, what role the two unharmed but agitated men had played, and holding the shoe in the victim's neck, he could not reach his radio for more help.

The scene was gruesome and chaotic.

But James had already called 911, not knowing Officer Burch would show up by chance, and soon more help arrived anyway. James Hernandez leaned over the victim, who was growing pinker and more alert, and urged him over and over to "hang in there, hang in there." And the Viet Nam vet with a severed carotid did hang in there. Paramedics arrived to relieve Officer Burch's effective but brutally makeshift first aid.

The big brother of the Remillard clan hung in there for six days more, but in the end, nothing as small as a rubber shoe or as big as a whole hospital could save him.

———————

Some six months or so earlier, Phoenix Police detective Clifton Jewell had been called out to a death scene. He found a woman who had obviously committed suicide, but he had a hard time figuring why. He traced her purchase of ammunition earlier in the day and found her cache of bullets. Accounting for what she had done to herself, several bullets were missing. He immediately went out to check on her family. He was greeted at the door, he was happy to see, by someone who was both alive and uninjured. But the person gestured behind him, to a television screen, where reporters were describing a bloody discovery in

Tolleson. Cliff's instincts had been correct—there had been murders before there was a suicide.

Cliff picked up the phone and called Ron Rock, the Tolleson detective he'd seen on the screen. "You looking for Naomi?" he said. "'Cuz I've got her."

Both veterans of their respective departments, this was the first time the two detectives had ever met. Their impression of each other was favorable, and just as in any other business, networking plays a role in police work. After David Estrada's death, Detective Ron Rock called Cliff Jewel and picked his brain a little on the subject of ballistics.

Ron Rock was also fielding calls from David's mother, who had saved various voice mails intended for her son, whose whereabouts she didn't know at the time the calls were received. Now the calls seemed sinister. Transients in the area began feeding to the detective stories of drug deals and debt collections. One informant sent him on a fruitless journey to a nonexistent address. A mysterious blue truck entered the story. It was tracked down; it belonged to a friend of David's, but the most they could learn here was that a female friend had been with David up until 11 p.m. the night of his death. She told detectives that David was avoiding going back home because he feared being institutionalized again. She thought he was headed to Mexico.

Others thought he was headed to San Francisco. David's friends from St. Mary's High School told various tales. The detectives drove up to Camp Verde, a half-day drive up and back, to lean on an investigative lead who was in custody up there for a hit-and-run. Turned out he had been behind bars since May 5 and had nothing to offer but rumors that were almost two months out of date with David's death. Everyone with a grudge against someone else phoned in theories. Everyone with a sin lied. Weapons were seized along the way, tested and eliminated from the investigation.

David's family went looking for leads themselves. A friend of David's had a dream about what had happened, and Rebecca sent one of her adult nephews out to look for the locale and characters described by the dreamer. An older stepson went to the crime scene and vigorously questioned local transients, collecting more vivid tales that went nowhere in the cold, hard light of day.

One sad entry in the police file reads, "I attended the funeral of David Estrada [today]," where a family member approached Rock in the halls of St. Francis Xavier with a list of names and phone numbers "that David had called from his mom's cell phone . . . and he thought we should have this information."

Months passed. The blistering summer turned into fall. Christmas came. No one was any closer to knowing what had happened to David.

Or to Reginald or to Tony, for that matter.

Or to a guy named Nathaniel Shoffner.

Chapter Three

I didn't want to get shot.

Stephanie Bartlett

At 6 p.m. on the evening of June 28, 2005, before David Estrada had arrived at his makeshift campsite on Eighty-third Avenue, about two miles away a commercial truck driver named Richard Bergman brought his kids out to see Sara Moon, the quarter horse he'd bought for them less than a year earlier. She was a beautiful deep bay color. He had her boarded at a wonderful little pasture on the outside edge of Tolsun Farms. The Bergmans drove over twice a day to pet her and see to her needs.

But before the Bergman family arrived for a visit the next morning, Sara Moon was found dead in her pasture, which was part of a rental property occupied by a City of Tolleson judge. When first discovered, the horse's cause of death wasn't immediately apparent. But when an experienced animal professional showed up, she recognized the signs of suffering around the horse's head, fluid from a punctured lung. The officer found the bullet holes in Sara Moon's body, four of them, and recovered .22 shell casings in the street, the side of the pasture that led to the exit from Tolsun Farms, out to Ninety-first Avenue. She called in the findings to the Tolleson detective squad, which was already hard at work on Estrada's case.

Tolleson detective Ron Rock says, "There was just the two of us, myself and my partner. Twenty-two shootings were uncommon. It was more typical to see nine-millimeters or three-eighties. I have two horses myself, I've had them for twelve years, but when the Sara Moon shooting came in, I had my hands full."

Sara Moon lived at the home of a local magistrate who had occasionally received threats related to cases. She also grazed along a major thoroughfare, Ninety-first Avenue. She was the first animal on what would become a long list, but no one knew that yet.

During the 1950s and '60s, a Reno woman named Velma B. Johnston had engaged in a battle that had her beloved in places as exotic as the Belgian Congo and hated in places as homey as Montana. One day Velma, who considered herself an average fifties Reno housewife, had followed a horse trailer dripping blood on the Nevada highway. Curious and concerned, she had hidden in the bushes to watch it be unloaded at a slaughterhouse. Shocked at the conditions she observed—the blood was coming from a live colt being trampled to death by the other horses packed suffocatingly thick inside the trailer—Johnston launched a several-year crusade that ended in an act of Congress.

A hostile rangeland bureaucrat had once dubbed Velma "Wild Horse Annie," and though the man had meant it as an insult, Velma embraced the moniker and eventually emerged the victor in their war, passing the Wild Horse Annie Law of 1959. She succeeded in outlawing the use of airplanes and motor vehicles to capture wild equines, as portrayed in the movie *The Misfits* (starring Marilyn Monroe and Clark Gable). But the callous conversion of the beautiful animals from America's wild and romantic past into canned dog food became her next target. It took another decade of fierce combat with cattlemen and other commercial interests, but Congress finally passed the Wild Free-Roaming Horses and Burros Act of 1971, which declared these animals "living symbols" of the "pioneer spirit" of the West. They were now to be free from "capture, branding, harassment or death." The days when screaming engines from the sky could start the terrible trek to the slaughterhouse and a crate of canned dog food were over.

Mandated by Congress, the Bureau of Land Management (BLM) took the herds in hand, defined, named and counted them, and when an individual herd grew too big for its own good or otherwise got into trouble, the bureau winnowed it out and offered the humanely captured animals to the public for adoption as pets.

Thirty years after Congress bowed to the public outcry whipped up by Wild Horse Annie and declared that wild horses and burros "enrich the lives of the American people," down in southern Arizona, a little north of the border of Mexico and right smack-dab on the California line, a jenny gave birth to a gangly and fuzzy little fellow. He had the characteristic oversized head, barrel chest and steep hoof of a burro. He was gray, or more salt-and-pepper when you could see him up close, and he had a black streak running down both shoulders, meeting at the withers and taking right angles to run up and down his spine. This distinctive black "cross" confirmed the sixty-six-pound newborn's heritage as a Nubian donkey, the kind that had his portrait painted by ancient Egyptians on the walls of hidden rooms in pyramids.

"I love burros," says Bureau of Land Management staffer Mary Pyles in the Phoenix office. "They are awesome." She tells the story of watching in horror as a burro had an argument with the gate of a corral. "It got both its front legs caught between the slats," she recalls. Since a horse would typically thrash itself to doom in such a situation, she naturally expressed her alarm and sense of impending catastrophe. But a more experienced burro man said calmly, "Wait. Just watch."

"Sure enough," she goes on, with admiration in her voice, "the burro stopped and thought about it. Shortly he balanced himself, then carefully he peeled one leg out, and then the other. He was fine!" As they watched the five-hundred-pound animal with the skinny legs trot away, Pyles's companion, a range management specialist, told her burros are so smart, "if they had thumbs, they'd have my job."

The young donkey down in the Yuma Proving Grounds proved as clever as the breed promised, and he found life was much easier when he could leisurely gorge to his heart's content on a field of domestic alfalfa. Farm crops are verboten to the wild burros.

"That's when we came and got him," says Roger Oyler, a specialist with the BLM's Wild Horse and Burro Program.

The 1971 law does allow helicopters to be used in captures for humane purposes, and it also allows for the protection of farmland. A helicopter was used to drive in several members of the Cibola-Trigo burro herd in the summer of 2004, but down on the ground, it was cowboys on horseback who got the wild animals to take those final steps into the trap, an enclosure built of mobile panels. They can't use a Judas animal, Oyler points out, because "donkeys don't care what anybody else thinks, they aren't following another animal's opinion about what spot is safe. Only the mamas and the babies ever really stick together."

A 1904 *New York Times* article playfully mocked a planned U.S. shipment of burros to Manila. The *Times* claimed the animals from the American West would spread "more spirit of liberty, insurrection and revolution" than had existed since the last rebel leader in those islands had been captured.

After being driven into the trap in 2004, the burros were separated by sex and transported up to Kingman, Arizona. "It's traumatic for them," says Oyler. "They don't know if we're going to eat them; all they know is they don't want to be there." But human hands inexorably come in to deliver vaccines and the freeze brand.

The whole process takes only sixty days, says veteran cowboy and rangeland expert Oyler, and by the time this salt-and-pepper burro was transported to Camp Verde, Arizona, for auction, he was still quite a feral animal with little human contact.

Stan and Linda Wilkinson both carry their Boston origins with them in their speech patterns, but in several decades of marriage they have lived everywhere from Costa Rica to Jamaica. As Christadelphians, a small Christian sect started in the first half of the nineteenth century, they felt a duty to do good works and spread the gospel abroad. In their autumn years they returned to the States, picking Arizona as the spot to settle, and took in foster children.

"We thought it might be good for these kids," Stan says on a sunbaked, 112-degree Arizona afternoon of the decision to take in a feral donkey. He and Linda and their two foster children made the drive up to Camp Verde, a mountain spot near Sedona, and attended a BLM adopt-a-burro auction.

"It cost more to have him transported down to the Valley," Stan laughs, "than he cost himself." His eyes glow with a re-membered smile as he talks about how the burro took to the children. "They say artistic children are special to them. You should have seen him follow those kids around."

They named the burro Buddy and moved him into the pasture that came with the house. They built him a shelter, as required by the BLM. He had a solid brick trough with running water. Buddy now had real salads of fresh, tender grass and his very own bales of alfalfa, properly purchased. He had regular veteri-nary care and all the affection a house full of children and mis-sionaries could supply. Assessing Buddy's new home, his one-time captor Roger Oyler says, "I think he probably feels he's died and gone to heaven." Buddy may have left the Choco-late Mountains, but in October 2004, he had stepped right into the sweet life. In the wild he could only expect to reach the age of nine or ten. Here in the Wilkinsons' back pasture, he could be expected to reach twenty-five or thirty. An awful lot of trouble had gone into getting him here, starting with Wild Horse Annie and ending in Roger Oyler.

Only eight months later, July of 2005, Linda Wilkinson re-turned from her morning visit to the pasture. "Buddy's acting like he's been hit in the head by a two by four," she said to Stan, as she stepped into the kitchen.

"It was a small-caliber bullet through the right ear into the base of the skull," says large animal veterinarian Dr. Traci Hulse. By the time Dr. Hulse pulled her truck up to the idyllic equestrian property, shady with trees and green and soft underfoot, Buddy had a high fever. The wound was bloody and infected. This burro, hanging his swollen head, eyes dull with pain, was a very sick boy.

Buddy was the only burro in the neighborhood, but several horses nearby were also shot around the same time. Some died, but Buddy lived. Stan and Linda speculate it was his feral nature and donkey soul. The docile horses took multiple bullets and must have made much better targets. Buddy only got hit by one bullet, and they believe it's because he recognized danger and knew to dodge and weave.

Dr. Hulse wonders who would do such a thing. It must be

someone with "serious problems," she says, "to do this. . . . for what? for . . . joy?"

_____

Buddy doesn't limp or show any signs of brain damage. Dr. Hulse says the bullet entered the skull but did not make an exit on the other side. "He was lucky," she says. "It never penetrated the brain. That is why he lived."

She sedated him. She anesthetized the wound. She cleaned it, she clipped the hair around it.

"Depressed, base of right ear swollen w/bullet hole on outside through base of ear & penetrating into base of skull," she wrote into her case file. She told the Wilkinsons two things were possible by the end of the week: he'd get better or he'd die. She prescribed anti-inflammatories and antibiotics and gave instructions on how to trick a donkey into taking medicine.

It wasn't easy. Stan ended up taking an electric drill and boring out the centers of carrots. The cavity held the medicine and the carrot fooled the burro. By the end of the week, Buddy was better. "These BLM donkeys are tough, tougher than your average horse," says Dr. Hulse.

"Still," Stan sighs, as he dips a finger into a pot of SWAT fly repellant, "he sure survived a lot of hardship out there in the wild just to have something like this happen here." He applies the ointment to Buddy's face. Stan leans over and wraps his arms around the animal's neck for a hug. Buddy leans in, too. His giant equine eyes close, looking like the savoring of sheer pleasure.

"I can't watch him drink," Stan goes on. Ever since that night, the big gray beast has seemed terrified of his custom-made solid brick running-water trough. Stan believes the stealthy rifle took aim at Buddy as he was drinking from the trough, relaxed and still, making a perfect target.

"He'll go a long time without drinking at all. Then he finally stands around looking at it, working up his nerve. Finally he'll dip his chin but immediately rear back out, doing nothing but splash water all down the brick. He'll do this over and over and over. It takes him twenty minutes to get any kind of water down his throat at all."

The hole cut through Buddy's ear has healed over and a small scar is visible on his fur. The bullet is still inside the cranium.

Rick Swier is a man with a large bronze statue of a horse at the front of his house, antique bridles mounted on the wall of his front hall and a silver belt buckle at his waist. He has two adult daughters living on their own and, in July 2005, also had a five-year-old daughter at home, as well as three happy dogs and a young painted horse named Apache.

Apache's irregular brown markings splashed down his side and under his belly and across his face, breaking up his otherwise snow white body, with a spray of black tail cascading down from a white cap. At two years old, Apache was just learning what his duties as a pet were going to be. He already had the scavenging for treats bit down pretty well. "He knew how to get into your pockets and really invade your space," Rick Swier says. It was the riding and training part that was something of a challenge. Rick grins and even giggles as he slowly, cowboy style, states, "He was pretty ornery." Ornery, apparently, is not unforgivable if you live in the backyard at the Swier house.

At dawn on July 20, 2005, the spirited young Apache was found lying down, bleeding, suffering. When veterinarian Dr. Mark Fink arrived, he took long stainless steel rods and carefully probed the wounds. Rick was not expecting the doctor's next words: "I think he's been shot."

"We had at that point already heard that another horse had been shot . . . [but] I don't think any of us really correlated the two together," Rick recalls, though some neighbors did begin to whisper about possible gang initiation rituals.

A bleeding Apache was loaded up and transported some thirty miles to Dr. Fink's facility in Chandler, for X-rays and treatment. "That was the worst part of his ordeal," Rick says softly. "That incision in his back trying to recover that bullet." Dr. Fink gave Apache a partial sedation, but the horse could still stand and would need to continue to, and not move, throughout the cutting. The doctor asked Rick to stand next to Apache and soothe him. A bullet had nicked the horse's lung. Breathing was difficult and painful. Having trouble breathing, the veterinarian points out, makes an animal panicky.

"I was wondering if it was all worth it," Rick recalls. "I was wondering what to do. With an animal . . ." His voice trails off.

What if vital organs were involved? How would the horse cope and function after this?

While he was making those tough decisions and standing by the animal as the doctor cut into his back, Rick remembers feeling sad for the horse. "It's hard to imagine someone would take such game just going around shooting other people's animals."

What would he like to say to the person who fired three bullets into his peacefully grazing painted horse, the pet of a five-year-old girl?

"How did life get so bad," Rick Swier says forcefully, "that you could make things so miserable for other people?"

Tolleson is a farming community more than ten miles from the heart of Phoenix. Just five thousand people live there, mingled with cotton fields and the occasional warehouse or shipping center. Just about a six- or eight-block strip forms the center of town, including the high school and city hall. The area where Apache, Sara Moon and the other horses were shot and where Buddy still lives is a small enclave of equestrian properties, less than a mile from the police department on the downtown strip. The small streets in this little precinct twist and turn, dead end here and dogleg there, and the sweetly grazing horses, behind white open rail fences, seem so beautiful and so . . . vulnerable.

In the summer of 2005, the neighbors in the borough expressed their rage to the *West Valley View*, a paper serving the small farming communities tickling the western edges of Phoenix proper, where a front page photo might be a granary truck loading for a dairy.

"Whoever is doing this to our animals is beyond description," wrote Julia Shepherd in a letter to the editor the summer of 2005. "Tomorrow I am moving my horses to a safer location."

In fact, Rick Swier did. After Apache was shot, he bought fourteen acres in northern Arizona and keeps the horses up there much of the year. He built a gated pen deep in the interior of his Tolleson property to lock the animals in, away from the road, at night. They no longer roam freely in the pasture the way Apache did on that July night.

Tolleson Police thought Sara Moon, the first horse shot, was perhaps collateral damage of some unrelated incident and got caught in the path of shenanigans not actually aimed at the horse. A second theory was that, even though the horse belonged to Richard Bergman and his children, she may have appeared to belong to the local judge who lived in the house on the property and therefore the shooting might be the act of someone with a grudge against a member of the bench.

But the second horse, Apache, was shot inside the little streets of the precinct where Buddy lives, and that seemed to rule out the idea of unrelated crossfire from a dispute likely to occur on a major thoroughfare. "It's looking more likely that someone was intending to shoot these horses," one officer, Jeff Pizzi of the Tolleson PD, told the *West Valley View*. "It's a very rare thing for a horse to get shot, especially two within a month."

———————

Five days later, Deborah Haddock, already grieving the recent loss of her mother, arrived at the property that she and her sister had just inherited. It was just after lunch. She walked through her mother's fruit trees and grapevines. In the tack room she picked up a bucket, filled it with carrots and apples, and trudged across the pasture to offer up a treat to her mother's little gray and cream miniature pony. With his coloring and small size, the horse could easily be lost to the eye, blending into the landscape. But within a moment or two, Deborah realized Little Man was unusually close to the ground, lying on his side, a rare position in which to find a horse. As she got closer, she noticed the horse did not seem to be moving.

As she came upon her late mother's pet, Deborah could see someone had put two bullets into him.

Her mother's Little Man would never gobble apples from her hand again.

———————

Five days after that, Stephanie Bartlett* stepped out her back door to head to a friend's Pampered Chef party. It was just dusk as she started to make her way across the small walkway that would take her to her car, parked deep inside the property, far

———————

*Denotes pseudonym.

back from the road. She looked up at her favorite view as she passed, the beautiful pair of chestnut horses in her back pasture, the one a very mature eighteen years, the other a two-year-old recently acquired to keep the senior horse company. Stephanie loved the pair. "I don't really know my neighbors, much," she says in a quiet voice, a voice likely more designed for horse whispering than for human discourse. "But I know all the horses around." In fact, Stephanie's devotion to the beautiful species even dictated her real estate decisions: she had chosen this particular property because it was the only one around where the pasture was in the interior of all the land. She did not want her horses to live exposed to a road. She thought that wouldn't be safe for them over the long term. She smiled at their loveliness in the dusky light as she walked.

Although it seemed surreal, what happened next she recognized right away: shots rang out, fired from a small-caliber weapon.

"The sound echoes around out here," she says, "so I couldn't tell where the shots were coming from. I didn't know if I was being shot at myself. I didn't want to get shot." So she ran back in the house, but not before she saw her own horses' behavior.

"They stopped, became motionless. They looked straight across all the pastures [of the neighboring houses on the block] and froze. Then they both wheeled around and ran away to the furthest northern end they could get."

Stephanie called the police, but by the time they arrived, it was fully dark and the officers could not connect the "shots fired" to anything or anybody.

The next morning, however, on the corner of the block, the story became clearer: a horse was found dead on the property due south from the pasture where Stephanie's two chestnuts live.

"I think they saw that horse fall," she says sadly. "I think they saw everything."

Now the Phoenix media itself began to take notice. Local television veteran Lew Ruggiero was actually present, doing a live shot about the three previous horse shootings, when the bullet in Buddy's head was discovered. Several TV trucks were collected on the pipe elbow turn in the street that afternoon when Stan mentioned Linda's remark about Buddy acting like he'd taken a "hit in the head by a two by four" to Lew. It was Lew who said, "Let's take a look." Experienced animal owner and neighbor Tony Morales joined them, pulled a clump of blood out of Buddy's ear and showed everyone the visible rim of a small-caliber bullet buried in the wound. They called Dr. Hulse and they called police. Lew had Buddy on TV within minutes.

Everyone in the little enclave was buzzing about the wounded and dead animals. Even the spotlight from urban Phoenix was aimed at the pastoral Westside. The Arizona Humane Society offered a reward of $5,000.

Live news trucks such as Lew Ruggeiero's from KPNX clustered in rural Tolleson to focus attention on the odd string of equine shootings, but the sad urban deaths of Reginald, Tony, and young David went unnoticed and unremarked by the area media. Phoenix remained dangerously unaware of what was really happening.

Chapter Four

Hey! Don't Shoot That Dog!

The weather is downright pleasant during November nights in the Valley of the Sun. It would have been balmy and beautiful on Veterans Day 2005 at midnight. A stray dog would have stretched out, comfortable for the first time in months. Or he might have found it an excellent time to scavenge, padding through the alleys without his paws getting burned by scorching pavement. With all the interesting smells of downtown, he might have been feeling very happy just to be alive, tail wagging, nose twitching, ears cocking.

Did the dog notice the car pulling up slowly? Nathaniel Shoffner did. Nathaniel would also have been enjoying the gentle evening weather. Midnight in summer can easily be one hundred degrees, or even more, in Phoenix. On this November night the mercury was around seventy-five degrees, making life on the streets so much more bearable, maybe even boosting a person's confidence.

Nathaniel Shoffner saw the car pull up and stop. He also saw something the dog couldn't understand no matter where his eyes were focused: a weapon taking aim. Nathaniel saw the dog's peril. Emboldened by the beer in his hand, Nathaniel stepped into view.

"Hey, what do you think you're doing?" he yelled at the driver.* "Leave that dog alone, you Bill Clinton–looking mother fucker!"

"What did you call me?" came a voice from the car.

Nathaniel drank more beer and exchanged more insults with the men in the car. The dog simply gamboled about, not attending to the human conversation.

Nathaniel didn't seem to mind that the rifle was now pointed directly at him.

Or that a trigger was pulled.

There was some swearing inside the car, though: the gun had jammed.

Nathaniel drank more and mocked more. He didn't put much stock in the bickering inside the car: one person wanted a shotgun, the other didn't think it would actually kill a man. No one knows if beer-soaked Nathaniel actually heard the words "I don't care! Just give it to me!"

Nathaniel was still tossing off boozy insults when the loud bang went off. The dog would have probably run off to hide under something, never knowing his life had been bought at the price of Nathaniel's.

An hour and a half earlier, in the northwestern city of Glendale, a different jurisdiction, two other dogs had had no Nathaniel Shoffner to defend them.

———————

Between 9:30 and 9:45 p.m., Issac Crudup was home watching TV. His two dogs, both large purebreds, were in the backyard. The older dog was Max, a German short-haired pointer, a beautiful speckled breed, liver and white. The younger of the pair was Shep, a blond Anatolian shepherd, much heavier and huskier and taller than the lithe and sleek Max. Only one year old, Shep might grow to almost 150 pounds when he filled out. At one year, he was the equivalent of a teenager, still more elbows than muscle. Anatolian shepherds have an ancient heritage as guard dogs for the flocks of Turkey. Deep in his blood, Shep felt

———————

*This conversation was repeated as secondhand information by Sam Dieteman; though no one will ever know what actually happened that night, his version matches perfectly with the known facts.

the need to patrol a perimeter, challenge intruders and guard his territory.

That evening Issac Crudup, an imposing man but with a quiet, focused manner, noticed his boisterous young Anatolian shepherd barking furiously. He had raised the big yellowish fellow from a puppy. The dog, he could tell from the sound, was at the south side of his property, the long fence that ran alongside a frontage road to Camelback. Camelback was a major thoroughfare. Issac heard that a vehicle had paused alongside about where Shep was barking. It was truly annoying how many unmaintained vehicles were on the road and how many of them ended up broken down near his house. Issac didn't get up to check. He knew the big dog was performing the job of his ancestors, defending his territory. But a few moments later, Issac heard a shot. Experienced with guns, he thought it sounded like a .22. Shep had also stopped barking. Instead, Issac could hear him crying, so he went outside to check, and found the dog at the opposite end of the large yard from Camelback Road. The animal was now whining and licking his right side.

At first Issac was puzzled. But then it sank in—the dog was licking a wound and that wound was just the size of a bullet. Issac brought the young yellow dog into the house, where he promptly sought out the underneath of a lamp table, a place he had been known to hide as a puppy but hadn't used since he'd grown bigger than the other dog.

Issac Crudup called the police.

He took a stoic but panting Shep to the vet. It turned out Shep was not the only dog there needing help with a bullet wound. It was an oddly busy night for the animal doctors.

Shep, who could have tackled a wolf or a lion, did not survive a one-ounce slug of lead.

Issac Crudup spent the rest of the night filling out police forms and talking to patrol officers. The next day, he returned to the veterinarian and asked for the bullet that had been removed from his exuberant adolescent dog. He could see he was right about the caliber; it was a .22. He sealed up the bullet in a container and drove it to the Glendale PD. But it was Saturday now and there was no one there on the weekend to receive it into evidence. Frustrated and grieving, Crudup did not want to let the death of his dog evaporate into bureaucracy so easily. He took

the sealed container home and locked it into a desk drawer. It sat
there for months.

David Cecena was looking for some privacy from the rest of the
family. On the evening of November 11, 2005, David, a big
thirteen-year-old with a sweet face and a soft voice, headed out
to the carport. His dog Irving, a three-year-old who'd been with
the family since he was a puppy, rushed up to greet him. Irving
was a joyful little mixed breed, with a hard coat, dark in color,
on a small terrier-sized body. David smiled at his pet, then
crawled into his brother's truck with his cell phone. The cab of
the Ford F-150 was roomy enough to be comfortable. The tinted
windows made him feel good and secluded. He'd not only have
his privacy from Mom and Dad, but not even the neighbors or a
stranger on the street could tell he was in there. A squat palm
tree was growing on the driver's side of the cab, shielding him
from the roadway. It felt like the perfect mini-hideaway for a
good, long chat.

At 9:48 p.m. David idly watched what he described as a blue
four-door sedan, a small model, drive past his house along the
road on the other side of the palm tree. He noticed it stop a few
yards past the house. David became more curious as the car
shifted into reverse and backed up to his own yard. He saw a
hand resting on the sill of the passenger side window, rolled
down on the cool November night.

Then, in disbelief, thirteen-year-old David saw a long barrel emerge from the car's interior and shoot his little pet twice.
He heard Irving give a sharp yelp and saw the dog start running
around on three legs. A third shot hit the truck David was sitting in.

The car sped off.

David jumped out of the truck and ran to the dog. The little
fellow was yelping and crying and, David could see, now that he
was up close in the dark, bleeding.

David ran into the house.

His father, Jose Cecena, was inside the house that evening.
His routine was disrupted when he thought he heard shots close
by, three of them. Then his son came running in the house upset
and calling for help. "Someone just shot our dog!" David cried
out. "Someone just shot him and I saw it happen!"

Glendale Police got another call.

At both Issac Crudup's and David Cecena's homes, about a mile apart, officers searched for bullet casings and other evidence on the night of the shootings. At both homes they'd asked about enemies or disputes or even if the homeowners might be involved in criminal activity themselves. But officers found nothing and the cases languished.

They did have David's description of a four-door vehicle. But, David said, because of the palm tree, he could not make out the plate number of the sedan.

Everyone in the family and the neighborhood and law enforcement said that because of the tinting on the windows and the palm tree shielding David from view, the perpetrators couldn't see there was a witness in the truck watching, or they probably wouldn't have shot the dog.

What nobody knew yet was that the tinting and palm tree instead may have saved David's own life.

When the four-door sedan moved to downtown Phoenix later that night, no tree or tinting was there to hide the next person keeping an eye on a dog.

Nathaniel Shoffner fell to the ground and bled. It was 10:20 p.m. An hour later, Christopher Scrantan and his wife drove through the dark streets near Twentieth and Monroe. They were on their way home from an evening out with friends. They had a babysitter waiting at home. When the couple's headlights lit up a man lying in the gutter, Scrantan's sense of professional duty fought with his feelings as a family man. By day, Scrantan was a Phoenix Police officer. But right now he was off duty and unarmed. He did make a U-turn to get a better look. When he stopped the car with the lights pointing at the man, he could see beer cans around him and fluid, probably vomit, filling out the scene. Twentieth Street and Monroe was not a nice place to be unarmed with your wife late at night. Scrantan's assessment from across the street, not wanting to leave his wife unattended in the car, was that the person was dead drunk. "He didn't seem to be in any danger; that is, he was not actually in the roadway," Scrantan says. "I just wanted to get him some assistance." Scrantan called it in. One for the drunk tank, he reported.

The babysitter was waiting. The corner was ominous. Officer

Scrantan had no weapon. Scrantan the husband and father put his foot on the pedal and got his wife out of that neighborhood. He did not wait for the reinforcements. The man in the street was left alone.

Just a few minutes later, on-duty officers did arrive. They also believed the man in the street to be passed out from alcohol. But paramedics were best suited to handle someone that drunk. When paramedics arrived, they could smell beer near the person, everyone on scene could see the beer cans scattered around, and the man was drenched. All were preparing for a rough ride to the drunk tank.

But when paramedics drew close and found the man utterly unresponsive, they reached for his shoulder and lifted. They turned the man over and discovered that he'd been lying in the gutter not vomiting from alcohol ingestion, but bleeding from a gun blast. The beer smelling up the scene had not been exhaled by a drunk but had spilled from unopened cans pierced by shotgun pellets.

The energy of the scene changed in an instant. The man was still alive. Rescue efforts commenced. Officers did not have time to shoo away a black dog with tan feet who had spied a bag of Cheetos and stolen it from the victim. By the time a detective arrived an hour later, the victim was long gone in an ambulance, but the dog was still there. It had managed to open the sealed cellophane packet and was gleefully strewing salty orange crumbs all about the crime scene. The detective scolded the officers, shooed off the dog and, for reasons he could never explain later, got a couple of photos of the dog as it slunk hopefully about the perimeter of the scene.

Turns out a shotgun *can* kill. But it does so painfully. Before midnight Nathaniel was transported to a hospital, where trauma specialists worked hard to undo the damage of flesh torn in dozens of spots. But little bits of metal traveling at high velocity are a formidable opponent. Of the pair who bickered with Nathaniel on November 11, and then with each other, the one who wanted that shotgun no matter what had won the argument. After twenty-seven painful hours, Nathaniel Shoffner breathed his last.

He may have had his difficulties and challenges, but Nathaniel Shoffner, at the close of a warm desert Veterans Day, died defending man's best friend.

Chapter Five

A Place to Live

In 2005, Hurricane Katrina wiped out New Orleans. Captured Iraqi dictator Saddam Hussein went on trial. And the San Antonio Spurs bested the Detroit Pistons four games to three to become NBA Champions for the year.

Ron Horton was trying to get out more, having buried himself in parenting his three boys alone, after his common-law wife had suddenly left, an action that surprised and grieved him. He helped the boys with their homework, made their lunches, and nursed them when they were sick. With all this on top of his construction job, his sense of self had been disappearing.

By all accounts, Ron poured himself into the job of dad until his own mother advised him to back off, give the boys some space, and himself a life outside of either cement mixers or Little League. Ron gravitated to some Westside bars, the Rib Shop, the Amber Inn, the Star Dust Inn and Stingers. He became a regular, shooting pool and swapping biker tales with a collection of buddies who had the same hobbies.

He became friends with Sam Dieteman,* a twenty-nine-year-old transplant from Minnesota, and a bartender at Pollack Joe's,

---

*Pronounced "DEET-mun".

one of the small, quiet pubs Ron frequented. Sammy was among the circle of amigos who collected around the pool tables, and Ron considered this bartender-slash-Honeywell-electrician-by-day a good friend, someone who would fall all over himself to pay you back for the slightest of favors. With a pool league to join and some bikers to raise a glass with, Ron had a burgeoning sense of camaraderie and contentment.

Sometime in 2005, Ron noticed that the young man from Minnesota was having a spot of trouble. No longer employed at Honeywell, Sam also lost the bartender job when Pollack Joe's closed down. His mother and stepfather lived out here in Arizona, but his mother's husband had recently kicked him out of the house. Ron heard about the divorced young father's need for a place to stay. Ron knew there were little girls back in the Midwest to support and he had a lot of sympathy for that. He offered Sammy what they could both consider a manly solution—in exchange for some work Ron needed done, he told Sam that he could come stay at his place and work it off in wiring.

It worked out well at Ron's house. He got some ceiling fans professionally installed and a houseguest who played easily with his growing boys. "I trusted him," Ron would later say. "He got along with my kids; that means a lot to me."

Sammy had a girlfriend at this time with a particular fondness for the Amber Inn, an unambitious joint with pool tables, a dart board and a restroom hallway dedicated to graffiti. Truth be known, by 2005, the electrician didn't need much excuse to go to a bar. In fact, he was sinking deep.

In October of 2005, Sammy's father arrived from Minnesota to celebrate his son's thirtieth birthday. Scott Dieteman had never had much of a relationship with his oldest son. Though Sam's mother and stepfather lived nearby in Arizona, his father really hadn't seen him in ten years. Scott Dieteman had remarried after splitting from Sammy's mother, and his son had felt displaced by the new stepchildren. Yet during this thirtieth birthday visit, Sammy managed to convince his father all was well, and Scott carried this amenable report back to all the relatives in Minnesota.

But Ron knew better and so did all the guys at the bar. More than one bar. The birthday boy—father of one young girl, stepfather to another—was now spending all his time at bars, first one there, last one to leave.

But it was the Amber Inn, in particular, where the lost Minnesotan would find a trajectory for the rest of his life. He had quit his job as an electrician at Honeywell. He had defiantly stormed out of his mother's house. He had stubbornly put on an act for his father visiting from Minnesota. But the most important thing Sam Dieteman did in the fall of 2005 was go to the Amber Inn with his girlfriend, where she introduced him to a guy named Jeff Hausner.

Chapter Six

I noticed a large blood smear.

Phoenix PD Report, December 29, 2005

December 29, 2005—the high temperature was in the sixties and the skies were collecting clouds on and off all day. Phoenicians call that kind of weather wintry, though the rest of the country might have another opinion.

It was a Thursday, and would-be bartenders were gathering at ABC Bartending School in Tempe, Arizona, for class. Among them was Annette Prince,* a woman with a past, trying to make a new start. She'd come a long way to escape violence, and had already risked so much. A new city, a new profession, a new life—she was preparing to meet the year fresh.

At 7 p.m., Annette was ready to leave class. She exited the building, took a few steps down the walk and froze: her car was riddled with bullets. A deep terror overtook Annette. The New Year would be nothing like she planned. Would she ever feel safe? She called a very private number. Later on, Tempe Police arrived. As soon as the officers were done, Annette rushed home and started packing.

---

*Denotes pseudonym.

Dr. Goudarz Vassigh had worked very hard to get where he was, and where he was was quite a drive from Annette. He was up in Phoenix at Thirty-second Street, north of Indian School. When he was almost sixteen years old, Goudarz had fled Iran with a passport set to expire within the hour. His parents, living in a suburb of Tehran, had set him off alone on a two-and-a-half-day bus trip to the border with Turkey, realizing that as soon as their son reached sixteen, the boy's passport would not be renewed, and he would be drafted into the war with Iraq, then led by a U.S.-backed Saddam Hussein. Goudarz's childhood had been set against the backdrop of the seizure of the U.S. Embassy and the headlines that dominated world news for years—a fiery eyed Ayatollah Khomeini, the burning effigies of U.S. presidents, and a dramatic Canadian rescue. What Goudarz remembers of the Khomeini revolution is the three-day lines for butane fuel where he and his sisters and parents would trade off shifts in the line, sleeping in it during the night.

Teenage Goudarz told the border guards he'd be in Istanbul for a short visit and would be back before his passport became invalid sixty minutes later. They waved him on, but the teenager headed west and never returned to become a soldier on the Iraqi front.

Eventually Goudarz made it all the way to America, learned English, graduated from chiropractic school and achieved his American dream—his own business. On this December 29, Goudarz was wrapping up his cases for the day and studying the latest research into insomnia and headaches when suddenly his American dream was shattered right through the front window. A bullet tore through the plate glass in front, the one painted with messages about massage, vitamins and the rest of his services. The bullet flew across the lobby where patients waited for him daily and lodged in the wall opposite the window.

Goudarz wearily called police and began answering the familiar questions about enemies and, in his case, due to his dark Persian looks and exotic name emblazoned on his window, questions about the possibility of a racially motivated hate crime. Goudarz didn't know what to think. He worried about the cost of the window and associated damage and the time lost to his business. He had worked very hard for that business.

Goudarz tried to maintain a calmness and sense of peace. After living through revolution and war and restless childhood nights in the butane line, he had a top priority of avoiding ugliness whenever he could and putting it behind him as soon as possible when he couldn't.

———————

Timmy Tordai had also traveled a long road, though a much different one. He'd gotten himself into trouble and now was working on his second chance. The forty-four-year-old, olive-skinned with a rich crown of softly curling dark brown hair, had a job at a cafeteria inside the main post office and a halfway house to come home to at night. The halfway house was called Life Cycles. It was an easy commute, just a straight shot down Van Buren by public transit. Saturday would be New Year's Eve and Timmy was looking forward to it. Tonight he had worked from 2 to 10:30 p.m, and at the end of his shift, Timmy caught a city bus home. He sipped a cold drink and yanked the overhead cable when the bus got near Ninth Avenue and Woodland. It was a brisk fifty degrees when he descended the steep steps of the bus into the night air. He didn't even hear the pneumatic whine of the vehicle's doors close behind him because he had popped earphones in and dialed up a favorite classic rock station to keep him company for the last few yards to home. Life Cycles was at the end of the block, Ninth Avenue and Adams. Timmy wasn't paying attention to his surroundings and he didn't hear someone calling out to him. He bobbed his head in time to the music and kept heading south.

The music stopped for Timmy when the headphones blew off and his body collapsed. "I thought I was having a heart attack," he says. "I couldn't move nothing but my head. But I was too scared to pass out. I prayed." He came out of his daze when he saw blood all over the sidewalk and realized it was coming from himself. "Then I knew I was shot."

Now he could feel the pain and his thoughts clarified. The blood was coming from his neck.

He snapped into survival mode. It would not be here on this sidewalk, he told himself, it would not be here that he met his death. He would not remain on this curb and let his life flow out.

"I forced myself up from the sidewalk and tried to make it home." His drink had spilled and his radio had cracked open. He was spewing blood but he could walk. Timmy pressed on, past an old brick church and a vacant lot, and finally, dripping blood at every step and feeling weaker and weaker, he made it to the Life Cycles lobby. He was never more thankful that home was a halfway house with a staffer on-site. He knocked on the door of the manager. "I think I've been shot," he said as the staffer opened the door.

All it took was the sight of blood and Timmy's stricken, staggering self—911 got dialed instantly. That 911 call set in motion some very sad discoveries.

———

Phoenix Police Homicide detective Cliff Jewell describes himself as a "scene guy." His four-person squad is always divided into (a) the case agent, who takes the long view and sees a case all the way through its prosecution, (b) the site detective, who takes charge of the scene of the crime, keeps it secure and gives a thorough scouring for forensic evidence and a lot of detail work, and (c) two officers who interview everyone at the scene and generally carry out the instructions of the site detective or the case agent. Cliff Jewell, a towering blond man, loves the details, and getting down into the nooks and crannies of a crime scene.

But on this night, out of nothing but random circumstance, when the 911 call about the man shot at Ninth and Woodland came in, Cliff Jewell caught the short stick and arrived on scene as case agent.

Ninth and Woodland was not a nice neighborhood. True, there was a pretty and historic brick church that Timmy had to stagger his way past, but it was protected by a chain-link fence and padlocked at night. One or two buildings on the block were outright abandoned. Empty infill took up the rest of the street. Running between Woodland, a small passageway, and the major thoroughfare of Van Buren was a tiny grassy area trying to be a park. It was more like a hot spot for streetwalkers and rough-looking men of no address. The dodgy blank spots of the neighborhood collected more of the same. Cliff Jewell was walking into a peculiar little society of its own.

When the first patrol officers arrived on the scene, denizens of the area approached them and guided them to nearby tableaus: a dead body at Tenth Avenue and Adams, and another one a block south at Tenth and Jefferson.

As detective Cliff Jewell walked around, his "scene guy" instincts told him the lost soul at his feet was connected to the man still fighting for his life with paramedics on the other side of the block. He thought all three of the shootings were connected. He had no forensics yet, no fingerprints, no witnesses—but his senses were tingling. His shrewd eyes scanned the area taking in the details of the night.

The bullet that wrecked Timmy Tordai's favorite song passed right through the soft tissue in his neck, entering from the back and exiting underneath his ear, over his shoulder. His lung had collapsed and was full of blood. By the time Cliff Jewell got to see him at Good Samaritan Hospital, he was full of morphine and angst. He talked a lot, but the detective could find little of value in the post-surgical ramblings.

One thing was certain: Timmy Tordai was lucky to be alive.

The same could not be said for Marco Carillo, who would never make it past the age of twenty-eight.

Or Jose Ortiz, who left this world at the age of forty-four on the same December 29.

Marco was found on the southwest corner of Tenth and Jefferson with two bullet wounds. Time of death was impossible to establish—more than minutes, less than days. Jose was found on Tenth just north of Adams. He had one bullet wound, and his time of death fit into the same time frame—but could not be narrowed down, either. No family came forward to claim either man; no friends were found who could tell their stories. The bodies sprawled across the urban terrain of concrete and asphalt, silent and solitary, their stories virtually unreadable—the only clues embedded in their chests for a medical examiner to recover.

Detective Jewell thought about the three men, his mind racing, trying on different theories and arranging the few facts in his head into varying configurations. He had no indication that the three men had known one another or had anything in common. But he strongly felt that they were united by the same evil. Two out of three dead. It was a terrible statistic and it sat heavy on his shoulders.

Across town, in a much nicer neighborhood, a pleasant residential precinct with gardens, playhouses, and friendly porches, a dog named Martin was cowering under the kitchen table, panting, crying, growling. Retired army lieutenant colonel Ronald Travis, a gravelly voiced man with a flag pin in his lapel, had been in the hobby room of the house working on family genealogy when he heard two pops and then a loud cry from the dog. He ran out to the backyard to find Martin curled up on the patio, bewildered, crying. The lieutenant colonel was just finding a bloody right shoulder on the animal they had taken in as a puppy in 2002, when he heard his wife, who had passed him and run farther into the yard, cry out, "Oh, Peyton." Peyton was a sleek, coal black Transylvanian hound, with floppy ears and a triangle head, who had been with the family since 1998. Mrs. Travis couldn't stop crying when she found the dog between the shed and the fence, whimpering and bleeding profusely. The Travis family called the police and tried to manage two dogs in crisis at once.

While officers were checking out Peyton and Martin, some few blocks away Ricardo Lopez and his wife were awakened by gunshots and wheels squealing. At first Ricardo kept low, afraid bullets would come through his bedroom window. Then he heard his dog crying. He ran outside to find Peanut, a German shepherd mix, chasing her tail in distress. As soon as she saw him, Peanut stopped her circling and began to lose her bowels. Ricardo's other dog, Chloe, ran to the far side of the yard and hid. "She was nervous," he says. "The dogs slept together, near that window." An angry Ricardo Lopez called in the crime against his pet and looked for an all-night emergency veterinary clinic. "We stayed with her till three a.m. She was suffering; X-rays showed bullets had fragmented inside her, and she was paralyzed; she lost more control, peed all over herself—it wasn't nice. She was drooling everywhere; she was in misery."

Before dawn, the order was given to end her suffering.

Marcia Wilson* had a hard time with relationships. She couldn't understand why her neighbors were after her all the time. She had a daughter and a brother who cared for her, but she had a way of causing unbearable trouble and alienation, and by the time authorities determined she needed a guardian, there was no one but the county itself to step forward to fill the role. The senior citizen with a beaming face and a blond pixie cut became a ward of the court; a long journey began, back to her hated medications and a measure of stability. The county took control of her beloved condominium, mired in an HOA lawsuit, and her other financial affairs. She was moved into an assisted living facility and given supervision that got her to her psychiatrist appointments and kept her psychotropic prescriptions current. She didn't always take the medication. Some years the guardian's report sounded discouraged, with accountings of Marcia's delusions and paranoias and even forays into violence, always motivated by her hallucinatory fears. After some time, though, the annual reports took an upturn as Marcia stabilized with more regular medicine intake and less paranoid ideation. After some years, Marcia "graduated" from the county guardianship. The county had saved her condominium from the HOA lawsuit. She had a home to return to and the mental stability to stay out of the worst sorts of trouble.

Marcia's grasp of reality and relationships would never be of the firmest sort. She called police often. Nothing was ever found to be wrong when they investigated.

Nevertheless, openheartedness runs deep in the community, and plenty of neighbors managed to look after Marcia. In 2005, Marcia had two dogs, an Australian shepherd named Cherokee and a little Chinese crested named Charlie. She knew many of the neighbors along the path she walked when she took the dogs from her house to the park.

On December 29, 2005, somewhere around 10 p.m., Marcia Wilson took that route. Los Olivos Park had mature trees and acres of grass and a playground. It sat in the middle of a nice neighborhood, with a church six blocks away, a certain chiro-

---

*Denotes pseudonym.

practor's office six blocks another direction, and everywhere else, comfortable single family houses. As she walked along the northern edge of the park, Marcia was doing pretty well on this nearly last day of 2005: a condo with equity, thanks to the county, a mind calmed by modern medicine, and two dogs to love.

Charlie, the little Chinese crested—a singular breed, hairless, showing off lavender patches of skin with tufts of cream hair at the crown and ankles—needed to take care of business just at the border between the front yard of one of Marcia's friends and the park itself. Charlie maneuvered himself a little inward, off the street. Marcia turned to Cherokee and asked her to "stay" where she was, barely inside the grass, just off the road. Ready with her plastic bag, she needed to focus on Charlie. Cherokee minded very well. All three of them were generally oriented westbound. Marcia noticed a small car approaching her from the east. "It swerved into the wrong lane, then 'boom!' Cherokee jumps two feet in the air and drops to the ground. I was so scared. The car backed up and I was afraid they might shoot me or Charlie next."

All the neighbors came pouring out of their houses and patrol officer Pedro Cano arrived moments later. He found Marcia "crying, fearful, hysterical" and the dog "pretty bloody, moaning, crying." He describes Cherokee's right rear leg as nearly "blasted" right off. She was lying on her left side.

One neighbor started up his car and drove Marcia and Cherokee to an emergency veterinary clinic. Another neighbor pulled out her credit card and assured the clinic she would pay for whatever Marcia's dog needed.

Dr. William Penn received Cherokee "bloody, with multiple wounds, no use of back legs, panting and suffering." He began emergency treatment on the Australian shepherd, but "Cherokee expired before we could do surgery."

In downtown Phoenix, hours later, someone mentioned it to the "pet detective."

Chapter Seven

Caliber: Twenty-two

If two-year-olds are known for something, it's putting their tiny little fingers where they don't belong, such as into fascinating objects with moving parts. When Detective Cliff Jewell was that age, he reached out for the tempting blades of a fan one day and got the lesson of his life. His left ring finger got snapped off at the tip. His mother gathered him and his finger up and scrambled for the car.

Mrs. Jewell first stopped at a physician's office in the vicinity. Incredibly, they were turned away. So Mrs. Jewell bundled up her bleeding little boy again and put her foot down on the gas hard.

Her luck seemed to sour again when she saw red and blue lights flashing behind her and she was forced to pull over for her obvious speeding.

The trooper in his black uniform and shiny accoutrements approached the Jewell family car. He seemed fantastically tall to the little boy in the passenger seat. The officer took one look at the bleeding child and put his ticket book away. He pulled out a radio instead and soon Mrs. Jewell and baby Cliff, with his bloody stump wrapped in a towel, had a personal escort, with shrieking sirens and strobing lights, to the nearest emergency room.

"I don't remember crying," says the adult Cliff, "but I remember those flashing red and blue lights. I was fascinated by them. I never forgot them. From that moment on, I never wanted to be anything else but the tall guy with the uniform and the flashing red and blue lights."

The tip of the finger did not survive that night, but his obsession with law enforcement never died.

As a young man, Cliff ended up in the Security Police of the army, a special unit not to be confused with the Military Police. The Security Police are soldiers charged with protecting, via the combined use of professional security and combat techniques, fellow soldiers as well as civilians who fall into harm's way in military-related venues. In March 1975 Cliff arrived in Thailand. A day or two later, his unit was assigned to rescue merchant mariners on the civilian ship USS *Mayaguez*. The *Mayaguez* had been seized by Viet Cong days after what was supposed to be the official end of the Viet Nam War. All the world held its breath as the infamous guerilla Communists tweaked the superpower, against the backdrop of the Cold War and its ever fragile balance of nuclear threats. A Communist satellite could not be allowed to grab U.S. civilians and assets. President Ford and the Joint Chiefs of Staff needed the most sophisticated soldiers, the most highly trained, the best of the best. Those were the men whom Cliff Jewell was numbered among, to defend the West in what would forever be known in the annals of major global crises as the *Mayaguez* Incident.

The soldiers climbed into a large chopper with their gear and their adrenaline, their thoughts and their training, each understanding the seriousness and danger of their mission. This was what they had trained for. This was their raison d'être. Their country needed them; indeed, the entire Western world needed them. They settled into the cargo bay of the chopper, leaning directly against the fuselage. At the last minute, a superior officer tapped Jewell on the shoulder and pulled him off the transport, saying his arrival in Thailand from Lackland hadn't been properly processed yet, so he couldn't be deployed until his paperwork caught up with him. Therefore, the strapping soldier of six years' experience looked on as a now famous photo was snapped. Cliff Jewell was standing near the photographer as all those inside the chopper faced him. The soldiers looked into the camera somberly, their sense of responsibility written on their faces.

The fat-bellied helicopter never reached open waters. An hour after Cliff was pulled off the transport, and waved good-bye to his closest buddies and colleagues, the helicopter disappeared over the jungles of Thailand, creating an international scandal that has lasted for decades. No survivor was ever recovered. Cliff Jewell, with his truncated ring finger, would be the only man from the group who would ever leave Southeast Asia.

Cliff retired from the U.S. Army the next year. He returned to Phoenix. As an experienced Security Police officer, he was a highly desirable hire for the Phoenix Police Department. At six foot three, it's likely he was also noticeably taller than the trooper who had seemed like such a giant to him on that day when he lost his fingertip.

Over the course of his years at Phoenix PD, Cliff became known as the "pet detective," thanks to his soft spot for animals. One day a relative who worked in a veterinary office called him with a sad tale of a dog that was slated for premature euthanasia. The veterinarian did not want to perform the procedure and his entire office was looking for a new home for the dog instead. The call to the "pet detective" brought their search to a happy close. Jewell rolls his eyes in self-exasperation for his own soft heart as he remembers bringing the dog home to join a household with two other dogs already in it. He allows himself a rare smile as he recalls that both he and the new dog had a limb in a sling at the same time, so they bonded while recovering together.

Since Cliff Jewell's love for pets was well known to everyone in the Phoenix Police, with two dead men on his hands and one halfway between this world and the next, on this hellish December night, someone thought to tell him, "Hey, Cliff, we had a dog shot out in the Squaw Peak precinct tonight. I dunno, I just thought maybe I'd mention it."

Cliff Jewell felt strongly that he had a bucketful of cases that were all related. It was a hard sell to others in law enforcement, though, because it was not a very distinct pattern in the known world of criminology. The incidents of December 29, 2005, involved widely divergent locales, from the well-groomed Arcadia district of Phoenix, to one of the scrungiest blocks of the urban downtown. What could be the connection between a downtown drifter and an Arcadia lady's pet? Phoenix PD, including Cliff Jewell, did not yet know about Annette Prince in Tempe at the ABC Bartending School or the Arcadia chiropractor Goudarz Vassigh.

Phoenix Police Headquarters, 620 West Washington, is a big square block of a building, the front lobby usually standing room only with ticketed drivers applying for the paperwork to get their licenses back. It's gray and a bit grimy and it's the biggest center of gravity in the law enforcement community in the Phoenix area. All officers from the farthest northeast bit of Scottsdale to the westernmost stretch of Buckeye refer to it simply as "620."

Cliff Jewell and everyone else who worked at 620 dutifully chased down leads. Someone called the tip line saying heatedly that his carpool partner hated the homeless and was certain to be the perpetrator of the shootings of the men downtown on and around Ninth Avenue. The two carpoolers worked at the post office. So Phoenix PD contacted the security department of the U.S. Postal Service and enlisted their professional assistance. In spite of the promising details offered by the tipster, the Postal Service quickly developed evidence that ruled out the carpool partner.

Not far from where Timmy Tordai was shot was a homeless shelter. One of its guests sought out police with information so detailed that he seemed to have been nearly an eyewitness to at least one of the shootings. The Phoenix PD sketch artist turned out a vivid portrait of the suspect the man described so fully and with such specificity. Posters of the drawing were distributed. Officers were nearly high-fiving one another with the triumph of a case solved so fast and the quick development of such a good witness. But Cliff Jewell tracked down the witness's movements and talked to officers who were stationed nearby the homeless shelter at critical times during the night of December 29. The officers could not support the man's version of events. Cliff made a call to the witness's probation officer and heard the bad news: "This man is a pathological liar. He can't stop making up elaborate stories. It's a violation of his probation for him to have been where he said he was that night."

The sketch artist posters were taken down, the witness was bounced back into custody for his probation violation, and investigators started over once again.

One of the things on Cliff Jewell's to-do list that harried weekend was to obtain security camera footage. On the night of the crimes, after the bodies of Marco Carillo and Jose Ortiz had been freshly discovered but still lay on the concrete, a Capitol Police patrol officer—the Capitol Police are a special detail commissioned to secure the complex of government buildings including the governor's office and the State Legislature—had pointed to a spot high above street level on a corner between the two bodies. The building was a parking garage for the Department of Environmental Quality (usually referred to as DEQ, it is an Arizona State agency roughly corresponding to the federal Environmental Protection Agency). Cliff was pleased to see that the security camera was right between his two crime scenes. He very much wanted to know what that camera might have seen.

———————

On Friday, December 30, Tolleson detective Ron Rock was feeling dispirited. It had been six months since he'd stood by for Mrs. Rebecca Estrada as she fell apart with the news of her son's murder. The case was a big priority for the two-man department. "For almost six months, we did not do anything else. But now the case had gone kinda stale. Nothing checked out. I had no suspects after investigating *more* than 'several' investigative leads. We had nowhere else to go with the investigation. After everything we looked at, his shooting appeared to be random." It's a terrible thing not to be able to give answers to a devoted mother, a woman you know is crying every day and living nightmares every night.

On December 30, Ron Rock turned on the car radio as he drove into work. He heard a lot of news stories about some shootings in downtown Phoenix. It gave him ideas. Soon he was dialing that detective he'd met on the suicide/murder from earlier in the year. He wasn't surprised to get voice mail, considering the night he knew his colleague had had. While Cliff Jewell and other Phoenix officers were talking to the U.S. Postal Service and the homeless shelter, Ron Rock left a message about David Estrada, as well as Apache and Buddy and other animals shot on the Westside six months earlier.

On Monday, January 2, after working the weekend nonstop, Cliff Jewell called him back. After hearing a quick summary of what Ron was dealing with on the Westside, he agreed they ought to talk. The two arranged to meet in the first week of the new year.

When they did, Detective Jewell caught a whiff of possible connection between their cases, and took a strong interest in the shootings from little Tolleson. The two detectives agreed to work together, and Cliff Jewell turned his attention toward stacks of files, looking for more potentially related cases.

On January 11, he found something very interesting. At least, he thought it was interesting. No one else seemed to want to take much notice. After all, it was in the far western farming town of Avondale, some fifteen miles and several magnitudes of difference in community type from the crime scene he was supposed to be investigating.

Detective Cliff Jewell entered into the log:

> *On 01-11-06 at about 100 hours, while researching a series of animal and human shootings in the Phoenix area, I came across this report. The report is very basic.*
>
> *I contacted the victim, Mrs. Zolcharnik, and determined that her dog had been put to sleep as a result of three .22 caliber bullet wounds. I asked if any shell casings were recovered at the scene. Mrs. Zolcharnik advised that the Phoenix officer that took the report contacted Tolleson PD since Tolleson was experiencing similar shootings. Det. Rock from Tolleson PD responded and seized two .22 caliber shell casings.*

So the case also involved his friend from tiny Tolleson PD, Ron Rock. Interesting indeed.

On the morning of July 20, 2005, slow-talking cowboy Rick Swier was just discovering some blood on his horse, the pretty painted Apache. He didn't know what to make of it yet. He also didn't know that several miles over into the next town, the Zolcharniks had already been up all night and they were just now coming to that most difficult of decisions a pet lover ever has to make.

Carl and Amy Zolcharnik were both in bed that hot summer night. Both disabled, the couple enjoyed having their grandchild with them, putting the little girl to bed in the corner bedroom. The little girl loved to play with their dogs, a beautiful dark reddish brown Akita with a black face, whimsically named Whiskey, and a much smaller Shiba Inu named Cody. Akitas were originally bred to be the Japanese fighting dog, but this one was great with kids. With the same general size of a tall collie, Akitas have medium short hair, powerful, trim figures and somewhat blocky triangular heads with upright ears. The Japanese have a story of legendary loyalty, of an Akita who went to the train station at the same time every day for fourteen years vainly trying to meet his beloved master who, beyond the dog's comprehension, would never come home again.

On this night, their sweet little granddaughter was not present in her corner bedroom, but Whiskey was sleeping in the yard, just beneath the bedroom's window. A few minutes past midnight, both Carl and Amy heard what they were certain were shots, coming from the street, toward the southeast corner of the house. They both ran outside and found their lovely Whiskey startled, panting, and bleeding. As bad as this was, they both looked at the window and shivered with relief that their granddaughter was not on the other side.

They found the first wound easily. Whiskey had a bloody paw. The second wound they found in the dog's torso, the rich brandy colored fur sticky, wet and red. They thought they'd heard three shots, but they couldn't tell where the third one might have gone.

Carl called the police and Amy bundled up the weakening dog and headed for the closest animal hospital she could find. At midnight, it just isn't easy to find a veterinarian. In a tiny rural burg, your options are even fewer. But Phoenix wasn't far, and Amy was able to find a twenty-four-hour veterinary emergency clinic in the metroplex. The unfortunate thing about twenty-four-hour emergency clinics, however, is that they are not set up for repeat customers. A pet owner may have a good relationship with the pet's regular vet, gaining the trust over time that means personal checks, even large ones, will be accepted at the front desk. But a twenty-four-hour clinic may require cash, especially if the outlook for your ailing pet is dire.

On the night of July 20, 2005, Amy Zolcharnik ran into that

policy. The clinic would need $1,200 before they would treat the beautiful, bleeding Akita. The Zolcharniks did not have $1,200 lying around the house or even in the bank.

"Whiskey was getting weaker and weaker," Amy recalls. "I was frantic." At one thirty in the morning she drove over to the home of her father-in-law, who without hesitation wrote her the check to cover the dog's emergency treatment. She raced back to the clinic, only to find that the clinic would not accept the third-party check. She drove to an ATM to deposit the check. Back at the clinic, they still would not treat Whiskey, because the large deposit would not process through the Zolcharniks' account during the night.

Amy was left with no option but to comfort the dog through the night.

"She was getting weaker all the time," Amy recalls sadly. "She was shaky and finding it harder and harder to get up or down. She was bleeding internally, and by now it was very uncertain if she could survive any surgery at all."

At 7 a.m., Amy's regular veterinarian, the one who knew the Zolcharniks and knew Whiskey, opened for business. Amy and Whiskey rushed over.

Seven hours after taking three bullets, Whiskey had sunk too far. Instead of going in for emergency surgery, the stalwart Akita with the deep streak of loyalty was put to sleep.

Cliff Jewell, the pet detective, reading bare bones details of the incident in a six-month-old report, called up Ron Rock and asked for the bullets from Whiskey. He submitted them to the National Integrated Ballistics Information Network. Later, Cliff was able to enter this into the log:

"A .22 caliber shell casing found at the 9th Avenue and Woodland scene has been matched to a shell casing found at this animal shooting."

On January 11, Cliff Jewell also went out to the Travis home. Peyton, the sleek Transylvanian hound, had not survived the night of December 29, 2005. Jewell asked Lieutenant Colonel Travis for permission to look around the backyard. Travis led him to the portion of fence near the shed where an immobile and whining Peyton had first been found by his wife. Jewell immediately spotted a hole in the back wall of the white shed. "Has this always been here?" he asked the homeowner. Ron Travis wasn't sure. Cliff thought he could see black dog hairs on the hole. He received permission to enter the shed, which was full of boxes and the various items a family stores long term. He says when he entered the shed, he intended to look both for bullets "and black widows."

He did find a bullet.

"It appeared to be a twenty-two-caliber to me." It also appeared to have flesh on it. He sent the mangled bit of lead to the Veterinary School at the University of California, Davis. They confirmed: the flesh on the bullet had come from a dog.

The bullet that killed Peyton had gone straight through her body and kept on traveling through a shed wall, not stopping until it got lost in the stacks of storage. And it wasn't found until Cliff Jewell went in there with the express intent of finding what he knew must be somewhere inside.

Although no one else seemed to take notice of his hodgepodge series of .22-caliber crimes, Cliff now wanted more than ever to dig deeper into the database of case files from jurisdictions all over the more than six hundred square miles known as the Valley of the Sun. He put out a call to all agencies and anyone who would listen: please send over your "injured animal" reports, especially involving small-caliber bullets.

He got nothing back.

But he had the bullet from Whiskey matching his shell casing from Ninth and Woodland.

Chapter Eight

Two Big Men and a Plainclothes Visit

According to Ron Horton, late in the year of 2005, Sam Dieteman had begun to mutter that he didn't deserve to live in Ron's house. He didn't deserve to live at all, probably. He had a way about him that made people want to help him, and his biker friends tried. No one understood where Sammy's dark thoughts were coming from and why he couldn't seem to get a toehold. Sometimes he slept in the back of a barmaid's car. Sometimes no one knew where he slept. Ron Horton was puzzled.

In November, Sammy left Ron's for good. He bounced around among other friends and even slept in the outdoors a few times. In January he moved in with his new friend from the Amber Inn, Jeff Hausner. Jeff and Sam would have made an imposing pair. Both were tall and husky. Sammy had a dark mop that varied in style and a beard that covered half his face. Jeff had brown hair that usually just tickled his ears and neck, and a matching, slightly too long mustache.

Jeff and Sam hunkered down in a small apartment in the far West Valley, just off Camelback. They drank a lot. And generally got on the nerves of a woman Jeff was reluctant to call his "girlfriend," Celeste Vance, who suffered from cerebral palsy. It was really Celeste's apartment, but if her big boyfriend wanted his big pal to live there, too, it was okay with her. Everything Jeff did was okay with Celeste. Also in the apartment was Celeste's teenage son, Travis. Jenny* Hausner, Jeff's teenage daughter, frequently came to visit.

In January 2006, the Pittsburgh Steelers were preparing to face off with the Seattle Seahawks in Detroit, the Fiesta Bowl was hosting Notre Dame and Ohio State, and Cliff Jewell was digging through case files.

Cliff Jewell discussed his and Ron Rock's findings with Phoenix Police public information officer Andy Hill. Sergeant Hill was one of the rare officers who agreed with Jewell that these cases might be related. They needed public input. And that was Andy Hill's specialty. On January 27, 2006, Phoenix Police sergeant Andy Hill invited Avondale and Tolleson Police Departments to join him in a press conference. They wanted informants and they also wanted people to protect themselves. After the January 27 press conference, stories began to appear about shootings on the Westside and downtown. For the first time, a series of strange shootings were linked publicly. Phoenicians were shocked and puzzled.

"It was hard to get my head around," remembers Katrin de Marneffe of Clear Channel Outdoor. "I mean, I've lived in New York. Nothing like this ever happened. This was *Phoenix*. I thought we were safe."

She could have been speaking for just about everybody. No one understood what the police were trying to say. None of it seemed to make sense. At the same time, the police had also begun talking about someone they called the Baseline Rapist. The locations the police mentioned were so far apart from each other, and the types of victims so divergent, it was difficult to reconcile.

The information had a stop-and-go quality to it. This paragraph from the January 27, 2006, *West Valley View* was typical: "The equestrian crime spree, which ultimately claimed the lives of four horses and left one mule injured, came to a halt after the final incident on July 30, 2005."

The paper reported a spree had come "to a halt." It was over, then?

Not at all. In fact, there were others (including the horse that

---

*Denotes pseudonym.

had died on July 30 as witnessed by the two horses owned by Stephanie Bartlett), which had not yet been linked or reported to the news media.

While it was difficult to process this sketchy and shocking information, everyone in Phoenix did take notice. The words "serial killer"—two of them, no less—had a way of making everyone sit up. It became a common topic of conversation at water coolers, bus benches and lunch lines as Valley residents compared notes and tried to process the alarming news. People became more alert in their surroundings, altered their schedules, and fewer ventured out alone at night.

One astute person popped up in the city of Glendale. Violent Crimes Squad case manager for the City of Glendale Police Maria Vida called Detective Cliff Jewell. Heeding both his alert to agencies and the press conference to the public, she had sifted through stacks of cases and found two that she thought he might be interested in. Two dogs, she said, shot on the same night. He drove out to Glendale the day she called, to take a look at what she had. It looked like his guy, he thought, as he read the files she had waiting for him. He focused in on the dog Shep. Maybe it was too late, maybe not. He wasted no time in finding out.

It was February 2, 2006, when Cliff Jewell drove out to Issac Crudup's house in Glendale. The chain-link fence through which big blond Shep had received a fatal .22 slug was gone. In its place, Mr. Crudup had erected a solid and high cinder-block wall. Cliff knocked on the door, but got no answer. He drove around the block and tried again.

This time, Mr. Crudup came to the door. He had arrived home during the time that Cliff was circling. He was surprised and relieved to meet the plainclothes detective in a civilian vehicle who wanted to talk about Shep. Did he still have the bullet he'd retrieved from the veterinarian after Shep's death? the detective wanted to know.

"It's in the filing cabinet in my desk," Issac Crudup said. He'd held it there for three months now. He would never forget the night his big Turkish guard dog had whimpered his way, bleeding, to hide under a table that was long since too small for him. Finally, someone was here to pursue justice. That it was a Homicide detective who showed up might have seemed unusual. But Issac had loved his dog, and he was glad to hand over the bullet to a professional who would pursue it.

Cliff Jewell also picked up the bullets retrieved from Irving, the little mixed breed dog who'd been shot right in front of a thirteen-year-old boy. Irving's bullets had been handed from the veterinarian directly to a Glendale PD officer at the animal hospital. Glendale PD was very interested in Cliff Jewell's theories. They asked him to brief all their relevant departments so they could help in his efforts. They also officially reassigned to him the cases of Shep and Irving.

Cliff was very happy to comply.

By now, Cliff had also spent a lot of time reviewing the security camera footage he had obtained from the DEQ camera on Tenth Avenue. What he saw there taunted him. He felt sure the black-and-white film held the image and identity of his serial killer. However, the limitations of technology kept him from seeing the face or tracking a license plate. The detective studied the video exhaustively, each time gleaning subtle new details he could add to his file. When he found the person he could place perfectly into what he saw in the small, blurry screen—a certain silvery Camry—he'd know he'd found the killer.

Chapter Nine

I was in an unhealthy relationship. I did it for him.

Clarissa Rowley

In late winter, while Phoenicians are savoring the last days of perfect weather, the very thing that makes the Valley of the Sun a tourism mecca for "snowbirds," Cliff got a call from an unexpected source but not a terribly unfamiliar one, considering his own history in military law enforcement: NCIS, the Naval Criminal Investigative Service, headquartered in Washington, D.C. The Naval Criminal Investigative Service declares:

> *NCIS is responsible for investigating a variety of high-impact felonies, including crimes such as rape, child physical and sexual abuse, burglary, robbery, the theft of government and personal property, and homicide. NCIS' Cold Case Homicide Unit deals exclusively with unresolved homicides, playing a key role in the resolution of 50 cases since its inception in 1995.*
>
> *Combating drug use among members of the Navy and Marine Corps is also a priority for NCIS. Special agents use relevant intelligence to stop illegal drugs at their source and to intercept drugs already on the street.*

It seems that, once in a while, marines do other things "on the street" besides drugs. When Cliff Jewell picked up the phone to find the storied naval unit on the other end of the line, he learned that the navy was seeking to turf out a lance corporal for, unbelievably, prostitution.

Thirty-five or so miles west of Baghdad is a former Saddam Hussein airfield seized by the United States and renamed Camp Ridgeway. While weapons of mass destruction have never been found in Iraq, the former dictator himself was found buried deep beneath the Mesopotamian sand, and at Camp Ridgeway, Russian MiGs and Iraqi fighter jets were found similarly hidden under the desert.

It was one of then Secretary of Defense Donald Rumsfeld's more memorable announcements. From his August 5, 2003, press briefing: "Something as big as an airplane that's within a stone's throw of where you're functioning, and you don't know it's there because you don't run around digging into everything on a discovery process. So until you find somebody who tells you where to look, or until nature clears some sand away and exposes something over time, we're simply not going to know."

When they cleared away the sand at Camp Ridgeway, they found several of the MiG-25s and Su-25s. There's a lot of sand there. As the former secretary of defense pointed out, who's to say that they have found them all.

By 2004 the strategies in Iraq were changing and Camp Ridgeway was rechristened Camp Taqaddum to put a local stamp on it.

It became one of the largest bases in Iraq, serving as a hub for military based anywhere in Anwar Province. Soldiers at "TQ," as it is now widely known through its military abbreviation, have amenities envied in smaller outposts—hot showers, real toilets, a PX.

And by 2005, a young girl from Topeka, Kansas, was working the food detail at Camp Taqaddum. Lance Corporal Clarissa Rowley had the blue-eyed blond look that could easily be found in corn-fed Kansas but would stand out anywhere off base in Iraq.

There might be "amenities" at TQ, but there was no way to forget this was the middle of a war zone, a dangerous place, a place where even the simple-looking sand could hold hidden perils as formidable as enemy fighter jets. The soldiers would have been glad for any chance to shake off the unceasing tension of their circumstances. For the young soldier from Topeka, a brief moment on stage, a chance to announce real entertainers, would have been a chance to feel the love of an audience that any performer can tell you about, a chance to be the hero, even for a few seconds. Lance Corporal Clarissa Rowley of the Third Marine Aircraft Wing got that chance in March 2005.

"On behalf of the United Services Organization and Armed Forces Entertainment, would you please put your hands to-gether," she told the crowd at TQ and then introduced a USO comedy tour.

One year earlier, Clarissa had been stationed in Japan. Barely out of her teens, she had an opportunity there, as well, to offer her cheerful service, and the navy was, once again, happy to showcase her, using her as an interview subject for a feel-good piece in the base newspaper, the *Torii Teller*. The article was about marines stepping up to help the planet on Earth Day.

Private Clarissa Rowley, a food specialist, said, "I am very happy to be here today. Cleaning up is something that helps out the environment."

The article is dated May 21, 2004. Rowley and fellow soldiers were volunteering. The article describes them as "cleaning up the sea wall," which apparently had become littered with debris and trash.

"Since we are ambassadors of the United States," Clarissa continues in the *Torii Teller*, "it is nice to show everyone that we also care. Also when Marines see this maybe it will make them also want to help out."

With the attention the U.S. Marines didn't mind tossing her way, Clarissa, having been duly promoted by the time she played emcee to a comedy show for soldiers at TQ in Iraq, seemed to have a future either in the marines or beyond.

Sometime in 2005, the Kansan got transferred out of Iraq and returned stateside. Clarissa was now based at the Yuma Proving Grounds, a good three-hour drive from Phoenix.

Which is apparently not too far of a ride to work the streets.

Not as a marine, not as an environmentalist, not as a food specialist or an emcee.

Clarissa Rowley was inexplicably journeying off the base to turn tricks.

In the aftermath of December 29, 2005, Cliff Jewell had heard about a young woman named "Clarissa Stevens" who'd been shot the same night some six miles or more from his own crime scene. She had survived the attack, and in the incident report that fell into Cliff's hands, she gave some tantalizing details. Cliff very much wanted to talk to her, but she was impossible to find. After she left the hospital, well before Cliff heard of her, she seemed to have vanished. He could not find even a trace of her.

Which is usually the point, when a person gives a false name.

Clarissa had been shot on East Van Buren Road, one of the most infamous stretches of Phoenix, probably the most infamous. Local teasing in the Phoenix area regularly uses a punch line something like "Where'd you get that, Van Buren?" In the wee hours along those blocks any female might be taken for a lady of the night. But Clarissa was a white girl, and the particular block where she was attacked was known as the turf of a pimp who ran black prostitutes. With her soldier day job, Clarissa might easily have avoided acquiring too much of the working girl "look." Needing to hide the incident from the marines and make it all go away as quickly as possible, she told police that she just happened to be on the sidewalk en route to a convenience store. It sounded plausible and she was a victim of a serious crime anyway, not someone they were looking to arrest. The police had no reason to hold her, but when they tried to follow up on her shooting, none of her contact information panned out.

And Cliff Jewell couldn't find her either, when he saw her report and suspected she might be part of something very big.

No one at Phoenix PD ever suspected that the girl shot on that ratty section of Van Buren was a soldier, an Iraq veteran, a U.S. Marine.

But eventually, in early 2006, NCIS caught up with their streetwalking lance corporal and started building a case to toss her out of the few and the proud. They called Phoenix PD wanting to know more about what happened on that December 29 night, because they had a pretty good idea what she was doing on Van Buren.

Now Cliff knew her real name and where to find her. Don't discharge her from the military, Cliff begged. He needed to know where to find her; there was a much bigger case going on and he needed her help. NCIS agreed to cooperate, and this time Clarissa Rowley, using her real name, not "Stevens," made the drive up from Yuma under NCIS escort for a chat with one Detective Cliff Jewell.

———————

Twenty-one-year-old Clarissa was now cooperating. She admitted to the tall investigator that she had been working the street that night. She went further and confessed that she was working two rival pimps, without the knowledge of either. "Do you think one figured it out and punished you?" Cliff asked. But Clarissa was sure they didn't know about each other.

Cliff thought Clarissa was playing a very dangerous game, but he agreed that the attack was unlikely to be from an enraged pimp. In his experience, an angry pimp gives the girl a very up-close-and-personal beating. An anonymous shotgun blast would accomplish little in a pimp's eyes.

Clarissa herself thought it might have been a "john." She had noticed the vehicle slowing down and had thought at first that her next "appointment" was lining up. But the car passed her by, and she saw it turn down a side street, then return up the same street back to Van Buren.

She watched it turn down Van Buren ahead of her, then do another U-turn to return to her yet again. She thought she'd have a new trick for sure. The car approached her, and as it drew near, it pulled in to the center lane, closer to her. She looked up, ready to smile and negotiate.

But if it was Clarissa the prostitute who looked up at the vehicle, it was Clarissa the Iraq veteran who saw the barrel of a shotgun rising up in the driver's side window. Her soldier training told her to take evasive action, and she held up her hands to shield her face, just in time for a shower of pellets to embed in her fingers and palms rather than in her eyes and mouth.

Clarissa's ordeal occurred half a dozen miles away from Detective Jewell's main crime scene, and as many more away from where Marcia Wilson's dog had been shot. The men at Ninth and Woodland had all taken .22 bullets. Clarissa and Cherokee took shotgun blasts.

"I made a copy of her report and put it in with my stuff," Detective Jewell says. "Even though others were seeing differences, the way she described it all, to me it seemed very much like my other cases."

Cliff felt, even with the change of guns, the wide spread of locales and the difference in type of victim, that Clarissa and the others all belonged together.

Chapter Ten

Sammy Gets a Job

Word spread that a Phoenix detective was looking for animal shootings. He didn't get too many from the Phoenix metroplex, but further reaches of the state began calling him. None of these leads went anywhere, but he spent a lot of time driving to Safford, Yuma and other far points of the state. The cases were sad, but Cliff mostly didn't feel they belonged. And they were very far afield geographically.

"While I was running around on all these animal cases, *America's Most Wanted* called me," Cliff explains. "I don't know how the case came to their attention, but I was interested to see if we could get some results. Unfortunately, some mistakes were made that I will regret the rest of my life.

"I was sitting there in the studio in Maryland watching the show live when a twenty-two-caliber rifle came on screen.

"They didn't tell me they were going to do that. I specifically asked them not to do that. 'Oh no!' I thought, 'now he's going to change guns, he's going to change caliber.'"

The show aired April 15, 2006.

On April 19, 2006, *America's Most Wanted* host John Walsh had appeared on *Larry King Live*, where the pair discussed the Serial Shooter case.

King: *We'll be right back with an amazing case from Phoenix.*

Announcer: *Phoenix has been in someone's crosshairs for months. Investigators believe they can connect as many as nineteen shootings of people and animals starting in the summer of 2005. If you know anything about these mysterious shootings in Phoenix, please call our hotline right now.*

King and Walsh spent several minutes bemoaning the nature of the news cycle and how the Phoenix case deserved much more national airtime. To his credit, John Walsh did give the case that big national platform, but he also started talking about a weapon that Cliff Jewell was not looking for.

Walsh: *There's been nineteen shootings, two people—the shooter shot two homeless guys, murdered them. Shot an innocent citizen right through the neck who survived. He shot five horses, he shot dogs. And they think he's got this bizarre survival gun. And this is a good tip for your viewers. It's a gun that shoots shotgun shells and it shoots twenty-two shells. So it's a very unique gun.*

Cliff Jewell found himself in the odd position of calling TV producers. He needed a retraction, he told them, he needed people looking for the right person and he really, really did *not* want the type of weapon talked about.

But he had a sinking feeling it was already too late. *The killer's changing weapons right now*, Cliff kept thinking. *He saw that show and he's making a change.*

During that spring Cliff also discovered that one of the reasons he was getting so few responses on his call for animal shootings was an issue of administrative codes. It turned out that most animal shootings were entered into the system as 651s, criminal damage. So when he asked for "animal shootings," hardly any were showing up, because hardly any were entered as such.

———

While Cliff was driving all over Arizona and giving seminars at other police stations, Sam Dieteman and Jeff Hausner, rooming together alongside Celeste Vance and young Travis, just off

Camelback on the Westside, were busier than either one of them had been in a long time.

The two big men were getting up quite a business in shoplifting together. Sammy got so adept at it, Jeff started bragging about him. "Sammy's as good as you are, sometimes better!" he would say to rib his own little brother, Dale. Even though Jeff was older and much, much bigger, Jeff looked up to Dale. Dale had a job. Dale had glamorous projects. Dale knew people. Dale knew a lot of stuff. And Dale was a hell of a shoplifter, the best he'd ever seen, until now.

Sammy heard a lot about Dale, too. He knew that Dale was the fence and the source of cash in exchange for the stolen goods he and Jeff lifted.

Sam settled right into Jeff's life and often tagged along with him to visit his elderly parents. In fact, it was often Sam who did the driving when they went. Jeff had an Oldsmobile, but it was Sam who would take the wheel during the visits to the old folks. Jeff, it seems, had panic attacks if he tried to drive while sober.* So Sam was a very convenient chauffeur to have around.

As for Sam's perspective, he was a stranger to his own father all the way back in Minnesota. His father had that other family, anyway. His mother had kicked Sam out of her house in Glendale. None of them needed him. His own little girls were back in Minnesota, too. So Sammy was fine going to visit Jeff's elderly parents in their Central Phoenix retirement medium-rise, on the south end of a park called Los Olivos. One day, on their way into the retirement apartments, they met Jeff's little brother, Dale, who was on his way out.

At long last, Sammy and Dale were introduced face-to-face.

"So you're the guy who's supposed to be so good," Dale chuckled.

Sam and Dale hit if off just fine. Dale wanted to see how good Sam was and began going out with him to Wal-Mart, Fry's, Sam's Club and their favorite, Costco. They believed Costco had the worst security. Sam admired Dale's cleverness and his systemization. Dale always bought something through the legitimate checkout and paid for it. And he even had specific orders to fill. Every night, at least two of the three men, sometimes all

---

*Court testimony.

three, would go out to eat and then go to "work." That is, shop-lifting. Liquor, particularly high-end specialty liquors, and CDs and DVDs were their mainstays. At the end of the night, Dale would peel off cash bills for his brother and for Sammy, always paying in advance, then load up the night's haul into his own car for resale to his customers.

The night's "work" was always done in either Dale's car or Jeff's—Sammy didn't have one. In fact, Jeff didn't actually have one, either. The Oldsmobile, like the apartment on West Camel-back, belonged to Celeste Vance.

———

Sometime that spring, Sammy ran into his old friend Ron Hor-ton. Ron was pleased to see Sammy looking more chipper than he'd last seen him, during his depression months of 2005. "Got a new friend," Sammy told him. "A guy who gave me a job."

Well, that certainly was good news, Ron congratulated him. Working a job was a very good thing for a man. He hoped Sam's new job was the right one, one that lasted longer than bartender or electrician had. Later, Ron ran into him again and the two sat down for a meal. This time Sammy was in a foul mood. He couldn't get along with his roommate's girlfriend. He didn't want to go home. Ron watched Sammy take some text mes-sages. Soon a man Ron had never seen before walked into the Rib Shop and came over to their table. Sammy seemed very glad to see him and eager to talk to him about the situation with his roommate and girlfriend, and promptly left with him. The man who picked up Sammy had struck Ron as a little odd.

Later that night Ron received a text message from Sammy. He said he was mad as hell and somebody was "going to get hurt."

Ron already knew his sometime houseguest was angry, but he didn't understand what he meant about someone getting hurt. He decided not to pay attention to it. Sammy could talk funny sometimes.

Chapter Eleven

It was a young woman, crawling into the street.

Daniel Brown

The northeast quadrant of the Phoenix metroplex is dominated by the wealthy, world-renowned town of Scottsdale. Scottsdale is the home of the Hayden Parkway, a miles-long, beautified greenbelt. Originally planned for flood abatement, the parkway was upgraded to a suburban playground where young moms with hundred-dollar manicures push kids on swings, retired millionaires compete in tiny races with radio-controlled miniature yachts, and still more millionaires arrive every February to take the field in MLB spring training.

When a world-class horse facility went bankrupt, the city of Scottsdale stepped in and purchased it. Now Scottsdale may be one of the only cities to offer a massive equestrian venue as a city amenity, a hundred-acre facility where the Scottsdale Arabian Show is held every year. The show is an event that features exhibitions ranging from old-fashioned fire wagons pulled by massive Percherons, to thoroughbred trotting events, to, of course, a parade of fully costumed Arabian horses, their bright robes flowing and silver medallions sparkling in their manes.

Scottsdale lives on tourists and millionaires, and therefore absolutely requires fine dining. Up on Scottsdale Road at Greenway is one of these restaurants, a freestanding and lovely building named Barcelona. It's a place where the grouper comes crab-encrusted and the broccoli comes with almond butter—à la carte.

Tuesday, May 2, 2006, was supposed to have been Claudia Gutierrez-Cruz's day off at Barcelona. Claudia, who had just turned twenty—her birthday was that week—had made her way up from Mexico shortly before Christmas and was working hard, sharing expenses and sending money home. She worked day shift at Inza Coffee, a Colombian bistro and coffeehouse even farther north in Scottsdale. She'd paid a coyote—an evil breed of human trafficker who escorts Latin Americans on a death-defying foot journey across hundreds of miles of open desert in order to avoid customs—nearly $2,000 for the chance to work two jobs back-to-back as a glass stacker. Claudia's days at Inza and nights at Barcelona kept her so busy she didn't even have time to go to church. She rarely saw her boyfriend, Felipe, whom she had known back home in Puebla, Mexico, before they got romantic here in Arizona. They were starting to talk about marriage. He had come to her birthday party on Sunday night, of course. Everyone was working during the week so they'd had to celebrate it early. Other than that, she mostly saw him when he'd pick her up from work.

Just about three weeks before, a hundred thousand—some estimates ranged up to two hundred thousand—Latinos had marched on Arizona's state capitol in support of immigration reform. It was the largest such march in the West, during a spring that saw a wave of grassroots immigration demonstrations across the nation. During that April 11 march, which Phoenix police called "unusually peaceful," Latino leaders called for a work stoppage on Monday, May 1, to show the country what a contribution their labor made to the U.S. economy.

Claudia hadn't been in this country long enough to develop opinions about such things. She'd only just paid off that coyote. She was here for one thing: to work. She was sending money home and recently she'd been talking to her sister, Adriana, about a Mother's Day gift for their mom back in Puebla, Mexico. Both sisters worked at Barcelona, though Adriana's second job was at Chipotle. Claudia did not march on April 11, and on May 1, a Monday, she did not avoid work.

But Tuesdays were Claudia's day off, at least at Barcelona. She worked her regular shift at Inza in the daytime that Tuesday.

She could have this evening to rest, maybe see Felipe. But late in the afternoon she got a call: please come into Barcelona tonight. It seemed work had backed up with so many participating in the Monday strike, which Claudia had stayed out of. Claudia didn't hesitate. She went to work.

Adriana was still working her day shift at Barcelona when Claudia arrived. Her sister was surprised to see her. "They called me in," she said, and promptly got to work.

Claudia was well liked at Barcelona. Her boss considered her punctual, courteous, reliable and hardworking. The boys considered her a great practical joker and fun to tease. The girls shared confidences. Everyone knew about her boyfriend, Felipe.

Claudia's normal shift at Barcelona ran all night, getting her out at two or three in the morning. Other shifts ended at the same time, and she could usually rely on getting a ride from someone leaving at the same time. Either that or her sister's boyfriend, Carlos (a close relative of Felipe's), would come to get them both. Felipe himself often came to get her. Claudia didn't like to ride the bus when she could avoid it, because rumors were rampant among her friends, mostly Mexican nationals, that Immigration raided bus stops.

But that Tuesday, Claudia wasn't needed the whole night, it turned out. She was able to clock out early, at 7:44 p.m. No one else was leaving at this time. It was the middle of a shift. Earlier in the afternoon Felipe had mentioned car troubles, so she knew he couldn't come for her. Claudia had no choice but to take the bus.

She climbed aboard at 8:05 p.m. and rode along as it headed straight south. She pulled the cable at Thomas Road. She would transfer on to the westbound Thomas Road bus, which would take her virtually to her doorstep, an apartment she shared with her sister and cousin.

What Claudia didn't know was that the last westbound bus from Scottsdale Road down Thomas had passed that corner just ten minutes before. It's uncertain how long Claudia waited around for a bus that would never come.

But sometime in the night, the pretty dark-haired girl, already worn out from one-and-a-half shifts at two busy restaurants, decided to walk more than three miles to her new American home. Claudia trudged along in the darkness. She was wearing blue jeans and a bulky jacket.

Daniel Brown, a mechanic with dark eyes, a mustache and a deep, calm voice, was on his way home from his girlfriend's. They'd hung out since late afternoon; at 10:30 p.m. it was time to call it a night. His route home was a "straight shot down Thomas." He was driving in the curb lane, north side of the street.

He noticed the car ahead of him, several car lengths farther west, swerve into the left lane, as if to miss an obstruction in the roadway. He couldn't see what it was yet, but he figured he'd better do the same. He looked and saw a shadowy figure, possibly a dog, half on the sidewalk, half in the street. He slowed down. It was very dark. There was no street lamp near the spot.

But as he got closer, he could see it was not an object, not a dog—what was lying in the roadway was a girl, a young woman who was crawling out into the street. If he hadn't seen the first car swerve, he would have struck her. Her feet were in the gutter, her head and arms halfway in the lane.

He rolled down his window, "Are you okay?" he asked.

Daniel knew very little Spanish. But he knew the word she cried out to him.

"*Ayúdame! Ayúdame!*"*

Daniel pulled over. He parked his car between the girl and the oncoming traffic behind him. Maybe his car would get wrecked, but she would be shielded. Two other people pulled over one minute later. These two could speak Spanish. Daniel called 911 while the others talked to Claudia and translated.

In the background of the 911 tape, Claudia's screams of agony can be heard. Nevertheless, she responds lucidly to several questions. She even gives out two phone numbers, begging her rescuers to call her boyfriend and her sister.

The suffering she was experiencing is nearly incomprehensible. This is what Daniel saw when he pulled over and started talking to the girl in the street:

"She was kind of lying on her side. Because I guess she wasn't able to use her legs at all so she, they were, she was kinda dragging them behind her. She was kinda supporting herself on

---

*"Help me! Help me!"

her hands kinda like almost in a bad push-up position with her hip on the ground, kind of on her side. And you know, she was kinda waving me down with one hand calling me to help out."

Claudia was crawling out into the street and trying to wave people down and speaking clearly. At first Daniel couldn't tell what was wrong with her because it was dark and he didn't see blood. But as his eyes adjusted and he looked closer, he understood:

"It was on her, her left side. . . . She had a bunch of, um, looked like organs or something spilling out the left side of her body."

Daniel didn't try to apply pressure because he couldn't see much blood. The injuries were so severe he feared any attempt he made at first aid would further harm the screaming girl.

"*Mi estómago!*" she cried again and again. "*No aguanto mi estómago!*"*

The 911 transcript (translated by Scottsdale PD) shows a Claudia quite conscious, desperate for her loved ones. She knows she's been shot, but she can't describe a suspect:

Operator: *Hello, this the Fire Department.*

(Claudia during the next couple of minutes is heard in the background yelling in agony.)

Claudia: (in Spanish) *Call my sister!*

Daniel: *She's not doing too well, she doesn't speak English.*

(Spanish speaker leans in to Claudia.)

Spanish Speaker: *What's wrong, what's wrong?*

Claudia: *I was shot!*

Daniel: *She got shot, she got shot?*

Operator: *She got shot? Do we know by whom?*

Claudia: *Ohhh* (moans). *Call my sister.*

Spanish Speaker: *Who shot you?*

Claudia: *I didn't see who did it.*

---

*"My stomach! My stomach! I can't take it!"

Spanish Speaker: *Where? Where?*

Claudia: *Here.*

Spanish Speaker: *Who shot you?*

Claudia: *I didn't see who did it.*

Spanish Speaker: *Where did they come from?*

Claudia: (moans) *Call my sister.*

Spanish Speaker: *Okay, give me the number?*

Claudia: (gives number) *I can't stand the pain!*

Spanish Speaker: *Hold on a little longer, they are coming! Don't move!*

Claudia: *I can't, I can't, I'm thirsty, I'm thirsty.*

Daniel: *Here they come, here they come.*

Claudia: (crying in agony)

(Police arrive. Lots of voices in the background.)

(End of 911 call.)

Felipe was already asleep when his roommate came rushing in and woke him up. "Claudia's been shot! We have to go! Get up! We have to go! Claudia's been shot!"

"What? How do you know this? What are you talking about?"

"A guy just called me, we have to go!"

"Who called you?"

"I don't know! Some guy! He said he was there with her!"

All the roommates, three young men, jumped into a car and headed for what they'd been told by a stranger was the location of Felipe's mysteriously injured girlfriend.

Carlos was just finishing up work. He started on his way to Adriana's. He saw his girlfriend a lot more often than Felipe saw his. Pretty much every day. He also saw that sweet little sister of hers probably more often than Felipe did. She was a very nice girl. Everybody loved her, and he knew Adriana loved her to pieces. Those sisters were very close. Well, he and Adriana were pretty close, too. Between the two of them, they only had one cell phone. Tonight he was using it. It was around ten thirty, probably a little bit later, when Carlos started to make his way to the girls' place. As he headed down Thomas Road, though, he saw flashing red and blue lights and orange traffic cones. The street was blocked off up ahead. Some kind of police mess. Looked like a pretty big deal. He turned south on to the detour, along with the rest of the diverted cars.

As he stepped through the door to Adriana's, his phone rang, the phone that was also considered Adriana's.

He couldn't believe what he was hearing. Some strangers on the phone told him something terrible about little Claudia. He rushed to the back of the apartment to wake up Adriana, and together they frantically left to find out whatever was happening to Claudia.

When officers arrived on the scene, they found pools of blood up on the grass berm that separated the grocery store parking lot from the sidewalk. Claudia was rushed to Scottsdale Memorial Hospital. The witnesses were separated and interviewed. Bits of Claudia's flesh strewn on the scene were found and recorded by several officers. The scene was so horrific, all were somber. All had arrived with sirens blaring. All noted in their reports the internal organs that were spilling out of her.

It was unclear to many of the officers on the scene what had happened to the young woman. Several assumed it was a hit-and-run. Others thought it was a stabbing. It wasn't until doctors received the young girl at the hospital that the nature of her injury became clear. Surgeons discovered pellets throughout her torso. Claudia had been shot with a shotgun.

The blast was so violent, surgeons estimated that the gun had been fired from no more than six feet away from her.

Birdshot or other grade pellets are packed into a shell with a wad or cup at the end. The gunpowder is behind the cup, pushing all the pellets out together. Shortly after leaving the barrel of the gun, the pellets continue on the ballistic trajectory, but the much larger and heavier cup will normally fall to the ground some distance from the target.

During surgery, as doctors struggled to organize the jumble that had become of the insides of Claudia, they came across and removed the shotgun wad from her body.

Claudia, a dedicated hard worker to the last moment of her life, as she pulled her dead legs and open viscera to the roadway, never had a chance.

Her loved ones were gathered in the lobby, all confused and frightened, none speaking much English. Sometime after midnight, Claudia's suffering ended. The work of Detective Pete Salazar now began:

"I next contacted SHC-Osborn* to assist with the notifying Adriana of Claudia's death. Due to the language barrier, SHC-Osborn had a translator do the notification. After they told Adriana that Claudia had died, Adriana dropped to the floor and began crying hysterically. Also present was Felipe and Carlos. Carlos was Adriana's boyfriend who had come with her to SHC-Osborn. Felipe and Carlos were also crying and appeared to be in disbelief of what occurred."

It would be a very, very long night.

Off to the east of the Phoenix metroplex, past Mesa, past Gilbert, even past Apache Junction, past where the desert takes over and the cacophony of city life recedes into the horizon, is a small town that never quite leapt out of the Old West. A place with a saloon, a hot bath, and a smile with a price tag on it for miners and ranch hands who lived at the northern edge of the Gadsden Purchase, the town of Florence sprang up along a crook of the Gila River in the eighteenth century.

Its people have always been a collection of miners, soldiers, explorers, Pimas, Apaches, and Mexicans fleeing revolution. Many of their descendants make up the population of the town today. In 1907, as the mines and ranches were staring hard at the twentieth century, the town got a welcome new industry as prisoners from the famous Old West Yuma Territorial Prison, featured so often for later generations in movie and television scripts, were shipped up to Florence to build themselves a new

---

*Scottsdale Healthcare-Osborn, the hospital to which Claudia had been transported.

prison. By 1909, all the modern Florence prison buildings were finished and the last inmate from Yuma had transferred in, leaving the old complex to the state parks department and the set designers from Hollywood.

By the turn of the next century, the word "Florence" had become synonymous with "prison" in the state of Arizona. Even prisoners of war were housed here, mostly Germans and Italians from the Africa campaign, during World War Two. The complex of incarceration buildings at the town has grown into at least nine different prisons—from federal to county—and employs just about everybody in town. "In that town we all make our way into law enforcement and we have two options: inside the walls or outside them," says Pete Salazar III, a Florence native and descendant of those Old West characters.

Salazar's dad spent twenty-six years with the Federal Bureau of Prisons. Young Pete remembers the lessons well. "Dad always said you have to treat [prisoners] with respect. We are there with authority to take away their freedom, but no right to take away their dignity. He was tough, but he always held that standard. When [Dad's] mother died in 1988, the prisoners on his block got together and sent flowers."

Public service in the Salazar family started at least a generation earlier, when Pete's grandfather—Pete Salazar I—performed such dedicated feats of maintenance and utilities for the town that they ended up naming a road for him. Salazar Road is the street that leads out to the cemetery.

The roadwork man's son, Lieutenant Colonel Pete Salazar of the Federal Bureau of Prisons, did not live long enough to see his own son graduate from the University of Arizona with a degree in Criminal Justice, or to see him end up playing a key role in the "case of a lifetime," as Scottsdale police detective Pete Salazar sat face-to-face with a serial killer and gained the confession that almost slipped away.

Young Pete had had a hard time gaining traction in the hometown industry. As a young graduate of UA, he put in his application for U.S. marshal just as Congress failed to pass a budget and all federal agencies went into deadlock, including the closing of national parks and hiring freezes everywhere else. Pete got hired at one of the prisons in Florence as a recreation director for the inmates. But no sooner had he signed the personnel paperwork than a prison riot led to a six-month lockdown. Young

Pete showed up to work in rec shorts . . . and did nothing. Frustrated at being shut out of real law enforcement yet again, he went on the rounds of filling out applications for Phoenix-area police departments. Others on the circuit warned him not to bother with Scottsdale PD; the tests were too hard and the chances too long. But after he got locked out of the physical fitness exam at Mesa PD by getting lost and showing up ten minutes late, the scion of Florence thought he had nothing left to lose. He pulled a wrinkled Scottsdale PD application out of his bag, filled it with blue ink cross-overs and Wite-Out and dropped it off. He was shocked when he got a call back in two days. In the winter of 1995, Pete Salazar entered the Arizona state police academy as a Scottsdale PD recruit.

After several years on patrol, Pete Salazar finally moved into the desk job he had always wanted. He became a detective on property crimes. During this time he cracked a case where suspects were stealing cell phones by the hundred. In April 2003, he transferred into Violent Crimes. His first case on his first day was a five-bullet homicide where one neighbor shot another over a barking dog. By the end of the day the suspect had jumped off of Camelback Mountain, and his body, murder weapon nearby, was found by officers, including Salazar, in full protective gear anticipating a shoot-out.

It was here that Salazar found his life's work. "There's no reason people should hurt each other. It angers me. Just do what we learned in kindergarten, 'keep your hands to yourself.'"

On May 2, 2006, thirty-seven-year-old Pete Salazar was at home, for once, with his wife and three young children. Around midnight he was in bed with his wife when he got a call to come in: someone had just died; the detective on duty had never handled a homicide as case agent before, and he needed help. In the family tradition of public service, Pete Salazar drove on in to Scottsdale Memorial Hospital as case agent.

Throughout the night interviews were conducted with witnesses, 911 callers, family members, surgeons . . . and by the time morning broke, Pete Salazar felt they had nothing. Absolutely nothing.

Phoenix detective Cliff Jewell had been very frustrated over the spring months. He had doggedly gone to every animal incident either the Humane Society or the Agriculture Department had told him about. He had spent some interesting time with Lance Corporal Clarissa Rowley and NCIS. He had been off to Maryland at the *America's Most Wanted* studios and scolded producers who wantonly aired information about a .22. His case was not getting solved, and he was very, very worried that his killer would change weapons now, after that broadcast.

On Wednesday, May 3, he was driving in to work with the car radio on. The news came on at the top of the hour. He heard a local story about a young woman shot on Thomas Road in Scottsdale. Cliff's stomach lurched. His killer was back. The quiet time was over.

Cliff went to his supervisor and said, "I need to meet with Scottsdale; this is one of mine."

In Scottsdale at that time, Detective Salazar and other investigators, including Detective Hugh Lockerby, were interviewing Adriana, Carlos, Felipe, Daniel Brown, all the witnesses, and all of Claudia's friends. They were contacting and interviewing all her coworkers. They were looking for someone named Carmen, the last name in her phone history. The fact that they couldn't find Carmen, and that her phone had already been disconnected, seemed sinister. The investigators were very interested in the coyotes who brought Adriana and Claudia, at different times, across the Arizona desert. Were the coyotes paid? the police asked over and over. Did Claudia owe the coyotes any money? No, Adriana replied through interpreters. They were paid off a long time ago. They hadn't seen anything of them since they got here.

Every person they found, investigators interrogated about Felipe. Was he violent? Was he jealous? Was he ever rough with Claudia? Was he angry with her?

What about Claudia? Were any of these boys at work in love with her? Was she two-timing Felipe?

Was Claudia involved with drugs or alcohol? Did she have enemies?

The answer to the questions over and over was that Claudia was a nice girl, everyone loved her.

"She was an awesome person," said coworker Alfredo, who

was finally given up on as a suspected love rival. "She was always happy."

Investigators even started in on Adriana. What was her relationship like with her little sister? Did they get along? Did Adriana owe money to someone like a coyote?

The family was frightened and grief-stricken and didn't understand the questions.

By Wednesday afternoon, the investigation took a new turn.

Pete Salazar received a phone call from an unexpected source: Phoenix Police Detective Cliff Jewell. Cliff Jewell notified him that he felt suspicious that their shooting on Thomas Road was related to a series of crimes he was investigating in Phoenix as well as on the Westside and in Glendale, Avondale and Tolleson. It was an unusual mix of locales, but so far Salazar and Lockerby were coming up empty on suspects for the murder of Claudia. Everyone around her seemed genuinely shocked. The girl had been well loved, had kept to herself and had even paid off her coyote promptly. The Scottsdale team agreed to a meeting with Jewell set for the next morning. Tolleson's Detective Ron Rock would also attend.

After the Scottsdale meeting, where he met Pete Salazar, Cliff went back to his supervisor and said that he wanted to call the FBI and get a profile. He got the green light.

That was Friday, May 5, 2006, that Detective Jewell called Quantico.

On Monday, May 8, a team of FBI profilers landed in Phoenix.

Cliff was very happy to see them and very gratified by the quick response. He told them everything he knew. He drove them out to Tolsun Farms, the little enclave of horse properties where Buddy and Apache and Sara Moon were shot. He took them to Ninth and Woodland. He took them out to Scottsdale.

In a couple of days, a meeting was scheduled where Detectives Pete Salazar and Hugh Lockerby from Scottsdale, Ron Rock from Tolleson, and Cliff Jewell could all hear what the famed FBI profilers would say about their suspect, the Serial Shooter. Before the meeting was convened, the FBI profilers chatted informally, tossing out their findings, such as that it was a white male, eighteen to twenty-four years old, acting alone, shooting out of both sides of the car. When the detectives in the room who had been treading in the footsteps of these crimes for nearly a year now heard the word "alone," they started shaking their heads. They told the FBI team that they felt there were two of them acting together. They thought that sometimes one shot, and sometimes the other, each from his own side of the car. The four local detectives had come to this conclusion based on the angles of gunfire, traffic patterns and timing and their own collective years of gut instinct. The profilers couldn't agree but said that, in their opinion, it wasn't two people acting together, but two separate people acting alone in two separate series of shootings. The FBI profilers felt the .22 shootings were committed by one perpetrator. They felt the shotgun shootings were committed by someone else. "In our experience," they told the Arizona detectives, "a serial killer does not change weapons in midseries." Cliff thought of the *America's Most Wanted* snafu, and he thought of Clarissa Rowley and the dog Cherokee—two shotgun victims on a night otherwise dominated by .22 victims. He was pretty sure he *did* have a serial killer who switched weapons, sometimes on the same night, and he was afraid he'd never get a chance to seize the .22. He was afraid he'd be seeing more and more of the shotgun pellets.

Detective Salazar remembers the three FBI profilers as very helpful. "They would have conducted a séance for us if we wanted." But what they actually did get from them, "well, those 'profiles' were just the kinda notes I already scribbled on a napkin," Salazar says with a shrug.

The meeting with the FBI never did get off the ground. The two sets of law enforcement could see they weren't going to get very far with each other, and the gathering sort of just fizzled out. The FBI flew back to Quantico and Cliff Jewell never saw them again.

But Cliff, Ron, Pete and Hugh started meeting regularly from this point. These four detectives formed the kernel of a group that would ultimately grow to two hundred law enforcement personnel. Ron Rock was the first one to apply the word "random" to the series of shootings that fell under his purview. Cliff Jewell officially connected the Phoenix shootings to the ones on the Westside and took over investigations from other jurisdictions. Pete Salazar and Hugh Lockerby endorsed the word "random," as well as the link between the shotgun and .22, and the connection between animal and human victims. By doing so and including their case, Claudia's shooting, in the pattern, they also extended the reach of the two other detectives—Rock and Jewell—to Scottsdale. From May 5, 2006, on, these four detectives never stopped working together. This was the team that was really convinced there were serial killers on the loose in Phoenix, killers who shot for sport.

Chapter Twelve

I was scared and panicky and frightened.

Kibili Tambadu

On the bulging western tip of Africa is a tiny little country first reached by Europeans some thirty years before Christopher Columbus ever sighted North America. It was a Portuguese ship that first spotted and named this place, calling it in Portuguese the Land of the Lion Mountains, later rendered into Italian as Sierra Leone. Although tiny, the place has had a lasting influence on the United States of America. It was from here that the famous rebel slave Joseph Cinque, Mende name Sengbe Pieh, was kidnapped from his farm by another African and later sold to Europeans and loaded onto the Spanish ship *La Amistad.*

The story was told in the Steven Spielberg film *Amistad*, with a cast of luminaries such as Anthony Hopkins, Matthew McConaughey, Morgan Freeman and, most notably, Djimon Hounsou as the defiant African who secretly loosed his own shackles to overtake the Spanish slavers and ended up in a complicated international case centered in an 1839 Connecticut jail. History records that Cinque galvanized the then disjointed and dispirited abolition movement as he continued to lead and inspire his fellow African captives even after he was separated from them. In court, he used his newly acquired limited English to shout, "Give us free! Give us free!"

A final court victory was achieved by an American founding

father, then seventy-three-year-old iconic former president John Adams, who was opposed in the case by policy and various diplomatic moves by the sitting president, Martin Van Buren. After Adams won the group's freedom both from slavery and from criminal charges, Cinque traveled the United States giving public appearances as quite a nineteenth-century celebrity, raising money for his group's passage back to Sierra Leone.

Cinque's star appeal and the tireless work of the Amistad Committee, comprised of both abolitionists and moderates, to educate and provide for the rebel-slaves-turned-refugees inspired an ongoing movement that led directly to the establishment of Howard and Fisk Universities, Talledega College and many others that are still educating thousands of Americans today.

When Cinque and his freed compatriots returned to Sierra Leone, after his fund-raising star tour in the United States, it was in the city of Freetown that they arrived and where they joined a complex community of native Africans, Europeans and freed or free blacks from London, Canada and the United States. Sierra Leone, with its jewel of a port, Freetown, would be an important cradle of the repatriation movement. A new language sprang up, Krio, a sort of pidgin American English mixed with French and with African languages, which was native to Freetown and spread throughout Sierra Leone as the language of commerce and trade. The history of Sierra Leone, then, is one of missions and reformers, slave trade and slave emancipation, pristine native tribes and colonial overlords.

Unfortunately, by the 1990s, Sierra Leone had become a war-torn country, a cauldron of evil where greed for diamonds was at the bottom of everything, and where children were kidnapped by rebels and turned into pint-sized killing machines while their fathers were kidnapped and enslaved in the diamond mines. These conditions were dramatically portrayed in another Djimon Hounsou film that hit theatres in 2006, *Blood Diamond.* Hounsou's character and his young son live out these devastating scenarios.

One person who knew firsthand how realistic that movie was was seventeen-year-old Kibili Tambadu of Phoenix, who during the civil war was the same age as the young boy in the film. Kibili was only two years old when his own father was slaughtered in front of him, yet somehow his mother successfully fled

Sierra Leone and eventually managed to get him, the baby of the family, as well as her older children into a refugee camp across the border, much like the mother in the film.

After years in the camp, Isatu Kabba, Kibili's mother, must have felt it a dream come true when passage to the United States became possible.

Speaking nothing but Krio, Kibili entered the fourth grade in a Phoenix public school. Through the medium of checkers, at which he became expert, the young boy began to learn English. He won the loyalty and admiration of his teachers as he progressed through the school system, and by the time he was a teenager, his English was indistinguishable from any other American kid's. But the family's ties to Africa were strong. Although Kibili wore shirts and sneakers like his schoolmates, his mother still wore African scarf headdresses and brightly printed sari-style African gowns. Their friends in Phoenix included Sierra Leoneans they had lived next to for years in the same refugee camp in Gambia as well as other Sierra Leoneans they had met here in Phoenix. Mrs. Kabba worked hard as a caregiver at a nursing home, and her children also all worked hard at learning English and doing their school lessons and pursuing individual professional goals as they matured.

When he came of age, Kibili also went out to work. He was a big boy with a baby face and wide open eyes. By the time he was a teenager, Kibili Tambadu, survivor of Sierra Leone's diamond wars, had gotten himself a job at a supremely American company, Burger King. As all the children did, Kibili turned over his earnings to his mother for the family's communal well-being. Mrs. Kabba had good reason to be proud of all her children, right down to the baby, in spite of the nearly unimaginable ordeal they had all been through.

The tragedies of Sierra Leone were well behind them in this land of opportunity, where you could go all day and all night without ever seeing a gun. Kibili had seen his father murdered, but he himself had not been conscripted as a child soldier. Nor had his brothers. This was a place to be grateful, a place to be safe, a place to be calm.

Even with all her children working as well as she herself, no one in the Tambadu/Kabba clan had a car. It was not uncommon for Kibili, a strapping youth, to walk where he wanted to go.

On the night of May 2, 2006, a Tuesday, Kibili was a little

restless and went out for a walk. He walked about two miles from his mother's small apartment. He stopped at Circle K to fill his water bottle, water bottles being ubiquitous in the dehydrating climate of Arizona.

Kibili's thoughts as he turned northward up Forty-fourth Street to head back home were undoubtedly a mix of normal teenage worries about girls and schoolwork, along with the heavier thoughts of his responsibilities at Burger King and his memories of Africa and the absence of the father he had not had a chance to know. Perhaps he was wishing that his father had been able to make it to America with them, to see and feel and experience the country where daily life is not a constant volley of raids and machine-gun fire, where walking down the street is peaceful.

Kibili was alone on the street with his thoughts. There were no other pedestrians near him and no traffic.

He was walking along the sidewalk that fronted a rather nice business park, had just passed signage for "KNXV TV15," when he heard a shot. This surprised and frightened him, so he looked around.

It was during the act of looking around in fear that Kibili saw blood. The blood dripping down was his own, to his astonishment, and now that he saw it, he felt the burning pain. Now he knew the shot had landed on his own body. He had no idea where the shot had come from, but he could now see and feel in the dark where it had landed, a confusingly wide swath of his own body—his arm, his back, his torso. He looked across the tall shrubbery and saw that a hotel was just inside the landscaping. He ran through the signage and the shrubs and the cactus, leaving blood the entire way, and staggered into the lobby of the Hotel Radisson.

It was 10:04 p.m. when dispatch received a 911 call from the Hotel Radisson. The address was Forty-fourth and Van Buren.

Kibili had made it out of the most miserable place on earth only to be attacked with a shotgun in the land of the free, on a street named after the president who had opposed the freeing of the *Amistad* Sierra Leoneans.

On the morning of May 4, Thursday, Phoenix detective Cliff Jewell and Tolleson detective Ron Rock and Scottsdale detectives Pete Salazar and Hugh Lockerby met to compare notes about the shotgun shootings of Claudia Gutierrez-Cruz and Clarissa Rowley, plus the dog Cherokee, and the .22 shootings of David Estrada, Timmy Tordai, Marco Carillo, and Jose Ortiz, as well as those of the animals Apache, Sara Moon, Buddy, Whiskey, Peyton, Martin, Peanut, Irving and Shep. They did not yet know about the other cases that would eventually also fit into what they called this "series."

Pete Salazar already felt his team had exhausted the possibilities on Claudia. No one had a reason to wish this hardworking, well-loved girl harm. Ron Rock had chased leads for a year on the also well-loved but troubled David Estrada. Nothing made any sense. None of the animal shootings could be traced to neighbor disputes or ownership quarrels. And Cliff Jewell, more than anybody, felt that his December 29 series of crimes pointed to what now could only be described as a serial killer, someone who killed for the sport of it. The four detectives from jurisdictions stretching from the far Southwest Valley to the northeast all agreed there was something to it, something random yet connected. They determined to work together from now on, and the first step they took would be to ask for those FBI profilers.

Claudia Gutierrez-Cruz's 911 call had come in shortly after 10:30 p.m.

What none of these four detectives knew that morning was that there was a living victim in a nearby hospital right that minute, his upper body swollen and painful with dozens of bloody little craters, another peaceful pedestrian, who'd been blasted by a shotgun at 10:04 p.m. the same night.

Two miles and twenty-five minutes from Claudia.

When the FBI profilers arrived on Monday, no one told them about Kibili Tambadu. None of these Homicide detectives had yet heard of the boy who had bled from the sidewalk, through the grass, past the cactus and all over the beautiful marbled lobby of the Radisson.

Chapter Thirteen

I was lit up pretty good, I made a great target.

Daryl Davies

In May, spring is threatening to turn into summer, which in Phoenix is a wicked misery. In 2006, Ron Horton was "buffing out." He spent a lot of time lifting weights and working out, but only when it didn't take time away from the boys. He hadn't heard from their mother in a while. That was too bad. The last time she left, he had convinced her to leave the two younger kids with him as well as the oldest one, who was Ron's only biological child. Biology didn't matter to him. He didn't want the boys broken up, and it was clear he was the parent who could provide stability. He doted on all of them equally. Debbie flittered up when she was able, but all the boys always had a home with him; he was in tune with each kid and others would see the all-male family break up into laughter when one of them set off a secret joke by a mere glance at another at a crowded dinner table. Cousins and aunts and uncles would be left wondering what Ron and his boys were laughing about. The closeness they shared was obvious to all.

One day when the boys were all at school, Ron ran into his old friend and houseguest Sam Dieteman at the Rib Shop. Sammy had a new swagger about him, but he also had the same old air of depression, perhaps with a new twist. Down in his cups as the two shared a meal, Sammy was talking not about killing himself this time, but about killing others.

"Do you know what it's like to kill a man?" he asked Ron.

"How would I know?" Ron answered idly, with a sense of mild irritation at such an oddball question.

"I didn't either," Sam rambled on, "until about a month ago."

Ron sopped up some barbecue sauce with a curly fry. He was thinking about his middle son's book report due Monday. Or maybe the little one's soccer practice that afternoon.

He looked up when he realized Sam was full-on crying now. "I didn't know it was a girl! I felt really bad when I realized it was a girl! I wouldn't have shot a girl if I had known! She looked like a man, I thought it was a man."

"What are you talking about?" Ron demanded.

"They'll never catch me, though." Sam turned defiant now. "They'll never catch me."

"Why's that?" Ron humored him. He bit into a succulent rib.

"Four-ten" said Sam.

"Huh?"

"Can't trace a four-ten. They'll never catch me. If you use a shotgun, they can't trace it. Little birdshot, four-hundred-and-ten caliber, them crime labs got nuthin', can't trace it, they can't get me on that."

Ron mentally clucked his tongue. Sam was really losing it. Whatever in the world he was talking about was pure delusion. Sam didn't have a shotgun. Sam was never sober enough to shoot anybody. Sam was just a big teddy bear, playful with the kids, good for a joke. This joke wasn't very funny, Ron didn't get whatever the punch line was supposed to be. He paid the bill for both of them, patted Sammy on the shoulder and wished him well as he walked out of the Rib Shop.

———————

On May 30, 2006, fifty-six-year-old James Hodge stepped out of his little apartment for a cigarette. It was about 11 p.m. and the evening temp was around sixty degrees. Jim lived on Camelback Road, in a sprawling single-story apartment complex that stretched from Eighty-seventh Avenue to Ninetieth. Part of the complex was cut off by an iron gate between parking areas and a concrete wall between buildings. Each apartment opened onto a tiny patio suitable for a hibachi-grilled dinner, a wind chime or an evening smoke. The western edge of the complex gave an Elm Street address to its residents, although Elm was really no more than a private roadway within the complex. Jim's apartment was on the eastern side of the iron gate, and he had an Eighty-ninth Avenue address.

Jim Hodge had a vaguely Santa Claus appearance, with his white beard, white hair and stocky build. However, he was more of a child himself, being under the conservatorship of his sister Marianne, who lived in her own house a little closer in to Phoenix. Like Reggie Remillard, Jim Hodge had served his country in Viet Nam, but Jim was airlifted out when demons invaded his mind. He spent the next thirty years trapped inside the paranoid hallucinations of a schizophrenic who did not always take his medication.

On this evening heading into the Memorial Day weekend, Jim stepped off the confines of his little patio out onto the grass and breathed in the comforting tobacco fumes. He wandered on down the grass in his slippers, to the north end of the building, along Camelback Road.

Moments later neighbors also poured out through their sliding glass doors, responding to two loud noises: a swift firearm blast and then ongoing moans and screams of pain.

The neighbors found the simpleminded Jim Hodge pacing, screaming and streaming with blood. Some called 911, others called his sister Marianne.

Two young men rushed over, one petite, red-haired, bearded and blue-eyed, the other dark-haired, burly and tall, and peppered the suffering Hodge with questions: How are you? What happened? How does it feel?

A nearby patrol car was almost instantaneously on the scene, but it had responded to an Elm Street 911 caller and found itself blocked by the iron gate as it went deeper into the complex. On the other side of the gate, officers saw a bantam-sized red-haired man with a full beard, who waved them in.

"Over here, Officer," the man called out. He pointed north. "There he is right there, hurry! Just hop the fence, he's right there, he's bleeding!" The redhead was very helpful. The officers were grateful for the assistance in the confusing layout of the complex and the frustrating gate blocking their way. Precious time was wasting while they were trapped in the maze; they had a bleeding victim who needed them immediately. As encouraged by the blue-eyed man, Officer John Cusson left his patrol car on the Elm Street side of the iron gate. He hopped over the concrete barrier at a point several feet lower than the gate. The spot had been pointed out to him by the helpful blue-eyed witness. Now on the east side of the barrier, Cusson could see the suffering victim.

On the other side of the barrier the patrol officers could now see "a white male, wearing no shirt, covered in blood." He was pacing up and down and the wounds were to his back. Officer John Cusson wrote more in the report: "I asked the male, later identified as V1* Jim, what happened and he was not able to tell me. Jim continued mumbling and stumbling, as if he was losing his balance."

By now, the patrol officers also had the name of that helpful redheaded man, who enters the record as W1. "I then recontacted W1 Dale," Cusson writes, "and I asked him if he could tell me what happened. Dale stated that while walking around with W2 Samuel looking for his cat, he heard V1 screaming. W1 Dale stated he found V1 standing in front of a condo, covered in blood. Dale asked V1 what had happened but that V1 was unable to tell him. Dale stated that at this time he heard tires squealing in the parking lot, [the same parking lot] where he was able to flag down police. I asked Dale if he knew V1 Jim, he stated no. I asked Dale if he heard gunshots, he stated no. I asked Dale if he observed any suspicious activity in the condominium and he stated no."

By now several of the officers on scene had had contact with the two witnesses who'd waved them over the fence and all understood them to be brothers. Officer Cusson's report continues: "I then contacted W1 Dale's brother W2 Samuel. Samuel stated that he and his brother were looking for Dale's cat at which time they heard screaming. Samuel stated that while in the parking lot they observed V1 Jim walking down a sidewalk, covered in blood. He and his brother both approached Jim and asked him

---

*V1 is the form's lingo for "first victim." V2 is the "second victim." W1 refers to "first witness." W2 to "second witness," etc.

what happened and he was unable to tell them. Samuel stated that at this time they heard tires squealing in the parking lot and his brother observed the police in the parking lot and flagged them down. I asked Samuel if he had heard gunshots in the condominium and he stated no. I asked him if he knew Jim, he stated no. I asked him if he observed any suspicious activity in the condominium, he stated no."

The helpful brothers easily gave police their names and personal information: "Dale Hausner, Race: W, Sex: M, Age: 33, DOB: 1973." Rather ambitiously, Dale's height was entered at "5'10"" and his weight at "170 pounds." He gave an address of "540 W. McKellips" and proudly listed his occupation as "aviation." He was confident of his civic duty: W1 responded "yes" he "will testify."

The name "Dietema, Samuel" appears on the incident report. It's not known how Sam's name got a bit nicked off. Cusson called in his report to a recording device, which was later transcribed by a secretary. The misspelling seems most likely to have been a typo.

W2 gave an accurate age of "30, DOB: 1975, Height: 6'1"" and a possibly flattering weight of 215. His contact info was also accurate, at least for that moment. W2 had no business name or occupation to give the officers, but he did pledge "will testify."

Marianne Thone had already gone to bed when her brother's neighbor called. She sleepily advised her to simply guide him back into his condominium if he was making a disturbance. She had often told the neighbors, "I'm trying to do my best." Marianne did visit her brother three or four times a week. This week she was working on getting him into an assisted living facility. But the neighbor insisted Marianne get in the car and come over right now, "something bad had happened." She wouldn't tell her what.

"When I arrived at the condominiums, I saw all the police vehicles. I immediately started hollering, 'Where's Jimmy?' Two men walked up to me and said, 'We tried to help your brother.' They are the ones who told me he had been shot. Then they kept talking about their cat they were looking for. I tried to be polite, I said, 'I appreciate your trying to help him,' but I wasn't interested in their cat, I was focused on trying to find my brother, but they kept trying to talk to me."

She shook them off and learned that her brother was no longer on the scene, that he'd already been taken away in an ambulance. She headed over to the hospital to join him.

The pair of helpful witnesses, although released by investigators, lingered until the last patrol car was out of sight. It wouldn't do to call attention to their vehicle, a silver Camry which was parked just yards away from the staggering victim. They had not told the officers about it. They had let them believe they were on foot, close to home. As soon as the last black-and-white was good and gone, the smaller man and the burly guy swung themselves over the fence and returned to the apartment where Jeff and Celeste and Travis lived, and Sam bunked. It was an address that happened to be a straight shot up Ninety-first Avenue from Tolsun Farms—where Sara Moon, Apache, another horse and Buddy had been shot the previous summer, almost a year earlier.

After some hours had passed, the two witnesses walked back to the gate—making certain once again that all emergency vehicles were gone—and said good night. It was still well before dawn. The smaller one then hopped the fence and returned to the parked car.

He turned on the ignition and drove the silver Camry away alone into the night.

———————

At 1:38 a.m. Miguel Rodriguez was walking down Indian School Road, one mile south of Camelback. He was right in front of a large sign spelling out the number 7002 at the entrance to an apartment complex, marking its Westside grid address—nineteen blocks farther into Phoenix than Jim Hodge had been. Miguel heard a gun blast, felt pain and staggered down the sidewalk several yards into landscaping gravel, where he collapsed. Several residents heard the shot and called 911. Some heard yelling for help. Inside the apartment complex, resident Ramon Lujan heard the screaming and went outside to find the bleeding man. Emergency responders soon arrived and Rodriguez was found "screaming in agony and pain, fearful, not knowing what to expect."

A gurney was lowered to the ground and Miguel was soon delivered to the care of Dr. John King at Good Samaritan.

While Miguel Rodriguez was still being tended on the gravel at 7200 West Indian School, officers heard another call: yet another shotgun victim, this one back up on Camelback, at the intersection of 8600, just three blocks from the Hodge shooting. Nine-one-one callers reported hearing a shot and seeing a man lying on the ground, screaming.

Daryl Davies, a lean and handsome man, about five-foot-eleven, with close-cropped salt-and-pepper hair, was under doctor's orders to walk as therapy for his chronic back injury. "I preferred to do my walking at night because of the heat," he says. On May 30 he'd had his cane in his right hand and a water bottle in his left as he started out along Camelback Road. "It was my intention to walk to Eighty-third and turn around there and come back home."

But when he entered the intersection at Eighty-sixth, he says, "I heard an extremely loud blast, it felt like I was in a tunnel. It knocked me almost to the other side of the road. Then my knees buckled and I smacked the concrete. I was dazed. All the animals in the neighborhood started barking. I was in excruciating pain. I realized I had to do something to get up, I had to remain calm, I didn't want to pass out. But I found I couldn't get up. I knew I was shot and needed help. I was screaming, but soon my lung was collapsed and I couldn't scream anymore. I was flip-flopping my cane in the air trying to attract attention."

Daryl estimates he lay on the ground for as long as thirty minutes before a homeowner at the end of the street noticed him and called 911. Soon a helicopter spotlight shone down on him from the sky, ambulances arrived, and Dr. King had yet another patient stippled with birdshot, someone else whose internal organs would never, ever function smoothly again.

Daryl was dumbfounded. He could not tell officers who would want to shoot him. He did not have enemies. He did not know anyone who would do such a terrible thing. He was also angry.

Daryl would remain hospitalized for two weeks. He had pellets in all his major organs and his left arm and left leg. Doctors decided not to remove the pellets. "I'm keepin' 'em," he says.

He urged investigators to pursue his attacker and promised his full cooperation.

Several weeks later, six of the evil pellets worked their way out of his skin. He put them carefully inside a pill bottle and called police. "Hey," he said, "you need some evidence? Here it is!"

When Cliff Jewell arrived to work on the morning of May 31, 2006, he immediately took note that three unrelated people had taken shotgun blasts in separate incidents during the night. He got the same shot of adrenaline he'd experienced four weeks earlier on May 3, when he heard about the shooting of Claudia Gutierrez-Cruz on the car radio as he drove into work that morning. *These are mine*, he thought. *This is my guy again. He had a busy, busy night.*

Jewell gathered up copies of the reports of the Hodge, Rodriguez and Davies shootings and set off for the hospital. By now it was midmorning, business hours. Each victim was several hours out from being shot and had received extensive medical care and surgery. When Jewell approached the bedside, each time, a groggy, morphined victim said, "A detective was already here, I already talked to a detective . . ." and drifted off.

Cliff Jewell returned to Phoenix Police Headquarters with a strong desire to talk to one Detective Clark Schwartzkopf.

None of the victims from May 30/31 had died. Although all were suffering, the terrible pellets blistering vital organs throughout each one's torso, trauma surgeon Dr. King was guardedly optimistic about their long-term survival. This series of crimes would be assigned to the Assault unit and Clark Schwartzkopf would be case agent.

Clark Schwartzkopf had not started his career as a law enforcement officer. When he graduated from college in Oregon, he went to work in finance, as an investment counselor. But ever since he was a little boy in Wyoming, he'd had a secret desire to wear a badge. His family had experienced a burglary and his own wallet had been pilfered. Ever since he lost the princely sum of "fifty dollars and change" at the age of eight, Clark Schwartzkopf wanted to put away the bad guys. In his midtwenties he walked away from his finance career and put on a uniform. By May of 2006, he was a veteran of some two decades. He was in the Assault Squad, a detective.

Cliff Jewell approached his colleague with his suspicion that the shotgun shootings of May 30/31 were related to a series of homicides from his own active case files.

"Let's see," said Schwartzkopf.

Cliff told him about the shootings on December 29: Timmy Tordai, Jose Ortiz and Marco Carillo.

"Downtown?" Clark said. "Mine are on the Westside."

"I got some on the Westside, too." Cliff told him about David Estrada and about the horses who had been shot in Tolleson and the dog in Avondale and the dogs in Glendale.

"Animals?" Clark looked skeptical.

"Well I've got some dogs on December 29, too." Cliff urged his colleague to consider the connections.

"But yours are twenty-twos?" Clark Schwartzkopf thought the ballistic variations were troubling. His assault victims were peppered with birdshot. He couldn't draw a connection to animal shootings.

"Sorry, Cliff, I just don't see it."

Detective Jewell told him about the shotgun homicide in Scottsdale. Now that incident, the unexplained murder of young restaurant worker Claudia Gutierrez-Cruz, did interest Detective Schwartzkopf, and he resolved to interface with the name Jewell gave him, Scottsdale case agent Pete Salazar. As a member of the Assault Squad, Clark had been briefed about a month ago on the shooting of a teenage boy, one Kibili Tambadu, but so many weeks later it wasn't something that came to mind, even when the date May 2 came up.

Clark Schwartzkopf appreciated the input of Homicide detective Cliff Jewell, but he was now ready to focus exclusively on the shotgun victims.

Cliff Jewell's thirty years of experience told him to keep at it. The blond investigator with the short ring finger doggedly kept abreast of the shotgun investigations—minus Kibili Tambadu, whom no one had yet mentioned to him—and continued to hammer his colleagues on the connections to his .22 shootings and the dogs and horses he had in his files. No one saw the connections but Cliff, but professional courtesy dictated he could attend the shotgun investigation confabs, if he could manage to figure out when they were meeting. Cliff went his own direction, continuing to cull through Humane Society leads on animal shootings, interviewing anyone he could find and reviewing that piece of videotape with the silver Camry in it over and over again.

Chapter Fourteen

If this has to happen, please, let it be quick.

Paul Patrick

Forty-five-year-old Paul Patrick was a dark-haired man with Irish good looks, a mustache and the muscles that come from working in the stocking section of a large grocery chain. He'd grown up in Phoenix and lived there most of his life. He had a grandfather who was a Baptist minister and remembered a childhood spent listening to his sermons. On his left forearm he proudly wore a tattoo signifying his time in the U.S. Army, having served as a medic for four years. Now he ran crews in the warehousing and distribution of groceries for Fry's, work that he loved. He was happy to be in a position to take care of his mother, who had just returned home that day after a stay in the hospital. His sister, Ruth, also lived with him and their mother in a house on the Westside of Phoenix.

Completing the family unit were two little dogs acquired as puppies from a cop. Playing off that fact, Paul had named the male Fella Nee and the female, Misty Meanor. The names made Paul laugh. Misty would go along with him when he jogged. Paul also had a girlfriend and a healthy love of baseball, and in June 2006, he was generally enjoying life, especially his job. "If you love your job, you'll never work a day in your life. Dad always taught me," he says. "Dad was really right."

For the last few weeks, Paul Patrick had been following the

case of the Serial Shooter closely. Like most of the rest of Phoenix, he had altered his habits, trying to keep out of harm's way. But June 8, 2006, was the last day before payday and he was out of smokes. He felt the tension familiar to many people on that last day, when the wallet feels thinnest. Even his beloved Diamondbacks had lost that day, to the Mets. Craig Counsell hit a double in the ninth inning, but it wasn't enough to come back, leaving the home team with an embarrassing final score of 7–1. Late in the evening that frustrating Thursday, Paul wanted a drag on a cigarette, but on a par with everything else that day, he found he was out. He thought he'd just go buy one pack with that last five spot in his pocket. He headed for the door several times. Each time, he turned back, remembering the danger on Phoenix streets after dark. The words "Serial Shooter" ricocheted around in his head. But the nicotine craving would rise and he'd step toward the door again, telling himself, as every human does, *It won't happen to me.* If he'd known what was going on at two Wal-Marts on his side of town that evening, he might have chosen to tough out the cravings, after all.

———————

Thursday night, at Camelback and Ninety-fifth Avenue, roughly one mile west and one mile north of the Patrick home, the world's largest retailer was open for business. This Wal-Mart Supercenter offered a full grocery, a pharmacy, clothing, bicycles, kitchen appliances—well, everything, right on down to houseplants, both real and artificial.

Customers strolled up long aisles, searching for the best bargains, grabbing up sale items and nabbing that certain object that couldn't wait for morning. But at 9:30 p.m., before Paul Patrick even felt his first nicotine craving, mayhem broke out at Wal-Mart. Smoke filled the building, sprinklers doused both merchandise and people, customers scrambled to flee, and employees tried to mobilize. Many cell phones were whipped out during the chaos. The 911 center was inundated with calls.

Emergency vehicles arrived. Smoke was visible from the street. More than 120 coughing and confused people clustered around fire trucks. Paramedics set up triage. Some people were transported to hospitals; some were treated at the scene. Even police and rescuers were unable to keep count; the official report simply states, "It is unknown how many victims were treated and released."

Unbelievably, at 10:15, a mere forty-five minutes later, the next Wal-Mart over, about eight miles away, also generated a flood of 911 calls. The scene was eerily identical—some seventy-five customers and employees fleeing, smoke rising, sprinklers spraying, victims going through triage, some to be hospitalized, others treated at the scene.

Mike Blair, a fire investigator from Glendale Fire, arrived at the first Wal-Mart at 10:25 p.m., still unaware that the second Wal-Mart was burning. Mike sifted through the soggy, sooty mess. He made his way to the back and stopped in the silk houseplants department. This is where it had started. "Silk plants are constructed of plastic," he wrote, "which is a petroleum product. The material is finally [sic]* divided by design, which promotes rapid burning."

Within moments, Mike learned of the second fire. He drove from one Wal-Mart to the next. When he arrived on the second scene, Mike found the center of the blaze to be in the same spot, the silk houseplants. The damage at the second store was worse. Later estimates would put the damage to merchandise and property at $25 million, the largest loss Wal-Mart had ever experienced in a single event. The company immediately posted security guards to patrol other area stores and closed some down. Mike searched among the crowd at both stores for witnesses, but found no one who had seen anything suspicious. One of the store managers did report having fired someone that day for getting into a scrape with a customer. However, the fellow had not been seen in the store at the time of the fire, and he was someone who would surely have been noticed and recognized by the entire staff. The name was dutifully written down, though, as the only investigative lead, even if a rather thin one.

But Wal-Mart, an institution that values its assets, had something much more important to offer investigators than tales of employee dismissals.

Both stores were riddled with security cameras, both inside and out.

---

*Finely.

Paul concedes what finally drove him out the door: "Nicotine's a bitch." He shut down the visions of the frightening Serial Shooter headlines from the last several months and finally pulled the door of the Patrick home shut behind him, ignorant of the scores of Wal-Mart customers clustered in local emergency rooms.

It had reached 107 degrees earlier that afternoon, and as Paul walked along after 11 p.m., it was still over 90 degrees. He was clad in a black Diamondbacks shirt and shorts. He crossed over the major thoroughfare of Indian School Road.

Paul was thinking about his ailing mother and a thousand other personal matters. He fingered the last five bucks in his pocket and pictured the soothing shot of nicotine he'd soon pick up at the corner gas station.

As if by sorcery, Paul suddenly felt a major impact in his right trunk area. He looked down and saw blood on his hands and, nightmarishly, his own entrails exposed and falling. He couldn't comprehend what had happened. Time stopped. Somewhere in a remote corner of his brain, he slowly processed the information that he'd heard a loud bang and seen a car pass. He wondered if something had been thrown at him, but, no, that loud bang, the car passing . . . *I'm shot.*

Paul began yelling for help but nothing happened.

He realized he was weakened. *I need to be louder*, he thought.

He tried.

Because he had been walking into the shot, instead of away from it, he was still standing. He tried to hold his viscera in his hands, keep them close to his body, prevent them from spilling all the way to the ground.

He tried to keep his lungs and his brain functioning, *help, help, help!*

Cars passed, some even slowing to look at him; none stopped.

He heard sounds as if he were inside a tin can. He felt his own blood soaking his shirt, his shorts, his hands, his legs, his shoes. The sensation in the wound was like a brick being pushed through him.

After long, miserable moments, alone on the sidewalk, bleeding, feeling the blackest of despair, he saw a man running toward him, a man with a gun.

Oh, Lord, he prayed to the Jehovah of his grandfather's faith, those childhood sermons rising up from the back layers of his memory, *if this has to happen, let it happen fast.*

––––––––

But the gun was not there to finish him off, it was there to defend him from further harm, if necessary. Even better, in the man's other hand was a first aid kit.

Paul Patrick's eyes flutter with emotion as he talks about the man. "Please," he says, "please, if you can, please make sure Saul Guerrero is thanked."

Just twenty-two years old, Saul Guerrero lived across the street. He'd heard the shot and the yells for help, stopped to call 911, then grabbed the tools of his trade and ran across the street.

"We have to get you down." Paul remembers hearing the words and being gently lowered to the ground as the young man took charge. Paul remembers feeling grateful he had the U.S. Army tattoo on his arm, because the young man reassuringly told the bleeding stranger, "I'm a U.S. Army medic, I can help you." Paul felt they were brothers; he could sink closer to unconsciousness knowing he was finally in not just good hands, the hands of a good Samaritan, but in the trained hands of a hero.

Saul administered to this man who could easily have been dying in his arms. He flicked his fingers lightly at Paul's eyelids, in what he considered to be an effective technique to stave off shock, holding him and reassuring him. Paul knew the young man was putting himself in danger and that he had no way of knowing why Paul, a stranger, was involved in this violence. "I could have been a 'bad guy,'" says Paul with emotion. "He didn't know. But he stayed with me. Many cars passed and did nothing, but Saul stayed there with me and kept me from dying. I owe him everything, everything."

Saul got Paul safely down before the Irishman could collapse on his own from loss of blood and loss of consciousness, but this also was a Phoenix summer night and both men were now being burned by the scorching pavement. It is the pain and blisters from the hot concrete that Paul remembers with most vehemence. "God bless those paramedics, Squad Forty," he recalls.

"The first thing they did was get something under me to protect me from the heat." His eyes flutter again with the memory of the pain, then the relief. "God bless Squad Forty. They knew just what to do." He also remembers becoming violent with the paramedics. "But they understood," he said. "Again, they knew how to handle it. They were gentle and didn't restrain me; they just sort of guided my arms rather than holding me down. I was down to the primeval—fight or flight—and they understood."

Paul's last memory is of being lifted onto the gurney.

Then everything went black.

Ruth Patrick, Paul's sister, was emotionally exhausted. This was her elderly mother's first day back home, in the house she shared with her two adult children. She'd just had a serious heart procedure performed on her in the hospital. Ruth had settled in for the night. It was unusually late when the doorbell rang. Paul would have to get it; he was the man of the house.

The bell rang again.

Ruth waspishly gathered up a robe and headed to the front door. *Why do I always have to get it*? she mumbled to herself in irritation.*

Ruth was startled to find police officers on her doorstep. "We are sorry to inform you," they said, "your brother Paul has been shot."

"That's impossible," she said, "he's just in the other room."

To her horror, Paul Patrick's little sister discovered she was wrong. She threw on some clothes and began phoning the rest of the family.

When detectives were turned away by the doctors at St. Joseph's Hospital, they approached the family members, gathered from far corners of the valley. Who were Paul's enemies? they asked. Who would want to do this to him?

The family was mystified.

An armed guard was placed at Paul's hospital door. A password was required to enter. Maybe someone didn't want him to survive; maybe someone would return to finish the job.

---

*As reported by the Patrick family.

Friday, June 9, Phoenix awoke to the news: two Wal-Marts ablaze, one man shot. The news stories had a tone of fear and wonder to them. Was Wal-Mart under attack by some enemy? Was this man who'd been shot while walking down the sidewalk connected to criminals?

Paul Patrick could not help the investigation. A detective had followed him to the hospital, but doctors turned him away. The victim would be in surgery for hours.

The family would not speak to Paul for weeks. They couldn't. The doctors had put him in an induced coma and did not know from moment to moment whether he would live through the day.

Misty, the little Chihuahua-dachshund mix, never left the front hall, waiting for her running partner to come home.

That summer, while Paul was fighting for his life, authorities gathered for press conferences. "Let me assure the public—and those who terrorize this community at the same time—that the Phoenix Police will work these cases hour after hour, day after day, and if necessary, year after year and never stop," an angry Phoenix mayor Phil Gordon told the city.

Phoenix Police chief Jack Harris put out the call for help. "Someone knows who these people are or has information that will lead us to them." He said he had more than a hundred officers and detectives on the multiple cases, at this time described as three separate and unrelated criminals—two random shooters, one operating last year, one operating right now, and one rapist/killer. He had not conjoined Cliff Jewell's string of .22 shootings with the shotgun series. It was frustrating, he said publicly, because there were no witnesses. None of the surviving shooting victims had seen anything.

No one should put themselves in dangerous situations, Harris said, but everyone should continue to lead their lives. The words were forceful, but confusing and slightly hollow because he was referring to two different sets of serial criminal activity. No one could quite understand how to stay out of the path of both.

Despite the crimes, residents should not be victims of fear, the mayor said. People should still go out.

On June 8, Paul Patrick had chosen to go out. He'd paid for it dearly.

Where could people be safe?

The mayor announced a hundred-thousand-dollar reward for information leading to the arrest of the shooter. Another hundred-thousand-dollar reward would go to anyone with information leading to the arrest of the Baseline Rapist. A community meeting would be held at an elementary school that night. Hundreds showed up. Frightened residents in an overflowing crowd demanded answers. It's very difficult, the police chief said, to find one or two or three guys in a valley of 3 million.

"For reasons most of us will never understand," Mayor Phil Gordon told the public several times over the course of that summer, "this world has always had its share of people with bad intentions. Right now it looks like we're chasing at least two of these monsters."

———————

Paul Patrick's mother began planning her son's funeral. Her out-of-state daughter said she'd rather come now, when Paul was still alive. Doctors had told the Patricks to keep talking to him, sometimes it helps. Paul's mother told him one day, "Colleen is coming." Somewhere, far away in the dark corners of his mind, the announcement registered. Mrs. Patrick was astonished to see her comatose son react. It was not a good reaction; he was somehow negative to the idea of his sister getting on a plane.

Paul Patrick's mother tried to make peace with her son's impending death. The surgeon could not accept the failure, and she found herself comforting the doctor, instead of the other way around.

Swollen nearly beyond recognition, covered in gauze and tubes, hooked up to a ventilator, Paul Patrick slept on.

Chapter Fifteen

He approached the city with an idea.

Katrin de Marneffe on John Jacobs

Clear Channel is a media conglomerate that owns dozens of radio stations and is heavily involved in the music industry. It also has a division for billboards, called Clear Channel Outdoor. An advantage to billboards, the sales staff likes to say to advertisers, is you can't turn them off. As long as people are on the road, they are going to see the billboard—no volume to mute, no fast forward button to press, no off switch to click, the billboard is one advertising opportunity that truly has a captive audience.

In Phoenix, Clear Channel is housed in a spanking new office building with beautiful tile floors and well-groomed landscaping. This building sprang up in an area sorely in need of redevelopment, transforming a dicey corner into a sparkling business park, including another major media venue, the local ABC television affiliate, with its active news department. Clear Channel also had its own radio stations inside the new building, with marked news trucks in the parking lot.

The corner this new business park had transformed was Forty-fourth Street and Van Buren. On May 2, although his name and details had never been released, seventeen-year-old Kibili Tambadu had been shot on the northeast edge of the corner, virtually underneath an "ABC15" sign. On June 20, a man named Tony Long was shot on the southeast corner of the same intersection. *Oh Lord, he got me, the Serial Shooter got me* was his first thought. "I took off running," he says. "I didn't know where that shot came from and I didn't want to get shot again." Two men helped him, his arms slung over their shoulders, to the same Circle K where Kibili had stopped for water a few weeks earlier. Several other shootings took place a few blocks farther both to the east and west along Van Buren.

"You couldn't help but be personally affected," relates Clear Channel Outdoor's Katrin de Marneffe. She remembers everyone in the building feeling especially afraid. She altered her own activities, stopping her hikes and carefully monitoring her daughter's activities.

One day in July, the management company of the beautiful new building that had transformed the corner from urban blight into prosperous business park issued all its tenants, including Clear Channel, guidelines developed in conjunction with the Phoenix Police Department. No one was to leave the building alone. No one was to walk along the sidewalk after dark. Tenants were to try to avoid coming to or leaving the building after dark, a particularly difficult goal for a media company.

The day the landlord came by with these restrictions, Katrin remembers her boss reaching a tipping point. John Jacobs wanted to take action. "We are part of the community," Katrin says. "He wanted to give back. He knew a way we could give back. John went to the city and offered over a hundred and fifty thousand dollars' worth of billboard space for the effort to find the two serial killers plaguing the valley. He had worked in Miami and successfully used billboards there to capture a rapist. He thought we could do the same thing here."

The city was thrilled. The police department worked to swiftly provide Clear Channel's art department with the details they wanted drivers to see.

The billboards went up immediately, with a big press conference. They called it the "Serial Killer Awareness Billboard Campaign."

The press release stated, "Clear Channel Outdoor has approached the city with a plan to launch a billboard campaign aimed at raising awareness and catching the serial killers plaguing the Valley. Clear Channel has agreed to donate the entire billboard campaign, which will consist of 12 large billboards throughout Phoenix developed in conjunction with Silent Witness."*

"It was open-ended," says de Marneffe. "John wanted the city to have these billboards for as long as they were needed. He gave them twelve billboards for as long as these terrible criminals were out there. We were a city under siege."

John Jacobs's campaign would have a lasting impact not only on Phoenix, but on the nation.

———

Ron Horton wasn't one to watch the news. But the odd things his friend Sammy Dieteman had been saying troubled him. When his coworkers started talking about the Serial Shooter, he asked them what they meant. They filled him in on the headlines. Ron was shocked. And Ron was very, very disturbed. That night he made a point of watching the news himself.

He was aghast at what he saw.

He reviewed in his mind over and over and over what Sammy had said.

Do you know what it feels like to kill a man?

They'd been at the Rib Shop. Ron knew Sammy; he was always half-drunk. He didn't think Sammy even knew what he was saying. Ron had simply dismissed the boozy talk.

I didn't either, until about a month ago, Sammy had said, then told him about a girl he had shot, and that he felt bad about it because he'd thought it was a man at first.

Ron had seen Sam defend women in various barroom situations before, so this had sounded like some kind of sloshy mixed-up memory of his. Then Sam started talking about using a .410 shotgun because it couldn't be traced forensically. Ron thought Sam was pretty far gone by then.

But after watching the news in July, Ron remembered something else peculiar Sam had said sometime earlier, in the spring, this time at Stingers, the night that "weird" guy had come to

---

*Silent Witness is the law enforcement program designed to attract tips from witnesses who wish to remain anonymous, usually because of fear of reprisal from suspected criminals. When the calls come in, law enforcement–trained operators rank the tips according to specificity and urgency, then funnel them to the appropriate detectives.

pick up Sam, the night Sam was so angry about a tiff with his roommate's girlfriend. He had talked about killing that night, too. He'd called it "RVing," which he said stood for "Random Recreational Violence." He seemed to be using this term to describe an entertainment that Sam and his new friends enjoyed. It amounted to going out and finding trouble together. But it sounded like that trouble could have very high stakes. And later, after he had left the Rib Shop with that other fellow who'd picked him up, he'd texted Ron that someone was going to "get hurt" that night.

Ron tried to remember what night that was. Had someone actually gotten hurt that night? Was Sammy not just telling drunken stories? For once in his life, could Sammy be telling the truth? Sammy, the big teddy bear who walked the barmaids out to their cars? Sammy, who played with Ron's own boys? Playful Sammy, who loved a joke and was so happy about his new job? Was "RVing" a real thing?

Could Sammy really and truly have been talking about killing people?

Ron was part of a biker community, and although Sammy didn't have a motorcycle, the unemployed electrician was accepted into the group as well. These bikers lived by a code, and that was you don't snitch on a bro. Ron didn't think anything that Sammy said could possibly have any truth to it. But why was he talking about things that sounded like what was on the news? If Ron turned over his concerns to the authorities, he would most likely be causing a bro a whole lot of trouble for no reason. It couldn't be true. Sammy couldn't be doing these things. But he had such a swagger these days, so different from last year when he felt so low he didn't feel worthy of living in a house, not even on Ron's couch. What were the chances Sammy might really have something to do with these terrible crimes?

Ron's ruminations finally came down to one terrifying, soul-crushing thought: if Sam really was killing people, blood would be on Ron's own hands if he did nothing.

He had little boys to raise, two of them not even his own. Ron Horton was not the kind of man to stand by while innocent people were getting shot, maimed and killed, if he could prevent it.

Ron carefully planned what he would say. He rehearsed it over and over. Then he looked up the number that was on all the billboards.

Chapter Sixteen

Skull of a Misfit

The city of Glendale, a charming Westside burg full of cottages converted to antiques shops; unique businesses, like a chocolate lover's candy factory open for tours; and lots of small town charisma, was smarting from the unprecedented crime wave of June 8 where two Wal-Marts were torched and one man was shot on the street, all within about an hour. The shooting victim lay in a coma and could not participate in the investigation. The Wal-Marts were another story. Executives from the retailer desired a resolution to these crimes that had cost so much in property loss and human suffering. They provided all the tapes they had from their hundreds of on-site cameras and kept up the pressure for investigation. Not only was Glendale Fire working hard on the case, but the federal Bureau of Alcohol, Tobacco, Firearms and Explosives stepped in.

At that time, Wal-Mart employed about thirty thousand people in Arizona, from the northwest Mogollon Rim high country down to the southwest desert of Yuma. In Dun & Bradstreet figures cited by the company, Wal-Mart accounts for another forty-two thousand Arizona jobs through its suppliers. It pays over 40 million dollars a year to Arizona tax collectors of its own accord and collects another 340 million from consumers as Arizona sales taxes. When two of its stores in the same small town were torched within an hour of each other, it affected a lot of people, not just the dozens who were in the buildings that night. Both locations were closed down for extended periods of time, for repair and the restocking of new merchandise to replace the aisles and aisles of items that were either drenched or smoke damaged or both.

The night of June 8, Wal-Mart's ace asset protection coordinator Patricia Davies had arrived at the stores, but found them "too smoky to go in." When firefighters finally allowed her inside, she saw that "we lost everything in the stores, the fire, the smoke, the soot—it went everywhere. You see black dirty water spread out through the floor." She spent the next two days laboriously scouring the scores of security tapes. She knew the layouts of both stores and she had an eagle eye. "I was looking for who started the fires," she says simply, underplaying the monumental task.

But her methodical review paid off. She dubbed off the relevant footage onto one disc, until the multiple camera angles told a sequential story. She showed it to ATF agent Kevin Shuster and Glendale Fire investigator Mike Blair. At the first store, a burly dark-haired man in a rugby T-shirt could be seen entering the store. At his side was a much smaller man in a bright yellow shirt. The pair were seen to grab a shopping cart and proceed through the store. They placed bedding into the cart. Mike Blair wrote into his report: "They are observed walking into the domestics area where they leave their cart. 60 seconds later smoke is visible in that area. Both exit the store and return to their car."

Now the agents popped in the tapes from the second Wal-Mart. Lo and behold, the same two men can be seen. Blair's report continued:

"They enter through the grocery entrance. Their actions are followed as they proceed to the domestics area. One of the men is observed leaving the fabrics area, which is proximity to area of origin. Approximately one minute later smoke is visible in the area.

"These were the only two people identified on the tapes that were at both stores during the time the fires originated. They can be seen in the immediate area where the second fire at Northern started."

The two suspects had distinct appearances. Especially the

larger man. His description is listed in the Glendale Fire report like this: "White male, dark brown hair, goatee, gray T-shirt with frontal design, blue cutoff jean shorts, brown boots, tattoo right forearm."

With millions of dollars of property lost, Wal-Mart wanted a photo still of the two men from the security camera circulated.

Blair's report went on to say: "Both fires received extensive media coverage, both locally and nationally due to the high dollar loss. During the days and weeks that followed a large number of calls were received from people who thought they might know who the suspects were. Some of the information received was discarded based on the limited facts provided by the callers. Most of the information received was considered possibly relevant and was followed up on."

It took nearly two weeks for the most relevant call of all to come in.

Joetta Gonzalez, an extremely thin woman with a blond ponytail, had been working bars for quite a while. She gravitated to the smaller taverns in the northwest Phoenix area, especially Glendale. She was friendly with her customers and considered the regulars her real friends. But the bar jobs came and went and so did the friendships.

One day in mid-June, 2006, her ex-husband called her on the phone. He was rather breathless as he urged her to turn on the news. She did as he asked and she saw a photo on-screen, a still from a video camera.

"Doesn't that look like your pal, that guy from the bar?"

Joetta stared at the screen and her mouth fell open. It certainly did look like him. One of her best buds from the old days at Pollack Joe's. She'd even dated him a little. In fact, she was sleeping with him while she was supposed to be his best friend's girlfriend. It had made for some fireworks and created a permanent rift between the two men.* Joetta reached for a pen and started scribbling down the number on the screen. Something about a fire, something about Wal-Mart. Yeah, that's right, those

---

*Testimony on the love triangle comes from the three parties involved—Joetta Gonzalez, Mike Lee (the boyfriend) and Sam Dieteman.

Wal-Mart fires that were all over the news. Son of a gun. There were two men in the photo on the news. She didn't know the little guy, but she was real sure she knew the big one.

Joetta dialed. Glendale Fire was very interested in what she had to say. She made an appointment to come in on the afternoon of June 20, 2006.

———————

Frederick Sena, fifty-seven, wanted to get that sign painted. The owner of A-1 Liquor had been good to him. The deal to paint the sign was good, too. A-1 had a little drive-thru, and Frederick, a man with high cheekbones and sad eyes, was going to give it fresh signage.

Frederick had his own ideas about when to work. It could be 115 degrees if he waited for daylight. It was the early hours of June 20—that's high summer. He'd work in the nighttime, when temperatures were somewhere around tolerable. If you have to work outside, you don't want it to be during the worst of the summer heat.

He had his toolbox. It was the kind that you can sit on or use as a stepstool. Frederick got out the paint and the brushes. He pried off the paint can's lid. He sat down on the multiuse toolbox and began to paint with bright yellow.

He looked up and noticed what he described as a smaller-sized bluish vehicle pass him on Indian School Road. There wasn't much on this little block besides A-1 Liquors. It wasn't the most prosperous stretch of urban Phoenix. Just down the way, though, there was the beautiful Indian School Park, closed for the night with big black gates, and the Veterans Administration Hospital just this side of the park. The VA and the park had adjoining grounds. Hospitalized veterans could often be found, especially on holidays, wheeled out to enjoy the park.

Now Frederick needed a new color. He rummaged in the toolbox for the can of white, pried it open, chose a new brush and started in again on the drive-thru sign.

Funny, he thought he saw the same blue car pass him again on Indian School Road. Maybe they were trying to see when the liquor store would open, looking for its hours painted around the front.

Frederick returned to the first brush, already wet with the yellow. He sat just to the right of a pre-made sign advertising

"Everyday Low Prices" on Budweiser. Over his head and across the drive-thru, mounted on the brick wall of the building proper, was a silver and black Bacardi ad.

Heck, might as well have some tunes while he was out here all by himself. Frederick flicked on the media player. Then he turned his back to the road.

He heard a loud bang.

Pain spread out from his head and neck down to his shoulders and upper back.

VA nurse Stephanie Bonficio was working the night shift at the hospital. It was 3 a.m. when the doors slid open and a thin man, about five-six, staggered in, bleeding from his head.

He said he'd been shot and he didn't know anything else.

Stephanie rushed to him and found his back side blistered with pellets and blood. But the VA is an urgent care facility, not a trauma center. The hospital had to call 911.

Firefighter Michelle Shantz arrived, moved the man to a spinal board and put a C collar on him. "Where do you hurt the most?" she asked him.

"My head," he responded.

They found a veteran's ID on him. When they X-rayed him, they counted thirty pellets. Another three were found inside a jagged two-inch gash on his hurting head.

Police found Frederick's blood-spattered toolbox near the half-painted drive-thru sign at A-1. Officers followed the blood trail across the parking lot, down the curb, over Indian School Road and all the way to the VA hospital two blocks away.

Frederick Sena didn't stay at the VA for long. His wounds were serious. He was transferred to St. Joseph's Hospital before dawn on June 20.

On March 8, about three months before Joetta sat down at the Glendale Police Department, Phoenix detective Cliff Jewell had made this entry into his files for the December 29, 2005, shootings:

At about 0800 hours I was informed by Commander Louis's office that patrol officers had taken an aggravated assault report on 3-7 at about 0130 hours on 4001 W. Camelback.

*Per the supplements in the system at the time I learned
that the victim, Timothy Boviall, was riding his bike home
from work. Mr. Boviall reported he heard what he thought
was a car backfire. He then felt pain in his buttocks. He was
transported to St. Joseph's Hospital [in downtown Phoenix]
where it was determined that the projectile had pierced his
rectum and he needed immediate surgery.*

*I drove to St. Joseph's Hospital where I learned that the
bullet was still in Mr. Boviall and there were no plans to remove it. I attempted to determine the size of the bullet by
viewing a CAT scan with the help of an anesthesiologist . . .
at the time of my visit, Mr. Boviall was heavily sedated.*

Detective Jewell left his business card with the doctors. He
wanted the bullet if it could be removed.

The tragic maiming of Tim Boviall was not linked publicly
or otherwise with the Serial Shooter except in the files of Cliff
Jewell.

Two months later, when he had just hooked up with Scottsdale's Pete Salazar on the Claudia Gutierrez-Cruz case, Cliff
Jewell was still thinking about Tim Boviall. He called Tim and
made an appointment to meet. From his files:

*I asked him to go over the events of the night he was shot.
Tim told me that he was eastbound on the south side of the
west Camelback Road near the entrance of the apartment
complex at 4000 W. Camelback when he heard a loud bang.
Tim told me that in the curb lane was a small four door foreign make sedan.*

*After the bang, Tim felt pain in his lower back. He reached
back and felt the area, which was wet. He brought his hand
back around and saw that it was bloody.*

*Tim is still currently undergoing treatment for his wounds.
He has to wear a colostomy bag until further surgery.*

Cliff advised Tim that he would very much like to have the
bullet if it was ever removed.

"Tim said he would advise the doctor and would prefer the
bullet is removed."

The bicyclist shot on the west end of Camelback had never

made the news. The story got its biggest play in the Amber Inn and in the file marked "December 29, 2005" maintained by Detective Jewell. Until Joetta Gonzalez showed up at Glendale Fire.

———————

At three o'clock on June 20, 2006, Joetta Gonzalez arrived at the Glendale Police station. It was only 105 degrees Fahrenheit, not bad for summer in Phoenix. The relative humidity was at 59, making the day a little humid. But there was no rain, just sticky heat as Joetta walked down the sidewalk to the department, a pretty redbrick building just around the corner from Glendale's cluster of antiques shops. She sat down with fire investigator Mike Blair and ATF agent Kevin Shuster.

Immediately she started talking about a man named Sammy. She said she knew him very well and she thought she'd seen him on TV. The two agents slid photos across the table to her.

Joetta tapped her finger on the tattoo on the large man's right forearm. "That tattoo," she said, "that's definitely him. I can tell you where that tattoo came from. It's a skull and it's from the Misfits album."

Joetta knew a lot about Sammy. She knew he was from Minnesota. She knew he was an electrician and once had a job at Honeywell. She knew his T-shirts were usually dark or black with screen printing on them. Some had swastikas. She said he drank a lot and didn't have a car. He was always catching rides from someone else. "Oh, yeah, he hangs out at the Star Dust Inn, and the Amber Inn and that other place, a biker bar, the Rib Shop."

"How do you get hold of Sammy?"

"Hard to say. He didn't have a place." Last time she saw him he was living with a guy. Funny thing, the last time she saw Sammy, about a month ago, he'd started to cry.

"Why would he do that?" the agents wanted to know.

Well, Sammy was asking her if she'd heard about the shooting of a man on a bicycle on Camelback, way out on the west side on Camelback, somewhere around Eighty-ninth Avenue. She really hadn't, and she really wasn't paying that much attention to Sammy—to tell you the truth, she said, he was a "major alcoholic." Used drugs, too. But he was crying and he was talking about having been out with someone, and together they'd shot the guy on the bike. Well, Sammy had shot him, but the other guy had told him to do it. They'd used a shotgun. And it wasn't the first time.

But Joetta was here about the Wal-Mart fire. She didn't really believe the other stuff. But she knew for sure that was him on the tape at the Wal-Mart.

On June 20, that overcast and sticky summer day, fire investigator Mike Blair and ATF agent Kevin Shuster weren't sure what to make of the barmaid's talk of shootings. She had an awful lot to say and it would all have to be checked out. But they were focused on the Wal-Mart fires. They played for her the store video of the vehicle the two suspects—her friend Sammy and the other unknown man—were seen using.

From their report: "At 20:53 hours (vcr time)* the suspects are seen arriving in a vehicle that resembles a light silver Toyota Camry at the 95 Avenue store."

Joetta didn't recognize the car. "Sammy doesn't have a car," she said. "He's always bumming rides." She didn't know anything about that silver Camry.

Twenty-seven-year-old Ashley Armenta, a pretty blond mom of three, knew cars. Her high school boyfriend "was really into cars," so she learned all about each new model and she could tell them all apart on the road. But now she'd been married for five years to dark-haired Javier with the easy smile. On the night of July 7, she put on a pretty pink top with cap sleeves and slid into the passenger seat of their car, Javier at the wheel, and headed out for a date with her husband. First, they had dropped off their children—a four-year-old girl, a two–year-old boy and a baby girl—at Javier's parents, just off Forty-fourth Street, north of Indian School. They went to dinner, then they went to a club. The couple closed the place down around 2 a.m. The young parents climbed back into their car and headed down Indian School to pick up their kids.

But after several hours on the town, including last call at the

---

*The VCR was not set to the correct time.

Coach House, Ashley and Javier, in the way of spouses every-where, found something to argue about. Ashley got madder and madder, so mad that she demanded Javier pull over and let her out. The stop was made at Forty-eighth Street and Indian School. It was only about a mile or so to the in-laws from here. She would walk the rest of the way, she flung at him. Her husband was just mad enough to let her do it. Ashley slammed the car door behind her.

It wasn't long before the pretty young woman, dressed for a date, attracted attention. Around Forty-sixth Street, a Jeep Cher-okee pulled up next to her and the driver asked her if she needed a ride. Ashley declined, but the incident pulled her out of her angry reverie. She watched the Jeep turn south on Forty-fourth Street. She was a little less furious now and feeling a little more foolish. She herself turned north on Forty-fourth street. Less interested in being alone at night on the streets, she pulled out her cell phone and called a girlfriend, Kelly. Ashley was also determined to remain more aware of her surroundings now. As she walked up the street, a major thoroughfare, she chatted with Kelly, telling her about the Jeep and asking her to stay on the phone with her for safety's sake. Ashley was walking up the east side of the road, which at this point formed the outer edge of a residential area with small side streets feeding onto Forty-fourth. She crossed one of them, Devonshire. As she took a few steps north, she sensed the presence of a car behind her. She was about thirty-five feet north of the corner when she turned around to look. With her onetime boyfriend's training in her head, she saw a "light blue, silver or metallic Toyota Camry." It was a 2000 model, or very close to that year. The Camry was on Devonshire, exiting the residential area and facing out westward toward the multilane Forty-fourth Street. Except that it wasn't exiting. It was just hovering there at the stop sign.

Ashley turned her face north again and took about five steps.

She heard a loud noise.

She felt stinging in her back and neck. She spoke into the phone, telling Kelly she thought someone had thrown something at her. Ashley turned around and watched the Camry pull slowly out of its perch at the Devonshire stop sign and turn south onto Forty-fourth Street, heading away from her.

Ashley put her hand up to the back of her neck and found blood.

Now she understood what had happened. She ran north as fast as she could.

In shock, she told Kelly that she'd been shot. Kelly told her to hang up and call Javier.

Javier Armenta had been having his own doubts about leaving his wife to storm home alone on the streets in the wee hours. He'd been at his parents' house, sitting in the driveway, for about ten minutes when he deeply regretted letting Ashley get out of the car. He left the sleeping children with their grandparents and headed back out to find her.

Ashley Armenta's cell phone records a call to him at 2:38 a.m., seconds after she hung up from Kelly. And just seconds after that, Javier was at her side. He'd already been southbound on Forty-fourth Street when she called. "Less than a quarter mile away," Javier says. "I was looking for her as we talked."

Wounded and frightened, Ashley had run north away from the Camry, but had fallen down at the next corner. Javier found her at Montecito and Forty-fourth Street. He saw the blood coming from the back of her head and all down her back.

Whatever they'd been arguing about earlier vanished into the night as the frantic young husband put his bloody wife in their car and drove her straight to the nearest hospital.

Miraculously, a police officer was in the ER finishing up work on a traffic accident when he overheard nurses working on a gunshot victim. He crossed the room and the investigation into Ashley's shooting began—and no one had even had the chance to call 911.

The spouse is always the first suspect, but Javier was easily cleared. Kelly was interviewed. Phone records confirmed the sequence of events. The blasted pink top was taken into evidence.

Ashley's hair was blood-soaked. She would not see her little kids as planned, at the end of a date with her husband. He stayed by her side as doctors spent the night tending to the birdshot in her scalp and neck and back. The pellets would be left where they were. Some would work their way out on their own, weeks later. She turned them over to police when they did.

Ashley Armenta would never, ever forget that silver Camry.

Joetta Gonzalez didn't know the silver Camry in the Wal-Mart video. No one in the room at Glendale PD knew about Tim Boviall. No one in the room was even thinking about Paul Patrick. All were focused on a major property crime.

Wheels were set in motion to find "Sammy," the man who looked very much like he was responsible for causing $25 million dollars in damage, with his suspicious cart full of bedding and the smoke rising as he left the area known to be the origin of the fire—twice, at two different stores, the same exact set of actions followed by the same billowing smoke and flooding floors. Joetta came up with a phone number for Sammy. By the next day, a judge had signed an order for trap trace on the cell phone. This does not include content, as in listening in, but only following the signals. Glendale PD closed in on the area of Camelback and Ninety-fifth Avenue and believed "Sammy" to be living there, based on the phone activity. This location was also suspiciously near the first Wal-Mart to burn on June 8.

Surveillance was set up at the Star Dust Inn, the Rib Shop and the Amber Inn, but the burly guy with the skull tattoo was never spotted.

They asked Joetta to give Sammy a call. She did reach him, but any hopes for a confession faded as it became obvious from the noisy background that Sammy was in a public place. They couldn't even make out what he was saying, over the din.

As part of the normal procedures of police work, ATF agent Shuster notified Phoenix PD of Joetta Gonzalez's claim that their arson suspect was involved in shootings.

Glendale Fire and the ATF began looking for "Sammy," a burly guy with a tattoo and an electrician by trade, in late June. Ron Horton had not yet flicked on the news. He was still blissfully unaware of the terror the rest of Phoenix was feeling. He was still running into his old houseguest Sam Dieteman from time to time at their mutual favorite haunts and vaguely tuning him out as the unemployed electrician rambled on about strange doings.

It was July 16—Glendale had been looking for Sam for about

three weeks—when Ron heard about the Serial Shooter, became horrified by Sam's statements, and decided he couldn't risk having blood on his own hands. It was July 16 that Ron Horton picked up the phone and dialed the tip line. His heart was pounding. He told the operator he didn't want to leave his name but he thought his friend "Sammy" might be involved in the Serial Shooter crimes. He hastily hung up the phone and paced around till his heart rate slowed down.

Tip line operators turned over the call to detectives. They had nowhere to go with the brief message, no way to contact the caller. But the name "Sammy" rang a bell.

The Glendale Fire investigation would soon dovetail with the Serial Shooter Task Force. Everyone wanted to find "Sammy." But how?

Chapter Seventeen

A White Cat and a Plane Ride

Ron Horton anxiously watched the news. He had managed to go a whole year without ever tuning in or buying a paper. Now the first thing he did every morning was check the paper; the last thing he did at night was watch the news.

Nothing.

He scoured each article—and there was always an article on the Serial Shooter—for some hint that his tip had led police to Sammy. He saw references to the shooting death of Claudia Gutierrez-Cruz, a young woman shot to death on Thomas Road. He agonized over whether or not it really could have been Sammy who killed her, Sammy who thought it was okay to kill her if she was a man, Sammy who had sobbed when he realized she wasn't.

He replayed those conversations over and over in his mind. Now that he knew about the case of the Serial Shooter, he was stunned he hadn't seen it before. It was everywhere—even on billboards. The more he kept up with it and followed it, the more sickened he was by Sammy's words. Ron berated himself for blithely standing by while people were getting killed.

Why hadn't he been paying attention?

What could he do now to redeem himself?

The rate of shootings stepped up dramatically as Phoenix sweated deeper into the summer months. At 1:23 a.m. on July 1, 2006, Dianna Bein stepped out of her temporary lodgings to seek a pack of cigarettes. The forty-seven-year-old was in hiding. A women's group had picked up the tab for her at a very humble motel where she could wait for a spot at a domestic violence shelter to open. As she walked down Van Buren toward a convenience store, she heard a loud noise and then felt pain "everywhere." She quickly realized she'd been shot. "I couldn't fall down," she states. "If I fell down, I would have been dead." She ran toward the nearest building she could see, another small motel, and banged on the manager's door. The manager opened it to the sight of a woman with blood running all down her face and head and body. When the ambulance came, it took her straight to the ICU.

Within half an hour, twenty-four-year-old Jeremy Ortiz turned up at a Circle K on McDowell Road about a mile north of Dianna. He had caught some buckshot on Sixteenth Street. He wasn't sure how. Phoenix Fire responded and started him on an IV. He had pellets in his face, chest, abdomen and arm.

The next day, July 2, nineteen-year-old Joseph Roberts rode his bike over to his cousin's and arrived around 5 p.m. Well past midnight, Joe decided it was time to head home. It would be a thirty to forty minute ride. When he was too far from his cousin's to turn back, one of the tires on his bike went flat. He forged ahead, simply holding the bicycle by the handle bars and walking alongside it. It was hot, even at 3 a.m. Joseph took off his shirt, throwing it over his right shoulder. Near Twenty-sixth Street and Indian School he noticed a four-door silver sedan slowing down as it approached him. The headlights were not on. But the driver's side window was down. Then Joseph saw a long-barreled weapon appear on the sill of the driver's window. "I heard a shot. It stung," the young man says nervously. "There was blood on my ribs and my leg." He slid down the wall of a nearby building. "The car took off fast. I got dizzy." He tried to wave down traffic. He doesn't remember much after that. An ambulance did come for him. He was hospitalized for a week. "They removed a third of my stomach."

Four days later, on July 7, 2006, David Perez was talking on his cell phone on the sidewalk in front of his own house in north Phoenix, on a little side street just off Twenty-seventh Avenue. A car passed, a loud noise occurred, the phone went dark and Perez dropped to the ground. A neighbor rushed out and called 911. Perez was bleeding from his neck. It was then discovered that both Perez and his phone had been struck by one or more shotgun pellets.

At 2:40 a.m., July 8, at around the same time that Ashley Armenta was shot on the opposite side of town on Forty-fourth Street near Devonshire, thirty-one-year-old Navajo Garry Begay was finishing up a late shift at the Circle K at Forty-eighth Street and Van Buren. He and his family had been worried about the Serial Shooter, and usually Garry caught a ride home from his sister-in-law. On this night, she called him up to ask if she should come get him. The slender and soft-spoken man remembers hesitating, then telling her, "No, I'll be all right." He started for home on foot. But right as he reached a classic Phoenix eatery, Honey Bear's Barbecue on Van Buren, he felt a car slow down behind him. He turned to look at it, because he thought it was making a left turn into the parking lot in front of him. Instead, he saw that the driver's side window was down, and a gun barrel was pointed at him.

Garry uses his fingers to illustrate what happened next. "I heard a 'pop.' A bright flash lit up the inside of the car," he flutters his fingers outward. "I saw a pale face." Now Garry's fingers flutter toward his own face. "Something hit me. I thought, 'Did I just get shot or what?'" His fingers flutter down his chest. "I started dripping blood. I was holding my blood. It was too far to go home, so I turned back toward work." When he reached Circle K, his coworkers called 911. His buckshot wounds kept him hospitalized four days. As with most of the victims, doctors decided against trying to remove the tiny lead pellets from his body.

From Saturday to Saturday, the Serial Shooter had racked up six victims in the first week of July.

Michael Cordrey was a big, blond, prosperous young divorce attorney, who was feeling a little too big on the night of July 11, 2006. "I'd just come back from two weeks' vacation and I ate too much," he says. He waited till the temperature dropped down to a passingly reasonable ninety-five degrees, clipped on headphones, tuned into talk radio and stepped out his door to take a slimming walk in his meticulously groomed and comfortable neighborhood. It was just after midnight.

The neighborhood was completely quiet. No other joggers were out, no dog walkers, nobody. Michael Cordrey was alone on the street.

After a half mile, he became aware of a "cast of light" behind him. He realized it must be headlights. But the headlights did not pass him. Darkness prevailed again as the headlights had been turned off.

"I turned to look and saw a four-door vehicle. It was slowing down near me, I thought it must be turning. The passenger window was down, but I couldn't see inside. It was eerily pitch black inside. I felt a cold chill. 'Something is wrong,' I thought. 'Why can't I see inside?'

"Then there was a loud boom and a bright flash. It was so loud it dazed me. When I could think again, I realized the car was very slowly moving on, very slowly. I took cover to see what this person was going to do next. I ran behind a van parked in a driveway. I crouched down. If they came back, I was going to start hopping fences. I watched the vehicle slowly drive off. At the end of the road, it turned south. I saw it had three tail-lights, deck-mounted."

Before he left the scene, Cordrey also looked around and actually found the shotgun wadding. He drove it straight to the Glendale Police Station, but like Issac Crudup before him, he found no one who would receive it. In the morning, Cordrey wondered what had really happened. Could he be making too much of, perhaps, a prank? Someone aiming low to scare him? Teenagers with firecrackers? He drove back to the scene. He found a cluster of sooty black dents in the cinder-block wall behind his position, about five feet from the ground. "When I found the bullet strike in the wall," he says, "I realized they were trying to kill me."

He told the senior partner in his law firm about the frightening incident. The senior partner took action. Glendale Police now kicked into gear.

The official Serial Shooter Task Force had formed three days before the Cordrey shooting. But it was Cliff Jewell who learned of the incident and drove out to Glendale to personally take custody of the wadding and add it to the Serial Shooter case files, which he still stubbornly believed should include his series of .22 victims. He glanced at the wadding sitting in an evidence Baggie on the passenger seat next to him as he drove back into Phoenix. He could tell it was from a 12-gauge shotgun, a very lethal weapon, indeed. His killer was using three weapons—a .410 shotgun, a .22-caliber rifle, and now a 12-gauge shotgun. Who was this person? From downtown urban blight to rural pastures to affluent suburbs, this killer had an appetite for everything. His victims were horses and dogs, men and women, white and black, Latino and Indian. The pattern here was loose, and it may be that only Cliff Jewell could see just how broad it was.

———————

While Arizona is all desert and dry dust, heat and sunshine, Minnesota, with its northern longitude and Lake Superior shoreline is all lushness and greenery, water and ice. This northern state is the "land of ten thousand lakes" and even the word "Minnesota" is believed to be Sioux for "sky water." Nowhere is the difference between the two landscapes more pointedly displayed than in the two state birds: Minnesota is represented by the loon, a waterbird with a graceful, long neck, which makes eerie cries as it floats across shimmery lakes. The Arizona state bird? A plain brown thing called the cactus wren, little enough to be comfy in its favorite hidey-hole, golfball-sized hollows in giant saguaros.

On July 11, just a couple of hours after Michael Cordrey crouched low for his life, two young girls in a small town in Minnesota awoke to morning temperatures in the sixties.

Out in Phoenix, on that day, Sam Dieteman the dad was getting a visit. Sam was just as fond of his former stepdaughter Lisa, age thirteen, as of his natural daughter Liane, age fourteen.* By now, Sam had quarreled with Celeste Vance for

———————

*Denotes pseudonym. Although "Lisa" is the daughter of his ex-wife Dorothy from a different relationship, Sam continues to consider her his own child as evidenced by his statements in court. He never differentiates between the status of the two girls. Neither does he ever refer to any other child, although they'd had a third daughter, who Dorothy says they put up for adoption.

the last time and had changed residences from Hausner, Jeff, to Hausner, Dale. The move had been accomplished over the Fourth of July weekend. Now Sam reoriented himself from the rural and blue collar Westside over to the religious and yuppie East Valley. Dale's address was 550 East McKellips—not 540 and not West as he'd reported to Officer John Cusson at the scene of the James Hodge shooting—and that was dozens of miles away from Jeff's, in the East Valley town of Mesa.

Dale was a heck of a lot tidier than Jeff. Dale did everything better than his brother, or than Sam, for that matter—he had a nicer car, he had a real job, he had his entrepreneurial enterprises, and his apartment was pretty nice. Sleeping on an air mattress on the floor of Dale's living room was cleaner than sleeping on a couch at Jeff's. And less crowded, especially now that Jeff and Celeste and Travis had moved out of their Elm Street place into an even smaller one.

As usual, Sam still had no car of his own. On July 11, his new roommate gave him a ride to the airport in his silver Camry. The slender little man dropped the electrician off at the curb and drove off. He had his own thoughts of fatherhood to occupy his mind. Dale hadn't married his daughter's mother, Linda, and it was a good thing; by now his relationship with Linda was pretty awful. But he considered himself a great father to little Mandy,* his tiny daughter with the feeding tube. When he'd bought the car he was driving right now, he had gotten the dealership to put on a benefit car wash to raise funds for Mandy. She had been considered a "failure to thrive" baby until the previous summer, when she was finally diagnosed with Von Gierke's disease, meaning she could not properly metabolize glycogen (which could lead to instances of critical low blood sugar and cause serious liver problems). The general manager of the dealership had even thrown in a generous personal donation. As a father, Dale was pretty good at getting people to offer financial assistance.

Sam Dieteman hadn't seen his daughters in years, but he did talk to them on the phone. Once a month, at best, according to

---

*Denotes pseudonym.

their mother, Sam's ex-wife, Dorothy. In a later interview she did with Scottsdale PD detective Pete Salazar,* she said, "The girls would call him and stuff but he did not answer phone calls." The girls would tell her, "Oh, we tried calling Dad" or "Oh, we talked to Dad." She recalled, "It varies, because sometimes he won't talk to them at all. Like for my daughter's [Lisa's] birthday or Liane's birthday, our daughter's birthday, he wouldn't have any contact at all." Sam's number changed often and it was the girls, Dorothy reported, who tried to keep track of it. When they did talk, Dorothy said Sam would often say, "Oh, I gotta go, I'm at work." She described her daughters' efforts to stay in touch with their father. "And I mean, I didn't never get— I never got to talk to him, so I don't know if he was actually at work or if he just said he was. I mean, some of these would be calls on Sunday during midafternoon."

When the girls had left Minnesota that morning, the humidity was a soggy 81 percent and the temperatures were cool. When they stepped off the plane in Phoenix, it must have been rather a shock to feel the 111-degree air, bone-dry at 19 percent humidity.

"I let them go out there [to Arizona] so that way they [could] see, basically, you know, him and their grandma and grandpa and their aunt that's out there," said Dorothy. "They [the grandparents and aunt] had bought the tickets and everything for them to fly out there." The girls would be staying at Sam's mother's for a week, since Sam didn't have a place of his own. His mother and his stepfather, Mary and Tom Monaghan, had also arranged for Sam himself to stay at their house while the girls visited. How else was he really going to see them? The Monaghans were off on the Westside, in Glendale, and Sam now bunked out in Mesa with Dale. That could be an hour drive, one way. He couldn't count on Dale to keep driving him back and forth every day.

After the reunion at the airport, the kids and Sam all rode with Sam's mom and her sister back out to Glendale on July 11. It was a Tuesday.

---

*Based on a transcript of Dorothy Ivorson Dieteman Kaiser August 15, 2006, interview with Scottsdale PD detective Pete Salazar. Case #0611485.

Michael Cordrey stood nearby while the senior partner from his law firm called Glendale Police. Michael was still dazed. He'd taken photos of the bullet strike that morning. The photos were spread out on his law partner's desk. The adrenaline from crouching low and watching the car slowly pass was still reverberating through his veins. He had stared at the bumper area, but he could not find a license plate. Either there was no plate, or the light above it had been killed, like the headlights themselves, as the vehicle trawled down Michael's street.

The photos showed a bullet strike at chest level. The cluster of soot was fist-sized, a very large fist. Michael had been very, very lucky.

The girls got to see Grandma and Grandpa and, especially, Dad.

And while the girls had visited, they had also met someone new. Dad's friend Dale gave Dad rides and also brought his own little baby girl over to the house and took photos of everyone. "When the girls were there, he [Dale] ended up coming over and taking pictures of them [all]," Dorothy said.

Dale's influence at the Monaghan household continued even while he was not present. "We did have nonstop texting," Sam testified. "'What are you doing, why aren't you texting me back?' Blah, blah, blah. It got annoying."

Sam stayed the night with them at his mother's on Tuesday. He stayed all day on Wednesday and slept over Wednesday night. But by Thursday morning, Sammy started saying he had to get out of there. He said it over and over again and he kept pacing and shaking and sweating.

"They told me after he was there for two nights and that half day with them," Dorothy related, "they just said that he was getting real sweaty and just real shaky while he was, while he was there and said that he had to get out of there. And he was kinda pacing the floor and stuff while he was there, too."

Liane and Lisa returned to Minnesota on Wednesday, July 19. They had visited Dad and his relatives for eight days. They hadn't seen him for years. Shortly after their return to Minnesota, they would see him on national television. Their deep feeling for him would come through in their reaction to the magnitude of the news. "My girls are blaming themselves," Dorothy reported, "because they were like, 'Mom, if we wouldn't have left, he probably wouldn't be like this.'"

Ron Horton had made his first call to the tip line on Sunday, July 16. The girls had arrived in Arizona the previous Tuesday.

While the girls were flying over Colorado, Nebraska and Iowa, the following Wednesday, Ron Horton was anxiously watching for news that his tip had been acted on and beginning to wonder if he should call the tip line again. He did make that second call, after the girls got back to the land of ten thousand lakes. It would be a long time before they'd ever get another chance to see Dad out in that desert, where the air is so dry and the birds live inside the cactus.

On Saturday, July 22, 2006, before dawn, Raul Garcia was riding his bike out in east Mesa, near Stapley Drive. He heard something loud. Down he went.

At 4:41 a.m. 911 received a call from an unknown man:

"There's a guy on the street laying down in the middle of the road. He won't get up. He's hurt."

When paramedics arrived, they found Raul peppered with buckshot. He had seen nothing. But the well-staffed Mesa Police Department immediately canvassed the area for security cameras. They found one at a nearby bank. Although nothing was actually visible on the tape, it was mistakenly reported in the East Valley *Tribune* that a suspect vehicle was seen.

When days went by and it seemed his tip to police had not helped any, Ron began to feel he himself was to blame. He had been too timid on the phone to the tip line. It wasn't Sammy's innocence or his cunning, it was Ron's own cowardice. He hadn't said enough—how could they do anything with that lame message he'd left?

Ron studied the articles and compared them to the conversations he'd had with Sam. One day he realized that none of the articles ever mentioned the caliber of weapon, but he had heard Sammy talk about a .410-gauge shotgun. A shotgun. Sammy had made a big deal about it. He said they used a shotgun during this infernal "RVing"—this crazy system of going out and causing trouble to anyone and anything they came across just for the fun of it—because birdshot couldn't be traced like a bullet could.

Now, that might be something useful, Ron thought. He waited until his boys were at school. He took the day off work. On July 28, he called the Silent Witness tip line again.

Was it really "silent," as all of the ads and billboards claimed the anonymous tip line program would be? What could happen to him? What could happen to his beloved little sons?

An operator answered.

Ron told her he thought he had information about the Serial Shooter, but he needed to know whether he could truly be anonymous.

Yes, she said, this information was only turned over to the detectives on the case.

Are you sure? he wanted to know. He wanted reassurance on the question of whether somebody could find out that he had done this.

Ron thought about the dead girl on Thomas Road. He felt nauseated.

He finally decided to go for it. He gave his full name, Ron Horton. He tentatively supplied the detail that the girl on Scottsdale Road named Claudia might have been killed with a .410-gauge shotgun.

The operator wanted to know how to reach him. This would be his last chance to keep some distance between himself and whatever records were kept by the Silent Witness program. He knew criminal defendants had a lot of access to law enforcement records when their cases came up. Attaching his phone number to his full name would probably kill any chances at real anonymity he had.

Ron thought about the girl, working an honest job, just trying to get home at the end of a long day. He thought about a weary bus ride down from tony Scottsdale, then a long trudge ahead on foot. He thought about the shocking loudness of a shotgun blast. He thought about the misery of dozens of tiny bits of metal tearing through the tender flesh of a young woman. He thought about the searing grief of a family who lost a twenty-year-old.

He gave the operator his number.

The use of a .410 shotgun had been flagged internally as an important marker for tip line operators. The tip from a man who mentioned the .410 got turned over to Detectives Clark Schwartz-kopf and Darrell Smith quickly. The detectives read through the report, and two more things jumped out at them: Ron's friend mentioning a "girl" being shot and the name "Sammy."

One of the squad made a quick call to Scottsdale's Pete Sala-zar. What was his victim wearing? Could she have been mis-taken for a man? Was she shot in a dark spot or in the glare of lighting?

She'd been nowhere near a street lamp, came the return in-formation. And, although she was very small with hair well past her ears, she had been wearing pants and a shapeless jacket over that.

Darrell Smith called the ATF. "Tell me again about that Wal-Mart fire you have. . . . A guy named "Sammy" who hangs out in bars? . . . Which bars? . . . The Star Dust Inn?" Check. "The Rib Shop?" Check. "What else can you tell me about him? . . . He was heard to be blubbering about shooting people with a shotgun?"

Before the day was through on July 28, Ron Horton had re-ceived the phone call he had been both anticipating and dread-ing. As soon as he could arrange care for the boys, he met up with Phoenix Police Department detectives Darrell Smith and Clark Schwartzkopf. Horton nervously arrived at the designated Mexican restaurant, one far off his usual circuit, a place where no fellow bikers or even Sammy himself would stroll in and wonder what in the hell Ronnie was doing talking with cops. One thing bikers don't do is snitch on each other. Not on a bro. Ron couldn't believe he was here. When he saw the two detec-tives, it felt worse than ever. Sammy couldn't have done this; everything inside Ron screamed that he was doing the wrong thing, he was breaking the code, causing everybody a lot of trouble just because ole Sammy got drunk and mouthy. *Who among us hasn't gotten drunk and mouthy?* he thought.

But then, there was that girl. He thought of his own kids. He'd kill anyone bare-fisted who harmed them. *Look*, he told himself, *if Sammy is innocent, it would be just as well to get this over with.* He'd listen to what the detectives had to say and he'd hear something that would let him mentally cross off his pal as a suspect. As long as no one saw him with the cops, he could tell them it was all a mistake and he could just go home and finally sleep again.

This could be a good thing—just satisfy for himself that there was nothing to the strange things Sammy had said; the detectives would surely know a lot of things that would end up ruling out the big electrician. That's what would happen, that would have to be it. Ron couldn't live in this torment any longer. He knew his soul would have no peace as long as he had doubts, so just go through with this and life can get back to normal.

Ron stepped into the dining room and slid into the booth where the detectives were.

———————————

Back at 620, Cliff Jewell was tapping play and pause buttons. He was watching the footage from the Department of Environmental Quality parking garage video of December 29. He had put out descriptions of every vehicle he could identify that came through the camera's field of vision—an unhitched semi cab, a white van, a dark pickup—but the one he was really interested in was a silver Camry. The camera was mounted on the fourth level of the garage, high atop the intersection of Tenth Avenue and Adams. Visible in its frame were the eastern and southern sections of the two roads and the sidewalks of the corresponding corner. You could see pedestrians pass through occasionally, but they did not appear to be acting suspiciously, and, most importantly, none of the people who casually walked through was carrying a .22 rifle. It was amazing what you could see, the detail even at that distance and in the dark—you could see white tennis shoes on the pedestrians and you could even see logos or designs on their T-shirts, though you couldn't make out what those logos or designs were.

Neither could you make out the license plate on that silver Camry, not with the camera pointed at a steep downward angle from the fourth floor. Cliff Jewell really wanted that license plate. For that Camry passed through the intersection four times in the space of ten minutes.

The first time the Camry appeared, it passed through the intersection and turned left, or westbound, onto Adams. The second time, two minutes later, it appeared to have circled the block and came into view from the same point, northbound on Tenth. This time, from the top of the camera's field of vision, a white cat was seen sauntering leisurely down the sidewalk, westbound on Adams. The cat was in no hurry. The animal had the air of an experienced alley cat who had little to fear, and the heft of one who knew where to get fed. But as the silver Camry proceeded out of the intersection and out of frame, the cat suddenly jumped straight into the air, changed direction and darted away at the speed of a cartoon character.

That was the view from DEQ parking garage camera 13.

Camera 9 happened to be mounted along the flat side of the structure, looking down at Adams Street, picking up vehicles as they left the intersection and headed west on Adams. On camera 9, at the time code where the cat was known to have perceived whatever gave it the startle, that silver Camry was seen to pause in the intersection, then accelerate slightly and proceed away, in a hurry, westbound on Adams.

On December 30, after first recovering this video from the DEQ security office, Cliff Jewell had gone to an awful lot of effort to find that cat. But the search was in vain. No bullet strike was found in the sidewalk, no blood trail, no shell casing, no spent cartridge and no cat.

But Cliff, the pet detective, watched the video over and over, and he felt sure he knew what would cause an otherwise confident and relaxed feline to jump so dramatically and flee in the exact opposite direction to the Camry.

Cliff sent the video to every tech department he could find, hoping for enhancements, but the compressed nature of the original imprint was intransigent. There would be no spectacular zoom-in à la television shows like *CSI* or *Numb3rs*. He was stuck with these pixels, in this size, in this dark light, at this steep angle.

Cliff did take in every detail about the Camry that he could. The distinctive hubcaps, the molded bumper guard, the side-view mirrors, the dark tinted windows, the B pillar (the design of the section separating the front windows from the back windows), the little opera window (the triangular window, usually operated manually, embedded in the design of the standard window) and, most of all, the deck-mounted taillights. There was red light visible down where most taillights were, but on this

Camry those were just reflectors. The actual taillights that came on and off as the Camry braked and moved were mounted inside the cab, behind the passenger seating, in the center. All of these features were common enough, but taken together, they made up a vehicle that could be described with a great deal of accuracy, to narrow down a small pool of suspect cars.

One more detail: a small lightbulb over the license plate. It was extremely frustrating. The numbers were there, bathed in light but still not visible because of the steep angle, almost deliberately taunting the detective.

There was one other detail that hit Cliff in the gut. The driver's side window was down and it was facing the camera. But the only thing visible was a hand, a white hand, a hand on the wheel, steering that Camry through the epicenter of a three-victim crime spree.

The first patrol car responding to the shooting of Timmy Tordai is seen passing through camera 13's view less than ten minutes after the Camry's last pass through. Timmy Tordai was, in fact, shot one block north and east of the camera.

Marco Carillo was found dead a block south.

And, worst of all, Jose Ortiz was found just a few yards north. If camera 13 had had about a thirty-degree wider lens, it most assuredly would have captured and recorded that murder as it happened.

Cliff Jewell played the footage over and over again.

He watched the cat jump.

He watched the silver Camry.

He watched the white hand.

Back in May of '05, Tony Mendez had died in the street of his Maryvale neighborhood, just a random half block ahead of his roommate. The .22 bullet had struck his heart and left him to collapse within seconds, the bicycle tipping over, spilling its trailer with tools and candles on the asphalt. The case agent had found no clue to go on. Mendez had had no money to steal. The roommate and owner of the bike trailer, grief-stricken Ricky Kemp, confirmed there was nothing missing from it. It had been a year now, and the case agent had nothing to offer the family, and didn't expect to.

When Cliff Jewell expressed an interest in the Mendez homicide, the case agent was only too happy to hand it over. The death of Tony Mendez by .22-caliber bullet with no leads was officially reassigned to Cliff Jewell. He put it with his December 29 shootings, Ron Rock's animal shootings, the death of David Estrada and the shooting of Tim Boviall, along with what he could recover from the case files on the Scottsdale murder of Claudia Gutierrez-Cruz, the Phoenix shotgun shooting of James Hodge, and all the other 2006 shotgun shootings that were being handled by Clark Schwartzkopf's Assault unit.

Since January he had submitted every .22-caliber gun he could get his hands on to the ballistics lab. By now, these tested guns numbered well into the dozens. Weapon after weapon after weapon came back negative. Cliff Jewell kept finding them and turning them in. More than fifty of them by July '06. Not one yet had come back even close to the gun that fired any of these .22-caliber bullets, let alone all of them.

The Assault unit wasn't interested in the .22s.

They were focused on buckshot.

Shotguns.

Of course, it was the mention of a shotgun that had got Ron Horton his sudden appointment with two detectives from the Assault unit of the Phoenix Police Department. And now here they were, tacos and chile relleno on the menu, and Ron Horton's stomach churning with the hope that he would leave here relieved of an unbearable burden, never see these cops again and be able to forget about the whole thing.

With the sounds of glasses of iced tea clinking and corn chips crunching about them, Ron Horton was handed a file. He opened it. His eyes fell on a still photo obviously made from video of a security camera.

Looking large as life on celluloid, there was Sam.

Sam.

It was Sam.

It was definitely Sam.

Now Ron was sick with both moral outrage and grief. He didn't understand yet what the still photo from a Wal-Mart had to do with the Serial Shooter case, but if these agents were showing it to him, it had to be very, very bad news. He would come to learn more details later. Right now the cops wanted to know everything he could tell them about Sammy. What was the man's last name?

Dieteman.

The name "Dietema, Samuel" was right in the case files of Clark Schwartzkopf from the James Hodge shooting, the first shooting that had pulled the detective into what had now become the infamous Serial Shooter case. Even after meeting with Ron Horton, though, when the name "Dieteman" was run through the computer, it kicked back nothing. Computers don't consider typos.

Ron told them Sammy's cell number changed often and he could be difficult to reach, and neither did he have a regular address.

What about the other guy? they wanted to know.

Ron didn't know him. Not at first. But after a closer look, his emotions roiling, Ron remembered the night Sam had been so worked up and later texted him that "someone was going to get hurt." That very night was one of the reasons he had called the tip line, why he was sitting here with these cops right now. That other guy in the Wal-Mart photo looked like that "weird" guy who had come to pick up Sam at the Rib Shop that night. No, he told the cops, he didn't know the guy's name or anything about him. Not a thing.

They showed him one last photo.

Looked like a silver Camry.

"Never seen it before," he told the cops. "Sammy doesn't have a car."

Chapter Eighteen

A Real Task Force

Detectives Clark Schwartzkopf and Darrell Smith urged Ron to phone Sam and try to arrange a social call with him. Ron wasn't sure. He had a lot to think about. It was too much to take in all at once. "Don't think too long," the detectives pleaded.

At this time on Clark Schwartzkopf's own desk were two different ways to reach Sam—the contact information provided by Sam himself and that provided by his "brother," Dale. But a typo, one little dropped off letter from an otherwise distinctive name, prevented the detective from realizing it.

Clark Schwartzkopf had made one visit to a morphined-up Paul Patrick. The man was now comatose. Clark did not expect to have a chance to interview him. He expected the next call he'd get would be from the medical examiner, summoning him to attend the man's autopsy.

Ashley Armenta still had a bloody and sore scalp, Michael Cordrey was turning in a 12-gauge shotgun cup, Raul Garcia was convalescing. Other victims, all with their unique stories, were still suffering. And heartbreakingly, other victims were at their final rest, and it was their relatives and loved ones who were suffering.

The Dieteman girls had been home from their visit with Dad one week.

Ron Horton had relatives who were making visits, too. He called his mom at her sister's in Boston, and told her confidentially that he was involved with something undercover with the police, something that involved homicide, and that, for her own good, he would be dropping out of her sight for a while.

———————

Robin Blasnek had been dating Tremain for years. But she'd grown frustrated with him by the summer of '06. They weren't kids anymore. She was turning twenty-three in a few weeks. They should get married. Tremain wasn't so sure. He loved Robin a lot, but he felt like he had a lot of life to live before he did something like settle down. They couldn't agree on how to proceed, so in late June, Robin had broken up with him. Right now they weren't seeing each other at all and he missed her very much. Robin was pretty busy. She had a lot of friends and a lot of activities and there were other boys. But after a few weeks of leaving Tremain to his own devices, Robin was missing him, too. She thought maybe this weekend she would see him and everything would be all right again. She just knew he'd learned his lesson. She began telling her friends that she was sure they'd get married after all. She began conjuring up wedding plans.

Saturday. She'd see him Saturday. Then he'd propose for real and she would start being a real bride. This was going to be the best summer ever!

———————

Around July 8, after Ashley Armenta's husband rushed her to the ER, Detective Jewell had heard on the radio about a "task force" to catch the Serial Shooter. The case was receiving intense publicity now. Not just locally, but CNN, NBC and other networks had headlines like "Millions in Phoenix hide behind locked doors." Cliff Jewell had been invited by the Arizona Homicide Investigators Board to put on a school, teaching other detectives the lessons he'd acquired over his long career. He'd been driving home from a long day of seminars, actually a long *week* of seminars, when he'd first heard the term "task force" on the Friday afternoon news.

Cliff called up Clark Schwartzkopf, who still wasn't much interested in the .22-caliber shootings or the animal cases—but now had been officially assigned as lead detective on the Serial Shooter.

"I have a task force?" Cliff asked Clark. "Should I be attending something?"

Cliff had already specifically asked at least four different agencies if they had any random small-caliber shootings. Later Cliff would be asked exactly what he'd meant by "random." Doubters wondered if the police were merely cleaning out their files by lumping their unsolved cases together and creating a mythical "serial killer," rather than working hard enough to find the real motive and suspect in each individual case. No, Cliff would be firm and clear: "'Random' means there is no apparent reason that person was targeted." Each case had been meticulously researched and other motives eliminated.

Two detectives had approached him and handed him the Reginald Remillard file. They had been scratching their heads over it for a year. This guy was just sitting on a bus bench, they told Cliff, he never hurt a flea. Twenty-two-caliber. Cliff was very interested in Reginald Remillard. The case was officially reassigned to him. He put it in the same huge pile with the December 29 shootings.

As early as January, the Avondale case of Whiskey the Akita had already been officially reassigned to Cliff Jewell.

In February, the cases Maria Vida found—little Irving, the three-year-old mixed breed dog shot in front of his thirteen-year-old owner, and Shep, the purebred Anatolian shepherd whose pain and bleeding led him to crawl into his former puppy hidey-hole under a lamp table—had also been officially reassigned by the City of Glendale to the big blond Phoenix detective who'd driven out to Issac Crudup's to retrieve the bullet kept locked in a desk drawer for months.

Later he officially was assigned to Tony Mendez's case, another one that had sat for a year, the hapless man on a bike with a trailer loaded with candles.

He had Tim Boviall, the biker who'd been shot in March, in his December 29 file. He had the marine prostitute Clarissa Rowley.

He also had Cherokee, the Australian shepherd dog, whose leg had been blown off at the edge of Los Olivos Park. He had Peyton and Martin, the dogs who belonged to a retired lieutenant colonel. And he had Peanut, the shepherd mix, whose death throes had left her chasing her tail and losing her bowels. He had the Westside horse shootings of Apache, Sara Moon, Little Man, and Buddy the burro.

And David Estrada, the beautiful young man with his guitar and his dreams and the big white house waiting for him at Squaw Peak.

These Westside shootings were still officially Detective Ron Rock's of Tolleson, but the two agreed they belonged in Cliff's big and ever burgeoning binders.

Even if no one else could see it yet, Cliff Jewell still believed that all these cases belonged with Clark Schwartzkopf's series of summer shotgun shootings.

In 2006, Cliff Jewell personally investigated thirty-four other homicides unrelated to the Serial Shooter, but in his off hours he showed up at 620 and sorted through the tips in the Task Force pile and followed up, and he made the rounds of other Valley agencies conducting briefings, urging them especially to be vigilant at night.

Cliff Jewell was going to be part of that task force whether they wanted him or not.

July is a damn good time to get out of Phoenix, if you can. It's hot. It's miserable. And the end is nowhere in sight.

While Raul Garcia was recuperating in a Mesa hospital, the two men who were now roommates and had once told police they were brothers managed to get out of Phoenix. They had heard on the news that a car had been identified on security cameras from a bank near a shooting on Stapley Road. They parked the silver Camry and drove a rental car up to Vegas for a few days. Not really much cooler than Phoenix, but, hey, gone is gone.

After meeting with Detectives Schwartzkopf and Smith, Ron Horton struggled with his conflicting emotions about his pal Sammy. He put in a call to the son of a bitch.

He waited.

On Friday afternoon, Stephen Blasnek picked up his youngest daughter Robin at her group home. She would spend the weekend, as always, at her real home on the little cul-de-sac just off Gilbert Road, the one with the custom-painted tile on the porch, the tile with the names of all four girls, including Rachel, who had already gone to heaven. Stephen Blasnek enjoyed the ride home with Robin. She chattered on about her week and all her friends at work, where she was a secretary. He knew she kept her little secrets, but he heard about her dinner plans for Sunday night at the Olive Garden and her special plans to see Tremain tomorrow. He tried his best to give her fatherly advice.

On Saturday, Ron still hadn't heard back from Sam. The detectives were calling him, but he had nothing to report.

On Saturday, Robin did meet up with Tremain. She was so glad to see him! And he was happy to see her. After all, three years together can't be thrown away just like that. But something went wrong. Soon the pair figured out they were not on the same page, after all. Robin thought he was ready to get married now. Tremain thought she was coming back to tell him she was ready to slow down. Tremain was sad when he saw his mistake. Robin, on the other hand, was mad. The couple split up again with some testy words.

Robin knew she'd get him back. But maybe she needed to teach him a few more lessons.

On Sunday, Robin went to church with her mom and dad, like always. On Sunday evening, she went to dinner at the Olive Garden with her posse of girlfriends.

On Sunday night, she pulled on her jammies and her fuzzy blue slippers and said good night to her mom and dad and disappeared into her bedroom.

At eleven, she slipped out the back door.

———————

Ron Horton got the call from Phoenix Police detective Darrell Smith early Monday morning. A young girl in Mesa had died overnight, blasted through her torso with a shotgun. She'd been out walking alone. The killer weapon was a .410 shotgun.

Ron Horton was distraught.

He had, indeed, heard from Sammy at last, and it was last night when he had done so. Sammy texted him that he'd been in Vegas and that's why he'd taken days to respond. He'd just gotten back to town.

Ron had felt a shot of adrenaline when he saw Sammy's name appear on his cell phone. But the old fondness surged forward, too, and his doubts about what he was doing roiled like swamp mist. He tried to engage Sammy in conversation, tried to seem casual, asked about the trip to Vegas. Sammy was in no hurry to talk. His answers came in slowly and tersely. "I lost," was one message. Usually Sammy talked up a storm.

Ron had felt he had done enough by finally connecting with the Minnesotan and reestablishing a friendly tie. That should do it for the night.

"*You're obviously busy*," he had texted in the 11 p.m. hour. "*Call me when you're free.*"

Chapter Nineteen

I believed they were the Serial Shooter that night.
They were hunting prey.

Phoenix PD sergeant Don M. Sherrard, on surveillance

Upon learning of the death of the twenty-two-year-old girl—
Robin had been pronounced dead in the wee hours of Monday
morning—Ron Horton was "beside himself."

He told Detectives Darrell Smith and Clark Schwartzkopf
that he knew "it was gonna continue" and it was up to him to
stop the killing. After the murder of Robin Blasnek while he,
Ron Horton, was dithering with Sammy, he felt blood was on his
own hands.

He now made an intense effort to connect with the electrician
and didn't quit until he had a date with Sam for Tuesday night—
just two days after Robin's death—to hang out at their favorite
bar, the Star Dust Inn. They'd shoot some pool and catch up.
Detectives wanted to flush out the other man on the Wal-Mart
video, so Ron did not offer to pick up the ride-less Dieteman. He
told him he had commitments related to the kids, could Sammy
get someone else to drop him off?

For weeks, officers had been staking out any place they could
think of that might look tempting to the Serial Shooter. This
included major intersections on poorly traveled nighttime areas
and dodgy blocks of abandoned buildings downtown. During
the Wal-Mart investigation, it had also included the Amber Inn,
the Rib Shop and the Star Dust Inn—but these bars at that time

were only associated with the arson suspect. As agents later put it, "information was fragmented, at best." Surveillance is taxing on manpower, and it was impossible to know if time would be better spent elsewhere. But on Tuesday, August 1, 2006, some ten or more units converged on that little hole-in-the-wall bar at the back of the strip mall at Forty-third Avenue and Olive, where Ron Horton was waiting for an appointment with their best Serial Shooter suspect so far.

Sitting in the parking lot at the Star Dust on Tuesday evening was Phoenix Police sergeant Don Sherrard. A beefy guy with a mustache and a flair for fashion, he'd spent about twenty years in public service, starting with stints as a firefighter in both Montana and Wyoming. Sherrard's expertise was in meth labs, and he was credited for, among many accomplishments in the field, developing the public awareness campaign "What's cookin' in your neighborhood, Meth?" But tonight, the dark-haired officer was all about the Serial Shooter. He had studied the Wal-Mart photos again and again, and when a silver Camry entered the parking lot where he was stationed, about 7 p.m. on that August evening, his senses tingled as he recognized the big-shouldered guy who emerged from it.

Radio traffic crackled across the multiple teams of watchers. There were two people in that Wal-Mart video. They felt they knew at least a little bit about Sammy—between the two informants, Ron Horton and Joetta Gonzalez—but the other guy was a complete mystery.

A silver Camry had appeared on the Wal-Mart video. Cliff Jewell was also rather obsessed with a silver Camry from the DEQ video from his December 29 shootings. And now here it was, big as life, with an unknown entity driving it, an entity that obviously had an association with their number one suspect. Don Sherrard watched the Camry wind through the parking lot and reenter traffic.

Sherrard turned the ignition key in his own unmarked vehicle and followed at a discreet distance.

Sam Dieteman made his way past the Siamese Kitchen, past the row of motorcycles, past the banner advertising "75¢ Long-necks!" to a door tucked away in the innermost corner of the collection of businesses and shops that could barely be called a strip mall. It was the door to the Star Dust Inn, where he would meet up with Ron Horton.

Sammy knew that his roommate Dale Hausner wanted to go "out" later tonight. In light of that, alcohol sounded like a great idea. In fact, a necessary one. He was glad that Ron had called. It would also be a chance to be free of Dale for a while. It was a funny thing, because although Dale had gone to bartending school and enjoyed mixing drinks at home and at private gigs, he really didn't like bars and usually even refused to enter them.

Sam stepped across the well-worn threshold and adjusted his eyes to the dark. Outside it was still full daylight, the desert sun just now softening into what would become the drama of an Arizona sunset. As his eyes settled into the dim room, he saw the pool tables, the dartboards, the little dance floor that he knew so well. To his left was a magazine rack, stocked with free specialty newspapers of interest to the Star Dust crowd, such as *Master Link*, for "all bikes, all riders," and the *Medallion*, "by dart players, for dart players!"

He saw a lot of familiar faces at this bar full of regulars, and quite a few faces he didn't know. The little Star Dust was doing pretty good business for a Tuesday night.

He saw Ron over there. He shambled up to his old buddy and ordered a rum and coke. The two exchanged greetings and began the process of catching up, aimless chatting and downing drinks. If Sam noticed that Ron wasn't drinking as fast as he was, he didn't say anything about it.

Something he did notice was the television over the bar. He lifted his head when the news came on.

And some of those unfamiliar faces around him would later record his actions in their official reports:

"[His] attention was concentrated on the news when the Serial Shooter case was being reported. He stood up and placed his hands behind his back as if he was handcuffed while watching intensely. He commented to the witness [Ron] stating words to the effect of 'They can't pin the shooting of the mental bitch on me, I used a small caliber shotgun on her.' He was referring to the murdered female victim in Mesa two days prior. He also made comments stating that he would not be caught and that the police are too stupid to link him to the killings."

Sam Dieteman's actions may not have caught the attention of the regulars in the bar, who were possibly preoccupied with their darts or cue sticks, but the man was surrounded by undercover officers who could overhear him just fine.

The undercover officers were so attentive that Ron Horton grew worried. Already as nervous as a cat on a hot tin roof, the informant used a brief bathroom break by Sam to urgently phone Detective Darrell Smith and have him call the undercover officers out of the bar because of what seemed to Ron's nervous eye to be their conspicuous consumption of water and suspiciously coplike appearance.

The radio traffic buzzed again, cell phones rang, and some of the faces unfamiliar to Sam inside the Star Dust quietly ended their patronage.

Sam didn't seem to share Ron's sense of high alert. He downed more rum and cokes, even bought a round for the house, and moved over to the pool tables for some three-ball.

Late in the evening, Sam climbed into Ron's white Ford pickup truck and they drove out to Wild Horse Pass casino. Ron's heart was pounding as he swung his leg up on the sideboard and pulled himself in behind the wheel. In the bar he'd known he was surrounded not only by friends, but by the coterie of law enforcement officers deployed nearby.

Here in the truck he was utterly alone with a serial killer.

He tried to make conversation again. He told himself not to finger the .38 he had under the seat. He thought about what Robin Blasnek's parents were doing right now, probably picking out her funeral clothes and talking to relatives and, of course, bawling their eyes out. He didn't think it was the right time, alone in this small space, just the cab of a pickup truck, to try to wrangle a more overt confession out of Sam. Ron was not wearing a wire. Of what possible use could a confession in the truck be? It would do nothing but endanger himself. He had his own kids to think about. Thank god.

Don Sherrard, the old firefighter, watched the silver Camry head over to Metro Center mall. The driver emerged, after parking the sedan, and now Don Sherrard could see his general characteristics, although he couldn't get a real good look, given that he had to maintain a certain distance lest the driver notice he was being tailed. Still, Sherrard could see that the driver was a male, much smaller than main suspect "Sammy," and he looked like he could very well be the guy seen on the Wal-Mart video. He was about the right size and build.

And he had the silver Camry.

Sergeant Sherrard watched him walk into Metro Center mall.

The decision was made to leave him be, but Sherrard did take the opportunity to have a Global Positioning System unit placed surreptitiously on the Camry. They did not have enough units to put someone on foot inside the mall; most of their resources were concentrated on the main suspect, that imposing bear of a man, the one who surely posed the real risk to public safety. Neither was the Serial Shooter prone to causing mayhem inside malls. If he were, it would have been much easier to catch him by now. No, the terror Phoenix felt was caused by the sheer stealthiness of the predator, moving unseen through dark streets.

The subject—by now they had tentatively ID'd him from the license plate as Dale S. Hausner—returned to the vehicle later with some mundane purchases, and Don Sherrard followed the Camry as it navigated the labyrinthine mall parking lot and reentered traffic. The vehicle soon turned onto I-17 and headed south. Sherrard hoped this would lead to something more interesting. The Camry exited the freeway in the heart of downtown. Now it cruised down Van Buren. All the radio units crackled as Sherrard informed the team of the vehicle's next move. It dropped down off Van Buren at Seventh Avenue, turned left on the small side street Adams and crossed slowly to Fourth Avenue, where it turned left again, placing itself back at Van Buren.

Everyone listening on the police radios tensed up. The Camry had sought out an inconvenient little bit of road on this mysterious side trip. There was no reason to enter that block of Adams unless one had business with the Phoenix Police Department. There's absolutely nothing there but the backside of 620. Had the Camry just taunted the police?

The sedan emerged from the odd little loop it had just made and reentered the eastbound traffic on Van Buren. It drove many, many miles out to the East Valley. Because the normal route would have been to stay on the freeway for the long ride, this behavior also interested the surveillance team. Van Buren had been hit hard by the Serial Shooter.

Don Sherrard was watching when the red-haired man parked his car at an apartment complex in Mesa and disappeared behind a door.

But he could not see the number on that door.

The tension of the night had gotten to Ron Horton. He didn't know what to do or what to say to Sam. He didn't want to be around him, but he didn't want to fall asleep at the wheel the way he felt he had on Sunday night, when a young girl ended up having her torso blown out while he played it cool. But now he had delivered his friend into a matrix of invisible police officers. He didn't want to be at the casino anymore. He didn't want to breathe the same air as Sam anymore. He wanted to go home and see his innocent sleeping boys.

He made a discreet call to Detective Darrell Smith and told him he wanted to leave.

That was fine, Smith told him, but don't give him a ride home if you can avoid it. We want the other guy to pick him up, if possible.

"That should be easy," Ron said. "They've been texting each other all night."

Ron sidled up to Sam and started talking about how weary he was.

"Where you living now?"

"Out in Mesa."

"Man, that's kind of a ways for me. I'm really feelin' it, man. Not as young as I used to be, you know?"

"No problem," replied the younger man, "Dale's comin' to get me."

"Well, then, be seein' ya! Good to see ya, man, don't be such a stranger."

Then Ron, probably with a very serious headache, left the scene.

Undercover officers inside the casino kept an eye on Sam's movements and knew just which door he exited through about 2 a.m. Out in the huge parking lot, Don Sherrard had followed the Camry in and watched it park. Secretly placed undercover officers on foot watched Sam scan the parking lot till he spotted his friend. The two men walked toward each other. When they met up, they were alone, no bar buddies like Ron or the bikers or the dart gamers around. They talked softly to each other; there would be no eavesdropping now, but many sets of eyes followed them as they strolled down the row and stopped at the silver Camry.

The smaller man opened the trunk. The linebacker-sized suspect pulled something out of it. It was a black duffel bag.

An object inside the bag appeared by its bulk to be about two-and-a-half feet long.

And now, incredibly, the smaller man was stroking the object through the canvas, petting it.

Sam now took the black bag and placed it in the right rear passenger seat.

If any of the surveillance team were harboring feelings of boredom or doubt or wondering if they were spending a night away from the comforts of home for yet another dead end, the sight of that black bag and the way the men treated it, especially the way the small guy was acting like it was a lover, galvanized them instantly.

The silver Camry drove away from the casino, but it did not return to the Mesa apartment where Sherrard had seen Sam's chauffeur disappear behind a door hours earlier. The Camry drove aimlessly about the neighborhoods and thoroughfares of Mesa, Chandler, Gilbert.

They slowed down by pedestrians and bicyclists, speeding up again when another car approached. Sometimes they did U-turns and passed a pedestrian twice. Sometimes they turned into side streets and entered neighborhoods.

"Apparently, they were, um," says Sherrard, searching for the only word that made sense, "hunting."

"They were going into areas where they didn't belong," he continues, "neighborhoods where they had no business. It was unnerving. We were hoping we could have stopped them if they started to shoot, but sometimes, in order to maintain stealth, all we could see were their taillights. You have to stay far back enough that they don't notice you, that's the whole point of surveillance. At best, we would be about five or six car lengths behind them.

"I now believed they were the Serial Shooter. That night, they were hunting prey. They were trying to find a target, an opportunity, then they intended to attack. We all felt it. My detectives were all feeling it."

Could they have intervened if the black object in the backseat was retrieved and came into view?

"Not necessarily. If they had stopped next to someone, we would have moved in."

By now there were at least ten unmarked police cars involved in the surveillance. Some would follow while others waited their turn in another grid. Even aircraft were deployed, and at times it was only the aircraft that had the Camry in sight.

"We were certain they were the Serial Shooter now. It was important they be taken off the street."

Detective Darren Udd, a commandingly physical man who moves with the power and grace of a boxer, takes over the story. "They were prowling for potential targets or victims; they drove away from pedestrians if they saw another vehicle. We were worried about public safety."

Detective Udd's opinion on the watchers' ability to intervene and save a life was much more pessimistic than Sherrard's. "It would be impossible for a surveillance officer to intervene."

And so was Clark Schwartzkopf's. Was any person in real danger that night? "Absolutely. There is absolutely no way the surveillance officers could have stopped a shooting. I don't care if they were right on the Camry's bumper. There is no way we could have stopped it."

Things were happening so fast that not everyone following the Camry knew why they were there. Tailing a vehicle takes a lot of manpower and various officers had been pulled in from other assignments without being briefed.

A full-time undercover officer from the Drug Bureau was one of these. Detective Bryan Benson keeps a very unpolicemanlike appearance in order to blend in with the crowd he normally infiltrates. Later, at trial, the media would be under strict court orders not to film or describe him. On this August night he assumed he'd been asked to follow a Camry involved in drug trafficking.

But when he saw the vehicle's behavior, he knew that couldn't be right. He believed, without being told by other officers, that he was following the Serial Shooter. "When I saw them pull up by a female pedestrian at Eighth and Main, I was just sick. I put

on my protective vest—I've never done that on any other surveillance. I thought, 'The public is at risk, something is gonna
happen!' I put on my protective vest in my car and got my gun
and my backup gun. They kept doing U-turns by people and
figure eights. I was beside myself, I was actually sick to my
stomach. It became a shell game. I stayed in sight of that car on
purpose, even if it meant our surveillance was 'burned.' We were
helpless, it was terrible. As soon as they'd drive away, I'd roll
down my window and I'm yelling, 'Go home! Get! Run away!
Get outta here!' I couldn't tell them who I was or what I was
doing—they must have thought I was a crazy person."

Benson describes one particularly terrible moment. The
Camry had wandered into a parking lot area where the unmarked
units could not follow. From their spot back a block or two from
the road, officers could see someone on a bicycle near the
Camry. "We were just sick about what was gonna happen," Benson recalls. Since they couldn't follow the Camry into such an
odd spot, the team had the air unit buzz the parking lot. Much
later, they would learn how important this move had been.

Up until this moment, there had been other possible answers to
the case of the Serial Shooter. "Sammy" became the most promising lead because he appeared in the Wal-Mart case as well as
in the Ron Horton tip, causing the two investigations to merge
and bringing the resources of the ATF into the Task Force. After
watching Sammy's companion "pet" the object in the black bag
and then witnessing Sammy place it within easy reach inside the
car, the entire team believed they were on the right track, and the
predatory driving behavior confirmed it. But they did not have
probable cause to make an arrest, much less evidence to make a
case. All it takes is an instant to pull a trigger from an unseen
lap, behind a tinted window. As Clark Schwartzkopf had said,
there was absolutely no way the officers could have intervened
to save a life that night, not even if "they were right on the Camry's bumper."

The surveillance units on the ground and in the air were all
relieved when the Camry seemed to be making its way back to
the apartment complex that Sherrard had now outfitted with undercover officers.

When the two men arrived home, they had a secret audience

watching Sam retrieve the black bag and carry it into the apartment, now pegged as number 1083.

Hidden in the bushes along their path was another full-time undercover officer, Detective Travis Bird—always out of uniform and looking nothing like a policeman—who overheard the pair talking. "Rain ruined the night," they were saying, as they passed his position.

Rain saved a life.

And now the entire Task Force kicked into high gear.

—————————

The apartment was never without its hidden army of observers after that. When Sammy, his loose bangs falling across his forehead and a wide goatee covering his fleshy cheeks, wandered out the next day with a black plastic Glad garbage bag and swung it into the Dumpster, one of these hidden soldiers emerged to fish it out as soon as Sam disappeared again behind the apartment door.

It was Travis Bird who climbed into the Dumpster from the spot where he'd been hiding in the bushes. He stashed the bag in his unmarked vehicle and drove away. A safe distance away from the suspect's apartment complex, Bird parked and turned his attention to the bag on the seat next to him.

The night had been electric with tension as the contingent of pursuing officers watched the Camry seem to "case" human targets, but there was still no evidence actually linking Dieteman or his companion to the dozens of shootings in the Serial Shooter case. Or to any shooting, for that matter. They couldn't go to trial based on nothing but informants with scraps of barroom bragging.

Arson, maybe, could be linked to the pair. They did have the Wal-Mart videotape.

Drunken, yet possibly empty, boasts to Ron and to Joetta, maybe.

But a pair of insomniacs out for a drive did not a killer make. It could never go to court like this.

Detective Bird opened up the bag of trash. What he saw made him start up the car again and speed back to Phoenix. Bird radioed his find ahead, and Detective Clark Schwartzkopf was waiting for him at 620.

Together they opened the bag again and fished out a map of

the Phoenix metro area. Red and blue dots and circles from felt tip pens marked up the map. Every single person in the room recognized the pattern: this was a map of the Serial Shooter's crimes.

The next item to be extracted from the black bag—an aluminum soda can, Cherry Vanilla Dr Pepper, and it was rattling. The can was picked up and tipped over. Out spilled a spent .410-gauge shotgun shell.

Any doubts anyone in the room still had went up in a flash of gunpowder. They stared at the shell. Everyone had the same thought—this was likely the very thing that had just killed sweet little Robin Blasnek in her pink tank top and fuzzy blue slippers only three days ago. She hadn't even been laid to rest yet. Every officer in the room felt they had just found her killers.

They couldn't start on the paperwork fast enough. Everyone scrambled to do his or her part—type out affidavits, lay out a case for an emergency wiretap and more search warrants.

They wanted those two guys.

No more innocents like Robin Blasnek or Claudia Gutierrez-Cruz falling to the malevolent blast of random birdshot. No more searching the city for an indistinct character who might be named "Sammy." No more dispatches in the middle of the night to find a bleeding victim peppered with tiny lead balls and breathing his or her last, moaning in pain. Detectives were sure they had the right men.

But search warrants do take time to arrange. Surveillance would continue while a team of detectives set about the lengthy paperwork required to invade the privacy of an American citizen.

The Serial Shooter never operated in the daylight, so they felt the city was safe enough while they typed and typed. As long as the sun was shining, they could get their case together.

The surveillance team reported that Sam didn't seem to have access to the car without the other man, who via the Camry registration was now known to be one Dale S. Hausner, thirty-three years old. More than once, Sam was watched as he walked away from the apartment to a convenience store or Wal-Mart. When he did so, he was sometimes standing right next to an undercover officer inside the store. He never caught on.

On Wednesday the men seemed to be having a quiet sort of day, lightly punctuated with errands. Neither one went to a job.

A SWAT team was assembled and ready to spring at a moment's notice. As the afternoon wore on and the sun got lower and lower, everyone felt the sense of impending danger return. Nighttime meant murder to these two. The Task Force did not want to spend another night fingering their triggers, anticipating what would most likely be a futile effort to save someone.

But, late in the day, Dale Hausner emerged from the apartment. He drove away from the complex. He was followed to a health clinic. He parked and went inside. When he came back out, surveillance officers were astonished to see what he had with him.

A baby.

Chapter Twenty

Wiretap

The baby had big blue eyes and a soft halo of gold curls. She was in diapers and appeared to be around two years old. The Kevlar vests and helmets worn by the waiting SWAT team suddenly seemed off-key. The presence of a baby turned this into an entirely new game.

None of the officers knew anything about her. No one knew how long the baby would stay. Perhaps he was just transporting her from one spot to another. Perhaps he would hand her over to someone else at his next stop. No one knew how this suspect might feel about the child. Could they even assume it was his own? How concerned would either of the suspects be for the safety of this child? If the Task Force made a false step, would this baby become a hostage? Or worse?

The decision was made that no arrest would be made until they could figure out the situation with the baby. A slew of detectives were working furiously on search warrants for wiretaps, and that would have to be the focus for now.

Surveillance officers were dismayed as they watched Hausner return to the Windscape Apartments and carry the baby into the apartment. The sun went down and the baby did not come out. This was an unsettling development. It looked very much like this baby would be staying the night.

An electronics crew arrived at the target address and first tackled the Camry. A microphone was installed in the cabin, in the rear deck behind the backseat. It was a spot that had once held a three-bulb taillight, a rather distinct taillight, a taillight they could tell had been removed.

Next, officers knocked on the door of the apartment adjacent to their target. Arrangements were made with the shocked tenants to use their home to install listening devices. Electronic surveillance is not the swift little game so often portrayed in fiction. It's more often a frustrating affair that takes hours to install, with disappointing results. This team experienced those frustrations, and it would be hours before the microphone embedded in the drywall of the common wall between Dale's place and the neighbor's would start to function, but when it finally did, officers from the Task Force had an unprecedented "get"— suspected serial killers talking freely and privately.

The police came to distinguish the voices of the people inside through the way they used each other's name and through Dale's interaction with the baby. Listening in, they could now tell she was Dale's child, and that her name was Mandy. He turned on the Disney movie *The Jungle Book* for her. The men also had a television on for themselves, tuned to the news. And the news contained several stories the two suspects were interested in. John Mohammed and Lee Malvo, the team that had once been known as the D.C. Sniper, were in the news that summer.

Detectives monitoring the apartment heard Sam Dieteman say, "The D.C. Sniper is more experienced than us with more technology and know-how." Hausner responded by asking when Sam had heard these things about the D.C. Sniper. About four thirty or five that morning, he answered. He then added, "On the five a.m. news, Phoenix and Mesa Police have linked the shooting death of the young Mesa woman to the serial killer, which now brings their total to six." Hausner was indignant. "The death toll is higher than that. What about that fuckin' guy I shot at Twenty-seventh Avenue in the yard?"

Dieteman continued, saying that the police were working with the feds in other states, looking for similar crimes and evidence. Dale took on a playacting voice and said gleefully, "Really? We're being copycatted, Sam? We're pioneers, Sam? We're leading the way for a better life for everyone, Sam?"

"They're searching other states."

Another news program came on then and reported that the Serial Shooter had killed twenty-seven people.* Dieteman interrupted. "Twenty-seven? We killed thirty-five."†

The news went on to show video of a community meeting held at LongFellow Elementary School where hundreds of frightened citizens showed up, asking police what the killers look like.

"Us," said Hausner.

Dieteman tossed in that he intended to kill "five hundred" people before he was through.

The pair discussed and fretted about the reports that a car had been identified on security video from the July 22 shooting. Then Hausner announced that the shooting on Sunday night, Robin Blasnek at the beginning of this very week, was not his favorite. But then he named something he did like, very much: "I love shooting people in the back. That's so much fun. That fuckin' old man I shot in the back."

Dieteman cherished something along the same lines: "My favorite thing is when someone is walking away and giving him a couple of seconds to aim without them looking. I get so paranoid when someone is walking toward you. I get paranoid when they are going to see you, well, not see me but the gun sticking out of the car window. I wait till the last second. I don't even get it to my eye but to where the barrel looks like it is pointed towards them."

Sam said he missed his own girls back in Minnesota. He'd like a hug from Mandy. Hausner was happy to comply; he urged

---

*The report Dieteman was reacting to on the television reflects the state of confusion and panic in Phoenix that summer. Police did not know how many cases to attribute to the Serial Shooter and neither did the press. Although there turned out to be well over twenty-seven cases of shootings, less than ten of them as of this writing have been identified as murders.

† Dieteman responded with a wild exaggeration of his own. But such talk made the police listening in wonder what was still out there to be discovered.

the baby to hug Sam. Sam was pessimistic. He said, "She won't hug me." But Hausner urged the toddler on and soon Sam was enveloped in the tender little arms.

"That was nice," he said to Hausner.

"Say 'Good night, Sam,'" Hausner continued to urge his baby daughter. "Say 'Good night, Sam' and say 'Don't kill anybody.'" The pair laughed as the baby's tiny voice repeated the syllables. Then they added on the phrase "in the morning." "It's too early [to kill] in the morning!" they advised the little girl to mock scold them.

————————

The SWAT team couldn't see how they could rush the apartment while this tiny child was inside it. Phone calls were made and several of the officers who were still performing the backup chores at 620, including such people as Scottsdale's Pete Salazar, were told to go home and catch some sleep, there would be no takedown that night.

Chapter Twenty-one

I have this image in my head.

Pete Salazar

Detective Pete Salazar of Scottsdale had been working nonstop since the suspects came into view on Tuesday night. Late Thursday night, August 3, 2006, the tall thirty-seven-year-old from Florence, Arizona, was at 620 helping with the search warrants, a process that involves a tremendous amount of paperwork. Getting a wiretap is a very serious thing, and several members of the Task Force were typing like maniacs making sure (a) they could get all the search warrants and wiretaps they needed and (b) the evidence they obtained in this way would not be thrown out at a later date by some error on their part. The guys at 620 were monitoring the surveillance team currently in play out in Mesa. Everyone was worried about the little baby in the house. No one knew when the "go" moment would come. Late on Thursday night, as Salazar remembers it, "'exhaustion' was not even close to describing" how he was feeling. Things had been "fast, furious and feverish." Late that Thursday night he was told the "don't pass go" moment had come and there would be no takedown tonight. He was told to go home and get some sleep. It took him the long drive home to come down from his professional rush, and by the time he crawled in next to his wife of eighteen years, he didn't need more than a moment to slide into much needed dreams for his sleep-starved body.

He well remembers the phone jolting him awake just fifteen minutes later.

"Takedown was under way! Come back!"

Just before midnight on Thursday night, shortly after many officers providing support services had been sent home for the night, the surveillance team out in Mesa watched the door to the apartment open.

A hulking figure emerged, carrying something, a bag.

The unseen juggernaut around him tensed up.

The big man stepped off the concrete walkway. He carried his burden out onto the black asphalt.

Earpieces vibrated, voices whispered, Kevlar vests rustled.

He was so close now that they could see that skull tattoo on his right arm. He was muscular and tall. The rain had dried out. Even though it was nearly midnight, the air was sultry, well over ninety degrees.

He ambled nonchalantly over to a large shape in the darkness, fetid, grimy. He swung his burden up and over. He let go. He turned back and lifted his feet in his last steps of freedom.

Go!

A SWAT team materialized out of the darkness and Samuel John Dieteman, thirty years old, father of three, murderer, tasted tarmac. Hands behind his back, the position he had mimed in the Star Dust Inn, knees in his back, hot asphalt in his face, Sammy's chance to up his kill count to five hundred ended right there.

Behind the door, little Mandy was now asleep, *The Jungle Book* long since silenced, her rosebud mouth no longer lisping talk of murder.

Her father puttered about the house, doodling with felt pens, scrolling through newspapers, scissoring along column inches. He began to wonder what was taking Sam so long. He should have been back by now.

Bang!

The front door crashed open, bright lights shined in.

He stood confused. He couldn't see the shape behind the light. Sam was always doing these practical jokes. He didn't know Sam had such a bright flashlight.

But the shouting, what was all the shouting?

Dale Shawn Hausner, thirty-three, now learned the hard way that it was not his pal joking with him. It was the real thing. A SWAT team had come for him, and now he was facedown on a hard floor, hands yanked together, knees in his back.

Dale wasn't upset. He launched into his ever-ready friendliness, putting a smile on his pink whisker-covered face and keeping his voice soft and cheerful. He started telling them about his little daughter in the other room. All friendly and sweet, he just wanted a few favors.

———————

All along the Task Force had assumed that the big man was the scary one. They had been looking for "Sammy" with the skull tattoo and the powerful build for weeks. He was the one to be heard bragging in bars about shooting people. He was the one in the Wal-Mart video who always walked ahead of the other guy. When they hid in bushes and lingered undercover at the casino, where the two men stood together in real life, they could see with their own eyes how much smaller the accomplice was. On the night of the takedown, after the arrests, the two men were kept separate and loaded, head down, into different vehicles. At the command station in Mesa, lead detective Clark Schwartzkopf took the first go at the little guy, the one everyone believed to be the sucker, the dupe, the one who would break easily.

But Clark spent hours with Dale, matching the man's ingratiating ways with confidence-building tactics of his own, without getting anything but repeated shock and denial over increasingly horrible allegations.

At last, Clark walked down the hall to the room in which the big guy, the intimidator, lurked.

And the case suddenly turned upside down.

———————

Nearly disoriented with fatigue and the brief flirtation with REM sleep, Detective Pete Salazar rushed back to the center of the action. He remembers watching the interview of Dale Hausner unfold. "He's toying with us," he concluded. "This is a game to him, he's trying to see how much we know."

Ten long hours had already gone by since Salazar left his wife's side, when he turned his attention to the other suspect, the big guy, the one who looked threatening but who had melted into a puddle of confession and contrition almost immediately.

The lead agent on the Task Force—the one that formed more than two months after Salazar and Lockerby had started meeting with Jewell and Rock—Detective Clark Schwartzkopf had entered Sam's interview room some hours after the arrest and dispensed with some polite preliminaries. Then he asked the simple question, "Do you have any idea why you're here?"

Schwartzkopf was dumbfounded at the response.

"Yeah, I believe it'd be the Serial Shooter case."

It was just moments before the big guy was volunteering the phrase "Serial Shooter" and confessing to awful misdeeds of murder and maiming.

But, as he admitted to heinous capital crimes with virtually no prodding, buried in Sam's sodden psyche were pockets of cunning resistance. The best way to lie, a good liar will tell you, is not to do it very often. Sam told a lot of truth that night. But it wasn't until Scottsdale's Pete Salazar, a disarmingly easygoing man with twinkling eyes and a bright smile, entered the interview room that Sam's story developed fissures. Pete Salazar was only responsible for one victim in the Serial Shooter case and he wasn't going home without buttoning up some justice for little Claudia Gutierrez-Cruz, a girl who just wanted to get home to her sister after a long day of work. Salazar's beautifully skillful interrogation sussed out the hidden lie like a Geiger counter.

Selections from the police transcript show how he accomplished it:*

Detective Pete Salazar: *I'm with Scottsdale Police Department. I work in the Violent Crimes Investigation Section. . . . Based on some of the things we've learned I have a feeling . . . that you guys were in Scottsdale one night and somethin' happened. Can you recall that night?*

---

*These selections from the official transcript have been edited for clarity and length.

Sam Dieteman: *We went through Scottsdale one night and was followin' this guy on roller skates but lost him. Otherwise we didn't really go in Scottsdale besides goin' to the casino there.*

PS: *You told Detective Schwartzkopf about an incident three months ago, almost three months ago to the day, where you and Dale were in the vicinity of 44th and Van Buren and what you described to be a heavier set male, you believe to be Hispanic. Do you remember describing that incident?*

SD: *Uh-huh. Yeah, that's the first time I ever went to stay at [Dale's] house.*

PS: *Okay.*

SD: *Spent the night over.*

PS: *Try to think a little more about what took place that night around the same time.*

SD: *We got him and got on the 202 and went over to his place and he made me a drink and took off to the store to get somethin'.*

PS: *Do you remember an incident involving one of the first females?*

SD: *Um.*

PS: *What other incidents do you remember involving a female?*

SD: *Um, down off of Van Buren there was a female walkin'. I don't remember what street it was on but, so he handed me the shotgun, "Here, get the whore, get the whore." So I shot at her and I missed, she ran into a club or somethin' that was open. That was the same night he shot some black guy somewhere.*

PS: *How many murders are you aware of? How many of 'em died?*

SD: *Well, the little girl in Mesa, uh, obviously five of 'em, that's what the paper said.*

PS: *Well, to your recollection.*

SD: *Uh, that's the only one that I read about. Like Dale told me that old guy [James Hodge] he shot over at his brother's place. That he died, but the guy was alive that night, he died in the hospital.**

PS: *Well, this one would have, uh, this one would have stood out, it received a lot of media attention, at [Dale's] apartment several newspaper articles were found reference this particular incident. That's why I'm tryin' to jog your memory as to what your recollection is.*

SD: *I don't know, he had like a shoebox full of obituaries and old clippings and stuff like that. He said he planned on gettin' rid of all of them.*

PS: *Now I know you've probably answered this question many times, it's been asked before so I don't want to harp on it but just for my clarification you never drove you were always the passenger or did you participate in driving?*

SD: *No, I was never allowed to drive his car.*

[Note: Later, in court, Sam would also pout that Dale wouldn't allow him to smoke inside the car, either.]

PS: *Never allowed to drive his car?*

SD: *No.*

PS: *This one, the, the incident I'm referring to, you, you should have some specific knowledge of having been the passenger.*

SD: *Somewhere in Scottsdale? I just remember a guy on the roller blades roller skating.*

PS: *Okay, let's take Scottsdale out of the equation because sometimes the borders get blurred and people think they're still in Phoenix and uh, don't really understand the distinction of how far west we go so that's, that's okay. Um, what do you remember about anything on Thomas Road? What type of incident do you recall on Thomas Road? It's even*

*Note: Sam is mistaken, James Hodge survived.

marked on this map [found in the trash]. Okay, this is uh, Scottsdale here in green. This is Thomas Road right here, runs all the way from the West Valley all the way to the East Valley.

SD: *Um-hum.*

PS: *Okay? So you see all this green and if you see how far we go west in this area of Thomas Road and you notice what you see right there on the border?*

SD: *Yeah, a dot there.*

PS: *Okay, do you know what that dot signifies?*

SD: *Um, obviously it would be some kind of shooting, there are dots on it.*

PS: *Do you have any recollection of it? . . . If you look along Thomas Road there's only one other dot that's even remotely close, so it's not like Indian School or Van Buren where there's multiple occurrences that you could be confused with. This would be very specific. The East Valley area, Thomas Road, right on the border into Scottsdale, three months ago. Do you remember any nights where you did multiple shootings in one night?*

SD: *Um, yeah. But Van Buren [was] where I missed that little girl and he got that black guy.*

PS: *Do you recall any other nights where there were more than one shooting?*

SD: *No. Yeah. Around where I used to live on 91st and Camelback I was with him for one of 'em but later I found he shot somebody after that on his way home.*

PS: *Do you know the area of 56th and Thomas? Do you know what's over there?*

SD: *Houses? Along Thomas.*

PS: *Oh, it's just the border. I'm trying to see if you have an idea what's, what type of businesses are in the area.*

SD: *I don't know Scottsdale, probably AJ's or something.*

[Note: Detective Salazar gained an important clue from Sam there. Sam had just admitted that he knew there was a grocery store at that location. It wasn't an AJ's, it was actually a Fry's, but of all the random buildings he could've named, it was telling that Sam picked a grocery store.]

PS: *You've done really well with your recollection and your, uh, sharing of information and this, this particular case uh, should have some sort of uh, memory to it based on the high profile nature . . .*

SD: *I don't know.*

Sam continued to use the map to direct attention to other spots where crimes were committed, crimes for which he knew at this point he would be facing the death penalty. But Detective Salazar persisted in encouraging him to remember Thomas Road.

PS: *So the night of this incident at 44th and Van Buren I believe somethin' else happened that night.**

SD: *I just remember him askin' me to lean back or somethin' then the guy started screamin'.*

PS: *It happened the same night, it happened the same night that the kid at 44th and Van Buren was shot. And based on that timeline there would have been no physical possible way for you to go back to McKellips, have a drink and head back out or for him to even drop you off and go do it by himself. There's no way possible. So the two of you had to have left the Van Buren incident and continued to look. . . . and you came upon her . . .*

SD: *I honestly don't remember. We were jumpin' on the 202 after that guy at 44th Street.*

PS: *Well, obviously you see it's a homicide. She, she's dead.*

SD: *Yeah.*

PS: *Twenty years old. Picture's familiar?*

---

*Note: Salazar is referring to the shooting of Kibili Tambadu.

SD: *The face is familiar. I think he showed me that.*

PS: *Are you having so much trouble with this because this is the one you shot, and you don't want to accept the fact that you killed somebody?*

Sam didn't react to this interesting accusation. He calmly repeated that he just didn't remember. The other detective jumped in at this point and tried to move things along, but Sam was resolute: they went straight home after shooting Kibili. They went straight home and Dale practiced his bartending skills on Sam. There was no shooting on Thomas Road. That's how it happened. Otherwise, he didn't remember.

It is spelled out for him that he has already confessed to capital crimes and one more would not make much difference in how things turned out for him.

Pete Salazar went back to where his internal Geiger counter started pinging:

PS: *You have been incredibly cooperative and provided great amounts of information. You've supported many statements and been extremely good about answering the questions that we have had, but I'm going to tell you this one more time that I, I've been very patient. I've been up, we've been up all night for days, okay, and (clears throat) I'm having a hard time with that because I think and I know based on the physical evidence that I have, that you just can't accept the fact that you shot and killed somebody and that's the problem and that's why you don't want to talk about this. But the best way to confront this is to deal with it and accept the fact and the truth of what happened that night.*

SD: *It's just . . .*

PS: *Same exact scenario as Van Buren, same exact scenario.*

SD: *I don't know what to say.*

PS: *Same type of shot . . . same type of gun, the ballistics, the characeristics, the MO, the way it happened, the way it went down, everything's the same. But this was your turn. He did the first one. And now it was your turn.*

SD: *I just don't remember bein' over there.*

PS: *And you don't remember telling Ron [Horton] about this incident?*

SD: *I don't know why I would trust him.*

PS: *Ron had specific information about this incident that you provided him. The ballistics, the characteristics, the shot pattern, the way it transpired, everything is indicative of what I've explained to you already and I want you to understand that withholding it, thinking it's gonna minimize your involvement . . . you're already up to your neck in it.*

SD: *I know. I just don't remember it. I just thought we jumped right on the 202.*

PS: *. . . well, you specifically told Ron shortly after this incident that you couldn't believe it was a female and you felt bad about shootin' and killin' a female. So that means to me that as you approached you were uncertain of the gender of the subject and then upon shootin' 'em you discovered that it was a female which is part of the remorse and guilt that you've been suffering through this. You even said yourself that if you could go back, you'd go all the way back to before you even met Jeff.*

SD: *That's what I would do.*

———————

Sam continued to deny involvement, saying over and over that he just didn't remember being there then, and that the only recollection he has of being in Scottsdale was when they followed the Rollerblader.

SD: *I just remember not headin' up that way, we jumped on the 202.*

PS: *You didn't. You didn't. You came north into Scottsdale. . . . There's no other explanation, none whatsoever.*

SD: *The only time I can remember bein' in Scottsdale was followin' that guy with the freakin' roller blades or roller skates or whatever.*

PS: *Well, I can't make it any more clear. There's nothing that* *you can do to prevent the avalanche that's already taken place.*

SD: *I know that.*

PS: *So by denying this or saying you don't recall does nothing to help your circumstances.*

SD: *I know. I don't remember.*

PS: *Think about it, Sam, think about it.*

SD: *I'm tryin' to.*

PS: *Do you seriously think it's gonna make you feel better if you stay in denial on this? You've done so much and come so far. And the thing that troubles me is I don't think you were tryin' to kill her. But you don't want to live with the fact that it happened. Denial's not gonna make her come back. It's not gonna make it better. She has a family that's devastated. You've been so remorseful to this point. This is your opportunity to the one person who you've took their life to be truly sympathetic and sorry for the loss.*

SD: *I just don't know what to say except that I don't remember headin' up to Scottsdale, we were jumpin' on the 202.*

PS: *Your recollection is so clear twenty minutes prior. You can describe the subject, you know your exact location, you described every action that took place in the passenger compartment of that vehicle and you expect me to believe that you have no memory twenty minutes from the time of shootin' the kid at 44th and Van Buren? It's not possible. It's not possible. What are you hoping to accomplish?*

SD: *I'm not tryin' to gain anything. I'm just tryin' to remember.*

PS: *What do you think happened? You got too close, used too much of a shot, too big a shot, what? What do you think happened? Describe the incident for me. Describe the neighborhood, the area where it took place. The publicity it received, you remember.*

SD: *I remember him showin' me that obituary.*

PS: *You were there and he coaxed you into doin' it. He's coaxed you into doin' all this and I don't think you wanted to participate in any of this but you said yourself you had too much to lose, you were going to lose a place to live, you were already down on your luck. He had a stronghold on you and he got you to do a lot of things you normally wouldn't do, in conjunction with the alcohol and methamphetamine. These things were causing you not to think straight, do irrational acts, it's not a rational act to shoot somebody. You were on Thomas Road, you see a target, you're trollin' . . . tell me what he said to you.*

SD: *I don't remember headin' up to Scottsdale.*

PS: *What did he say to you before you shot her? I have this image in my head. I think I see what is taking place in the cab of the vehicle because I see you struggling with it right now and you struggled with it then. But if there's one last way you can make this right . . .*

SD: *Ah, if you want to say I did it, that's fine.*

PS: *Own up to your actions. Tell me how it happened. Tell me what he said to you. Tell me how he got into your mind and handed you that gun when you did this.*

SD: *I just don't think that one was us, that obituary, I don't know why he had it.*

PS: *Well, we've been studying these cases and following everything that's transpired in this valley for a long time. There isn't anybody else runnin' around town doin' this. There isn't anybody else. You told Ron that you felt bad about this and that clearly indicates that you do have some remorse for this. And the final act of remorse should be to own up to it and just tell me how it happened. Tell me what took place in the car, what conversation took place and what your reaction was afterward 'cuz I know you felt bad. You felt bad shootin' a girl. You were just too damn close.*

SD: *I didn't try shootin' her. I tried shootin' at her and missing, like the other people.*

At long last, there it is. Sam Dieteman, under Pete Salazar's artful prodding, finally admits he did shoot Claudia and he does remember it and he would never forget it. Salazar proceeded to get many corroborating details from Sam after this point in the interview. And now that he had his case all buttoned up, Salazar asked, "How did you feel after you realized that you did hit her?"

"Kinda like I wasn't in my own body anymore. I slept away the next few days."

"Does it still haunt ya?"

"I gotta get drunk to get to sleep."

"Is there anything you'd like me to tell the family?"

"I wouldn't know where to begin."

"I'd do that courtesy for you."

"Besides 'sorry,' I just wouldn't know where to begin."

"My heart went out to [Claudia]," Salazar recounts. "I had a job to do, I had to stay focused, I could not get emotional. It was like a chess game or a poker match: you've got to know your next ten moves, but don't give 'em any idea where you're gonna go. Sam was a beaten man, he was all slumped over, it was my goal to keep him talking to me. I had a job to do," he says. "What people do to each other, it blows my mind."

Chapter Twenty-two

Inside the Lair

Cindy McGillivray and her family lived next door to Dale Hausner in Mesa. "If we opened our screen doors at the same time, they would smack each other." She remembers when Dale moved in; it was spring of 2005. She was friendly with her neighbor and took great delight in his daughter, Mandy, a toddler who was running and exploring and learning to talk. Cindy's own grandson would often come by, and the two little ones loved playing together. "She couldn't say his name, 'Ethan,' so she called him 'Ee-wee.' We all thought that was so cute," she says with a fond smile. Sometimes Dale's own mother, Rosemarie, would come over to babysit, and the two grandmothers would sit on the porch together watching Ee-wee and Mandy play.

Although Mandy appeared typical of any small child and blended well with Ee-wee, she would often disappear from Dale's apartment for long periods of time. "She's in the hospital," Dale would say when Cindy inquired. Cindy knew about Mandy's strange blood sugar disease and marveled how she could appear to be doing so well on one day and then disappear for a week or more into a hospitalization. It was such a shame.

In the middle of the night of August 3 to August 4, 2006, the McGillivray family heard a commotion. Cindy stuck her head outside and found the distressing sight of swarms of law enforcement personnel and vehicles, all seeming to center on her neighbor Dale's apartment. She couldn't imagine what trouble could involve the dedicated young father, but her thoughts immediately turned to Ee-wee's playmate, the little girl who could go from rosy-cheeked giggles to a long hospitalization in the blink of an eye. Cindy hurried outside and approached a member of the SWAT team. She told him, "You folks need to know there's a little girl inside. I'm worried about the baby, she's not well." The officer told her the little girl was fine—she had already been "delivered to her mother."

"I was astonished," Cindy says, "because I didn't think there was a mother. Dale had always led me to believe he was her parent and that's it—there was nobody else."

Amanda, in fact, very much had a mother, Linda Swaney. Although the child *had* been hospitalized once or twice during the last year, most of her "disappearances" from Dale's apartment were merely her regular stays at her full-time home with Mom. Linda, a fortysomething divorced mother of two and an ultrasound technician at an East Valley medical center, had first been introduced to Dale at Adventures 2000, a singles activities group. At one of their parties in 2002 she'd met the engaging younger man and then fallen in love. The pair did not marry, but a pregnancy resulted from their relationship and Dale moved into her new house. Amanda was born on January 4, 2004.

By July 4, 2004, Dale was out.

Linda had learned not to trust him and had even become afraid of him. "He was always getting even with people. He said he could ruin a pool real quick by throwing some oil in it. I had a pool. . . . I wanted him out, but I wanted to 'play nice' with him because I was scared of what he would do in retaliation."

Over the next two years she maintained an uneasy alliance with Dale, occasionally going to family events together. He kept a key to her house, and sometimes she'd come home from work to find him there with the baby. He usually had her on his days off, and he'd pick her up from the day care where Linda had left the child early in the morning. When Linda had foot surgery, Dale moved back in to help her out. However, she found this a frustrating arrangement because he often stayed out until two thirty or three in the morning and she'd be alone, crippled and in pain, with a crawling baby to care for.

In July of 2006, Dale brought over a friend and asked Linda to hire him to do some electrical work at her house because he was down on his luck and Dale wanted to help him. So Linda agreed to have Dale's tall friend Sammy install some ceiling fans in her house and rewire the pool. She gave cash to Dale to pass on to Sam. She had no idea where Sammy lived. She had no reason to care.

But during this time, Linda felt Dale was acting more and more unpredictable. He retrieved their daughter for fewer and fewer visits—sometimes day care would call her in distress saying Amanda had not been picked up by anyone yet. One day her former lover dyed his hair red and asked her what she thought. He was also experimenting with a beard. The more unreliable and quirky he became, the more her daughter suffered the consequences. Mandy was beginning to repeat strange things she'd heard at her dad's house. When Linda asked him about it, he got angry.

Neighbor Cindy McGillivray also describes a change in Dale in the weeks leading up to August 4, 2006. Whereas he had once been gregarious and outgoing, he was no longer even friendly. A big guy named Sam had moved in, and Sam was never friendly to begin with. Furthermore, Cindy hardly ever saw Ee-wee's playmate anymore.

One day she stepped out onto the walkway her apartment shared with Dale's and, seeing him there, attempted to greet him. But he did not respond. Suddenly, he jumped as if something had frightened him. "He turned and looked at me as if he were seeing me for the first time," she says. "'Have you heard about the Serial Shooter?' he asked me. 'Just on the news,' I said. Then he just stared at me real weird for a moment and turned and darted back into his own apartment. It was very odd."

By the summer of 2006, Linda Swaney's own frustrations with Dale had hit their breaking point. She thought Amanda was not safe with Dale. She filed for an order of protection against him. . . . She was not as lucky in this effort as a woman previously in Dale's life had been. Karen Hausner, Dale's second wife, had successfully obtained an Arizona order of protection against him some years earlier. But this time, a court wasn't as impressed by Linda's point of view. On July 16, 2006, a judge filled out a form with "DENIED" stamped across it. Unless she wanted to become a lawbreaker herself, the mother who had finally seen through the sympathy-seeking craftiness of her erst-while lover would have to continue handing over her baby, feeding tube and all, to Dale's care for unsupervised overnight visits. The reason for the judge's decision? There would be no restraining order against Dale Hausner because the judge had deemed him "not violent."

Less than three weeks later, the same Dale Hausner would be arrested as a serial killer.

———————

When the SWAT team busted in the apartment door, they found an arsenal. Law enforcement found many weapons strewn throughout Dale's apartment, often within easy reach of a curious toddler. Many were firearms: a shotgun, sawed off at the butt, on the floor; a 12-gauge leaning against the door; more than a dozen guns stored anywhere from behind the couch in the living room to on the floor in the bedroom. Everywhere the officers looked they found fanny packs, Tupperware bowls and beer boxes full of rounds and rounds and rounds of live bullets. Other items in the grisly inventory were blade weaponry—ice picks, awls and buck knives. There were fistfuls of plastic cigarette lighters, some in bowls, some in Baggies, some in special wooden boxes, all the lighters in the color orange.

Mandy, a child who could walk and crawl, with growing little hands that had learned to reach and grasp, had just spent the night inside this jumbled, unfettered, overstocked armory.

Linda had never been inside this apartment. Nor had Cindy. Very few people ever had. Dale would tell detectives later that day that "no one" came to his apartment, and he liked it that way, to "avoid problems."

The Hausner apartment was also stocked with other things.

Officers came across small bags of crystal meth, sitting on the television in plain sight, and in the kitchen, a glass pipe. The front part of the small apartment also had dozens of rows of neatly arranged hard liquor. The place was filled with multiple shelves of DVDs and CDs, their shrink-wrap seals unbroken.

On the coffee table was a book called *Stupid Criminals*, about the antics of people who'd been caught in their misdeeds, and another, a how-to book for various acts of revenge, titled *Getting Even*. There was also a satanic Bible.

But none of the writings in the apartment excited the investigators quite as much as a handwritten note they found in the kitchen.

Scrawled across the back of a flier for a boxing event was a message they felt had come straight from the mind of a serial killer. Interrogations and perhaps even testimony lay ahead of the pair that had been cuffed and hauled away in tonight's takedown, but whatever statements the two made from now on would always be for an audience—a detective, a family member, a jury. But this note was composed while a man thought no one was looking, and seemed to hold a bald declaration of self.

In black pen in hand-printed letters, the note proclaimed, "He who asks about the $5 bill is a homicidal maniac, thief, arsonist, destroyer of property, drug taking God among mortals."

No one knows for sure to what the "$5 bill" portion of the note refers. Did the killer lure in a victim by offering a five-dollar bill? Some speculate that the note may have been written in regards to the killings of Jose Ortiz or Marco Carillo or David Estrada, whose gunshot wounds were consistent with having been leaning over a car window or bending over. The note was written on the back of a boxing match flier—had there been an incident at the cash box, perhaps a humiliating one? Had the note been written to savor the writer's secret superiority over the annoying cashier?

Whatever happened with the five-dollar bill, the rest of the statement was a full catalogue of the crimes that would be laid at the doorstep of the Serial Shooter. Most importantly, it gave the justification for the deeds—the person was a "God," one who moved among "mortals."

No one else counted.

Incredulous at the find, the investigators dropped the note into an evidence bag. Of paramount importance to them now would be obtaining writing samples to compare Dale's handwriting to that on the note, and they knew they'd be booking a handwriting expert for trial.

Before the case was over, they would, indeed, have an expert tell them who wrote the note. And they would also find out that it couldn't have been further from a message written by the same person some years earlier.

Chapter Twenty-three

What Becomes a Killer Most

Stepping off a plane in a large city is often a wearying experience. The time spent in cramped quarters with recirculated air, the endless struggle with overhead bins and carry-on items makes the traveler tense and irritable. The din of the strange terminal engulfs him in yet a new layer of confusion and pressure.

At Phoenix Sky Harbor, that would definitely be the traveler's experience if he landed at Terminal 4, the biggest, most prestigious terminal, named after the state's biggest, most prestigious statesman, Barry M. Goldwater.

But the traveler who was lucky enough to be routed to tiny four-gate Terminal 2, built in the forties, would find a charming relic, a cozy little concourse where the lucky traveler would not be swept up in an anonymous tumult but rather gently embraced by contented emissaries of the city, such as a baby-faced janitor.

That janitor might just sidle up to you and tell you about his personal philosophies, like "Hug more and take lots of photos." After all, Terminal 2 was "like one of those small towns in Texas—without the accent," he'd say.* He'd worked in its carpeted

---

*Said to *Arizona Republic* reporter Angela Pancrazio on April 12, 2006.

snugness for two years, but he'd worked at the airport itself for a total of eight. If you were famous, he'd pull out a camera stashed—against the rules, but harmless, yeah?—in his custodial cart and pose with you.

That genial janitor had big ambitions for those rolls of film. He had a second career going, one that promised glamour. Not a single boxer ever came through Terminal 2 during Dale Hausner's shift who was not captured by the custodian's furtive lens. When he wasn't wheeling the cart through the outdated little airport concourse, Dale Hausner was hanging out at boxing gyms and matches. He worked his shutter and his charm in the sweaty, violent rooms until he became a fixture at the Hard Knocks Gym on Northern Avenue. The world of boxing from Phoenix to Vegas knew Dale Hausner. He got himself press credentials to the fights, albeit with iffy consistency, often offering to work for free. His shots of fighters appeared in such magazines as *Ringsports* and *Ringmaster*. Dale admired the eloquence of muscles. "He let his fists do the talking," wrote Dale of legendary pugilist Joe Louis. "They spoke volumes."

At five foot nine on a good day,* with a rather spindly build, Dale's own fists did not have much to say. Instead, he worked hard at ingratiating himself with men who *did* carry clout in their sinews.

Dale grew up in Nebraska as the youngest and smallest of five boys, the sons of auto mechanic and handyman Eugene Hausner.

Eugene Hausner had come from a big family, with at least twelve siblings, and had graduated from Technical High School in Omaha, Nebraska, in 1954. Married to Rosemarie, Eugene provided a modest but stable home for his children. Education was not a priority in their rough-and-tumble boys' world, but religion was, and so was loyalty. When the baby of the family, little Dale, was about five, the family moved to Arizona, except for the oldest son, Gregory, who was an adult by then and stayed in Nebraska.

---

*Dale's height is not certain. In some criminal court filings, he is listed as five-ten. In others, five-nine. But in some of his divorce filings he is reported as being five-eight. In person, Dale appears to be no more than five-eight and could be shorter.

Veteran Phoenix homicide detective Cliff Jewell with his own dogs. He paid close attention to animal cases he found. He built a matrix of cases that closed in on a serial killer.
Camille Kimball

ABOVE RIGHT:
Detective Ron Rock of the tiny Tolleson Police Department made an important phone call the last Friday of 2005.
Tolleson Police Department

LEFT:
Scottsdale PD detective Pete Salazar thought Sam had more to say. He wouldn't let go until Sam revealed his buried nightmare.
Scottsdale Police Department

Twenty-year-old self-taught guitarist David Estrada sang "Blackbird" by the Beatles to his mother. He was murdered eight weeks after this photo was taken.
Courtesy of Rebecca Estrada ("In loving memory of our beloved David.")

Claudia Gutierrez-Cruz used her dying breath to ask for her sister. The twenty-year-old was walking home from a long day of work at two different jobs because she missed the last bus.
From the files of the Scottsdale Police Department

After being in a coma for three weeks, Paul Patrick slowly came back to life. His dog, Misty, waited at the front door for him the whole time. Paul still had eighty pellets inside his torso and used a cane when not on his scooter.

Camille Kimball

Twenty-two-year-old Robin Blasnek was the last of the Serial Shooter victims. She died surrounded by good-hearted people who tried to help, bringing her blankets and towels and comfort.

*From the files of the
Mesa Police Department*

"He was always getting himself into trouble," says Rick Swier of his horse Apache. "I didn't think much when I first saw the blood on him." It was the vet, Dr. Mark Fink, who determined the horse had been shot.
Courtesy of Rick and Deb Swier

Buddy leans in for some love. Owner Stanley Wilkinson rubs the right spot. The wild burro still has a bullet embedded in his skull. He was shot at the beginning of the Serial Shooter spree.
Camille Kimball

A security camera at the top of a building captured what is believed to be Dale Hausner's silver Camry passing through several times at the time of the murders on December 29, 2005. Detective Jewell picked up important clues about the car and the person driving it.
Arizona Department of Environmental Quality

Phoenix homicide detective Cliff Jewell believed the .22-caliber shootings were connected to the shotgun shootings even though others didn't. The body of Marco Carillo was found at the far end of this sidewalk, the body of Jose Ortiz where the detective stands. The security camera at the corner of the building behind the detective missed capturing the Ortiz shooting by a few degrees. Timmy Tordai, shot one block over, survived a bullet through the neck.
Camille Kimball

ClearChannel's John Jacobs. He made Phoenix's misery count for something. Now the entire nation benefits from his program to dedicate billboard space to law enforcement needs. He passed away while Dale Hausner's trial was in jury selection.

Courtesy of the John Jacobs family

The killings stopped here. After he stepped across the grimy threshold of the Star Dust Inn, Sam was never out of sight of surveillance teams though he traversed the six hundred square miles of the Phoenix metroplex from end to end and side to side.

Spencer E. Lyman

Sam Dieteman testifies that he was truthful with officers the night he was arrested, "Until it came to the part about a life that I had taken. I had a hard time admitting to that." He took the stand against former roommate and killing partner, Dale Hausner.
Tom Tingle, The Arizona Republic

Jeff Hausner formally used his Fifth Amendment right not to incriminate himself by testifying in his brother's trial on January 22, 2009. He was dressed in jail stripes and shackles. From the gallery, his mother mouthed words to him.
Pat Shannahan, The Arizona Republic

Dale watches prosecutor Laura Reckart present evidence against him. He wrote a letter to the judge complaining about her "facial gestures," which he claimed were meant to mock him. He was very actively involved in his own defense. At the end of the proceedings, he told jurors, "I've never been so tired in my life."
Pat Shannahan, The Arizona Republic

Under friendly questioning from his own lawyer, Dale demonstrates how he holds a long barreled weapon and why he had the butt of a shotgun sawed off. Jurors later stated he did himself no favors when he took the stand.
Tom Tingle, The Arizona Republic

Later, Gregory would repeatedly travel back to Phoenix from his Omaha home to attend Dale's court proceedings and would eventually move back to Phoenix. Second son Kristopher, developmentally disabled, would write to the court in support of the family. Third son Jeff, the one who had introduced Sam Dieteman to Dale, hung out with Dale quite a bit and looked up to his younger brother. Fourth son Randy looked up to Dale, too. Randy also worked as a janitor at the airport, and for some time the two brothers lived in the same small apartment complex a few blocks from a church, the one at Glenrosa and Campbell, less than a quarter mile from Los Olivos Park, where Cherokee was shot and killed on December 29, and equally close to the chiropractor's office also shot that night.

Randy was always immaculately groomed. He had ambitious goals. He took on the unforgiving world of stand-up comedy. He learned to take the stage and make a crowd laugh, and he became deeply involved in the business of comedy. His life also revolved around his church, and he put his considerable promoting and organizing skills into developing singles events.

Randy's relationship with his baby brother was strong. Dale would use his boxing connections to obtain fight tickets and then donate them as prizes for the comedy tournaments that Randy put on.

Dale didn't appear to have too much trouble attracting women, first marrying at age nineteen and never seeming to stop thereafter.

At the time of his arrest, Dale seemed to have several girlfriends. One day at Terminal 2, he met a sophisticated lady passenger, Marianne Lescher, a nationally respected educator who had even been quoted in the *New York Times*. She was on the adjunct faculty at the Arizona State University School of Education, in the field of curriculum development, and her full-time job was as principal of an elementary school. The ingratiating janitor met her in the airport as her marriage was ending. He swept her off her feet with dinners at nice restaurants, tickets to pro hockey games and trips to Vegas. She never knew the romancing was financed by his professional shoplifting. Nor did she know that sometimes when he left her bed, he allegedly went out and shot living things.

Dale took photos of his prize girlfriend. She appears pretty and blond, older than him by fifteen years, and happy. Neither was he averse to stepping in front of the camera. One photo displays him in a pose that can only be described as meant for seduction. A formal portrait, in it Dale reclines suavely on the floor, clean shaven, shoulders back, leaning on his arm. He's wearing a black dinner jacket, collar open, his tie loosened by several inches and splayed wantonly across his chest, his coif studiously groomed, his eyes suggestive. He seems very much the dandy, almost as if he expects the phone to ring at any moment with *Gentlemen's Quarterly* on the line.

Although Dale was a fellow well able to seduce a series of women into weddings and serious relationships, in fact neither he nor his brothers seemed able to repeat Dad's success when it came to marriage. Eugene and Rosemarie were still going strong in a marriage that had lasted several decades, but Randy hadn't yet found the right girl, and Dale and middle brother Jeff had both become familiar with divorce court. Through it all, the Hausners displayed a remarkable streak of softheartedness as well as devotion to one another. Randy entertained underprivileged children. Dale had his mother's name published in a boxing magazine, asking for prayers to see her through an illness. Middle brother Jeff was known for taking in stray dogs and stray people.

One of Jeff's drifters was a burly fellow, an electrician by trade, Sam Dieteman.

Hard times came and went, but the Hausner tribe saw one another often and stayed interconnected. Dale and Randy both ventured into broadcasting, Randy guesting on comedy shows and Dale purchasing airtime for something he titled "Fist City," on his favorite topic, boxing. Dale also briefly hosted a cable television show on that sport.

Dale never missed a weigh-in, often bringing the capstone females in his life—his elderly mother and his infant daughter—to the arena, passing the baby around for beefy cuddles and introducing Mom to muscle-bound boxers.

Dale wasn't afraid to share his private life in that world of steel jaws and brass-knuckle brawn. In addition to the prayer request for his mother, *Ringsports* managing editor Rusty Rubin once put out an appeal on Dale's own behalf: "Prayers are requested for Ringsports.com photo journalist Dale Hausner of

Arizona, who is having problems with cancer."* Hard Knocks Gym trainer Clement Vierra began organizing a fund-raiser to help Dale with Mandy's doctor bills. It's not known how the tally compared to the one held by Camelback Toyota.

Dale made sure everyone knew how much he adored the petite princess.

"She is my little sweetie and I love her with all my heart," he wrote in an e-mail sent to his large network of contacts and co-workers. He placed her in the arms of boxers and snapped away. *"There is no such thing as too many pictures,"* he counseled in that e-mail.

After all, photos were all he had left of two other toddlers, babies whose memory had inspired that letter in the first place.

Tracie Hazelett, nineteen years old and pregnant, was the first female to agree to become Dale Hausner's wife. Her boy, Donovan, was born a few weeks after she became Mrs. Hausner. The nineteen-year-old groom welcomed him, even though the baby was the child of another man and would have a different last name. Soon Dale and Tracie gave Donovan a little brother. Jeremiah Hausner was born in 1992.

Tracie thought she had lucked into a romantic man who would love her and shelter her babies. But the dream melted away. After just eighteen months, she had filed for divorce and Dale was zeroing in on the second Mrs. Hausner. The day after the divorce with Tracie came through in 1994, Dale, then twenty-one, took another bride.

Karen Hausner was devoted not just to her husband, not just to his son by another woman, but also to little Donovan, who was no blood relation to either of them. Karen and Dale wandered out

---

*What this appeal refers to is unclear. Dale may have been asking for help for his daughter, his mother, his father or himself. Dale's enthusiasm for charitable fund-raisers does not always match the facts of his life. At one point he claimed to have had "six surgeries for skin cancer," but documentation has not been produced, nor did his lifestyle or work record seem to substantiate claims of his having a disabling cancer, nor does he have any visible scars.

to Texas to make their fortune as soon as they were married. But Dale was not the kind of guy to walk out of his children's lives. None of the Hausner men ever did that. In November 1994, just six months after the wedding to Karen and six-months-plus-one-day after the dissolution of the first marriage, cherubic eighteen-month-old Jeremiah and spunky preschooler Donovan were staying with Dale and their new stepmother in the Lone Star state.

———————

Corsicana, Texas, is a small town about forty-five minutes south of Dallas. Maybe it's one of those "small Texas towns" Dale was talking about when he described the hominess of Terminal 2. Corsicana's main attractions are a synagogue abandoned to the administration of the city, which was willing to take it on thanks to its "unique" onion-domed architecture, and the Russell Stover candy factory. In the 1990 census, 23,911 persons claimed Corsicana as home. If you're on your way to Houston, about two or three hours away, you'll cruise down Interstate 45 from Corsicana, and before long you'll cross Richland Creek, a wetland recreation area that loops across the highway. With a proper permit, feral hogs, woodcock and hare can be hunted there all year long. And don't forget the purple gallinule, a large ducklike marsh fowl, which, in proper Texan contrarian fashion, actually sports feathers that are blue and green, not purple. The area is rough; four-wheel drive is recommended at Richland Creek, warns the state's Parks Department.

In the predawn hours of a Saturday in early November 1994, Dale Hausner's uniquely blended new family—new wife, new son from an old marriage, and stepson from a previous relationship of the ex-wife's—was traveling along Interstate 45. Dallas, the destination, was little more than an hour away now. They'd been driving all night. Karen was at the wheel. The boys were asleep. So was Dale.

And, to the horror of all, soon Karen would be, too. The young stepmother drifted off the pavement right as I-45 passed over the marshy, winter waters of Richland Creek.

The car plunged twenty-five feet over the side.

"*My boys drowned in a filthy, freezing, cold body of water,*" Dale wrote in an e-mail on the tenth anniversary of the accident.

"I tried to get them out but the current was awful and the water was freezing and I almost died trying to find them."

It took all day for rescue crews from Corsicana to find two-year-old Donovan. His body wasn't recovered until three o'clock in the afternoon.

Corsicana crews wouldn't find baby Jeremiah for three days, until Tuesday morning. His little body washed up on the banks, in thick foliage, about ten miles south of town.

Dale and Karen suffered minor injuries and a lifetime of grief.

"Remember to hug and kiss your loved ones as I wish I could do to my two boys, Donovan and Jeremiah," Dale wrote in the e-mail. *"Life is short and your life can change as fast as mine did."*

Chapter Twenty-four

We act like we're demigods and gods. You know?

Dale Hausner

Now, in August 2006, Dale's life was about to undergo another swift change. On Thursday, August 3, he put his daughter to bed as a full-time professional shoplifter, a part-time professional photographer, a City of Phoenix janitorial employee and a certified bartender. Before she woke up the next morning, he was in custody as the Serial Shooter and he would likely never see her again. In fact, he himself would probably never see the outside of a jail or courtroom for the rest of his life.

But not for nothing did Dale's older brothers admire him. Wearing only gym shorts and handcuffs, Dale Hausner began his first interrogation in the interview room with an attitude of confidence and cheerfulness. The following sections are from the interview's transcript.*

Detective Clark Schwarzkopf: *Morning.*

Dale Hausner: *Morning! How are you?*

CS: *Good. How are you?*

DH: *Pretty good.*

---

*The transcript has been edited for length and clarity.

CS: *Dale, I'm Detective Schwartzkopf. I'm with the Phoenix Police Department. Um, I, ah, asked you to be brought down today, I have some questions I have to ask you about some stuff.*

DH: *No problem!*

(Detective Schwartzkopf delivers Dale's Miranda rights.)

DH: *You need my height, weight, anything like that?*

CS: *No, that's okay, I'll get it.*

DH: *Like I told the other officers, I'll be more than willing to talk to you, about anything you guys wanna know about . . . so . . .*

CS: *Great.*

DH: *I'm not gonna hide anything, give you a hard time.*

CS: *Fantastic! I appreciate that. I apologize for having to sit around for so long.* *

DH: *Oh no, this is, they were real nice about [everything] and they were very nice and I, I appreciate that.*

CS: *You have a roommate?*

DH: *Not really a roommate. I told him he could stay with me for a little bit until he gets on his feet cause he had nowhere else to go so . . . Sam's a pretty good guy.*

CS: *Do you own a vehicle?*

DH: *Yes, I do. It's a 1998 Toyota Camry. It's license is RHZ-537. And it's blue.† I bought it February 3rd of '05. The day before my birthday. Happy birthday to me. Before that I owned a 1988 Buick.*

CS: *[After discussion of baby Amanda and her mother] You have a cordial relationship with the mother? Let me ask you another thing. I found out there was an issue of, uhm, did she try to take a restraining order on you for some reason?*

---

*Note: It is midmorning. Dale has been in custody since midnight.

† The exact color of the car would become a complicated issue at trial.

DH: *No, what it is is um, she gets—she apparently, typical woman, I don't know what you think, but she, she gets mad at me because I don't, I didn't want a committed relationship even though we have a baby together. And she'd get mad at me for not wanting to be with her. And then she would fight and she'd call me names and I'd hang up on her and she'd call me back and so, um, we got into a fight, let's see, I don't, can't remember exactly, two weeks ago we got into a big fight. I told her to fuck off, I'm tired of listening to you, I've been nice, but, you know, you've been calling me all these names—fuck you. And I told her I never want to be with you, I'm not gonna be with you. The hell with you and everything you stand for. Hung up on her. And then two or three days later somebody knocked on my door and said, court order papers, and what it was was she wants to change [Amanda's] last name back to Swaney. A good kick in the ass for me.*

CS: *I understand.*

DH: *She knows I fuckin' hate that! And then she said she also wants me to have to go to, uh, some parenting classes, as does she, in the paper it says that her and I both have to go these classes. She also wants me to pay child support even though, this pisses me off, I pay more than I should right now for all the crap I buy for her. I'm paying more and, uh, she also wants me to be tested constantly for methamphetamine* [Note: Less than five minutes earlier, Dale had admitted to Detective Schwartzkopf that he might have smoked some meth either the previous night or the night before.] *and I told her 'I'll go to all your classes, I'll do all your stuff.' I've passed all her drug tests she's ever given me, and I told her 'I have no problem doing all that stuff you want me to.'*

CS: *So this is a bitter issue?*

DH: *Yeah, we just go back and forth. She just gets pissed off cause you know I didn't I didn't wanna marry her, I never really wanted to marry her and she figured that out, I didn't want a marriage, just wanted to have a baby because I had two kids before that passed away in a car wreck in 1994. I guess when she realized I wasn't coming around to wanting to move back in with her cause I lived with her for about a* *year, um, when she found out I'd been smoking methamphet-amine, she gave me the boot and I, ah, left.*

CS: *I understand. Do you have any idea why you're down here today?*

DH: *I think so.*

CS: *Do you?*

DH: *Sam, Sam and I were at the casino about a week and a half or two weeks ago and they pulled us in there and read us the riot act. They said we were slashing a bunch of tires out in the parking lot, which is a filthy lie. . . . I don't know what their problem was, but they grilled us, they took our pictures, they just looked through my car . . . found my ice pick, cause I'm also a bartender, and they gave us a bunch of shit about that and said you're never allowed back on the casino prop-erty. 'We have you on tape slashing tires.' I told 'em, I come here to relax. If I lose money I'm not mad at anybody else.*

CS: *You don't blame it on anybody else?*

DH: *Yeah, I'm like, look . . . you know, "I'll answer all your questions* (as if addressing casino personnel) *you don't need a search warrant, check in my car for anything you wanna check." They found a knife. I said that's what I use to cut my limes. They found an awl, that's what Sam uses, and then they found an ice pick.*

CS: *Did they say anything about this incident being captured on video?*

DH: *Yes, they did. They said, "We have, we know it was you, we have it on video but we're not gonna prosecute you." And I'm like, "If you have it on video and you knew it was us, don't think I wouldn't know you wouldn't prosecute me!" [sic] I have a feeling that they decided to bluff our ass on it so, I'm pretty sure that's what it is. This. This is kind of severe for the SWAT team to come out, I think. I mean, Jesus Christ, scared the shit out of me!*

CS: *Alright.*

DH: *Uhm, the only thing I could think of was maybe they found* *out I was using drugs or something or their great big ass sting or something so . . . It's either one of those two things. That's the only thing I can think of.*

CS: *Alright. Well. It's a little more complicated than that.*

● ● ●

CS: *Have you been following at all what's going on in the city of Phoenix lately?*

DH: *Absolutely. I've been following the Baseline Rapist and I've been following the Serial Killer.**

CS: *What do you, what do you know?*

DH: *I know everything that's in the newspapers because I even clipped them out and saved them. I have all the clippings at the house, that's the reason, I even have some back dated stuff, I keep track, I know that they're looking for a black guy with a wig.† . . . he's 25 to 30, he's five foot ten to six foot, he's a hundred and seventy pounds. And I keep track of the Serial Killer, the other guy that's going around shooting people. . . . um . . .*

CS: *What do you know about that particular case?*

DH: *Thirty-five people shot‡ ah, animals, horses, dogs, um, five, six people dead.§ Ummmm . . . several cities, counties, what-*

---

*It's interesting to see how Dale referred to the perpetrator alleged to be himself. He seemed to immediately want to group the Serial Shooter in with those national figures who were already considered "serial killers." At times he used the term "serial killer" in a way that led the detective to believe he might've been referring to the other serial killer plaguing the valley at the time, the Baseline Rapist, possibly in an attempt to obfuscate or elicit information.

† Note: This refers to the Baseline Rapist.

‡ Note: This is a figure not used on the news but heard on the wiretap when the two men corrected the news to this higher figure.

§ The Serial Shooter could never be sure whether his victim lived or died. If the case made the news, Dale tracked it carefully. But many incidents did not make the news. The tallies that Dale threw around on the wiretaps and in his police interviews were products of his own math, his own imagination, and possible knowledge of crimes still unknown to the police.

*ever you call 'em, been shot up . . . ummm . . . let me think . . .
Serial Killer . . . I guess that's about it.*

CS: *Okay. Is there any particular reason why you've taken such
an interest in these?*

DH: *I just, I find it interesting. I have a movie called* The History of Violence. *I also have the movie* Starkweather *which
was the first time, I don't know if you know any of this stuff.
Stark—Charles Starkweather was the first person to ever
even go on a serial killing spree in America. He was from
Nebraska, which is, you know, my home town [sic].*

• • •

CS: *My problem here is that a person has come forward and
actually given me information that, um, Mr. Dieteman has
been, has been bragging about being the shooter in this particular series of crimes. Does that shock you?*

DH: *Yeah! That does! I can't believe that! I, I, I, I . . . don't
know.*

CS: *Do you think it's possible that he could do something like
that?*

DH: *I don't really think that he—been in trouble with the law a
lot, I'm sure you have his rap sheet for violence and stuff, but
I don't know if he's ever . . .*

CS: *How does he earn his money? What's he do?*

DH: *I have no idea.**

CS: *Why do you think he would even mention the fact that he
was—that he was involved in some kind of—*

DH: *Okay, let's say I'm Sam in a bar. I'm talking shit and his
buddy, say, Dale—even though it's not me sittin' next to
him—Hey, I'm out shootin' people! Why would he do that?!*

---

*Note: In fact, Sam considered Dale his employer, having been trained by
him in professional shoplifting, been transported by him to and from shoplifting sites, and had his goods fenced by Dale.

Mmmmm. . . . Maybe self esteem problems. Maybe the kid doesn't have . . .

CS: *Does he have a self esteem issue?*

DH: *Yeah, he doesn't have self-esteem. He tells me he's worthless, you know, he—*

CS: *He said that to you? He thinks he's worthless?*

DH: *Yeah, he said he can't wait to die and stuff and he just says, uh, he says, you know "I wish I could be like you." You know, "you got a job, a car, a house, a kid." You know, and "You get to see your kid all the time. My kids are in Minnesota, I never get to see my kids. I'm just worthless." I'd go "No, you're not worthless, man!" He'd go, "Yeah, I am. Just a fuckin' drain on society," you know, and I'm like, "Whatever," you know, so. Maybe if he was gonna, I—I don't think, you know, what—why he would do that, but if you ask me why would somebody do that? Why would somebody say something to strike fear, maybe make people afraid of you or to in a sick way boost yourself up, you know, "I'm the killer," you know, "Here I am."*

• • •

CS: *Has Sam ever, when you guys are watching all this stuff [news coverage of the Serial Shooter], has he ever come out and said, "That's cool"?*

DH: *We joke around. Sometimes I'll say, you know, we'll be watching on TV and I'll say, "Man, that's what you fucking get when you walk down the street at three am! Man, someone's gonna drive [by] and shoot you in the ass." People just don't listen, you know? People take this shit as a joke. You will never find me walking around at four am. Down a dark street. That's the kind of stuff we talk about. It was back and forth and we talk about, you know, "How can you have a hundred fifty fucking cops on this and not have any kind of clues theirselves and we have no idea for doing all that! Jesus Christ!!!! How hard can it be to catch somebody doing this shit, you know?"*

CS: *How stupid are we . . . ?*

DH: *Yeah! And it's like why don't they put—I'm not trying to . . .*

CS: *No, no, no. That's fine!*

DH: *Really, I'm not—I don't want you to be insulted.*

CS: *No, I'm not! I'm not at all!*

DH: *I mean, and I'm not a genius or anything, but, um, we was talkin' about this sh—couldn't be this hard. I mean, maybe it is this hard to catch people. . . .*

CS: *Maybe the person's just really good.*

DH: *Could be.*

• • •

CS: *Okay, so you guys were actually physically at one of these scenes? That kind of piques my curiosity.*

DH: *I gave my ID and everything to the police officer, gave a full statement. Stayed around as long as I could.*

CS: *Okay, so you guys are out looking for your cat . . .*

DH: *"Come here, Tinky!" We saw some guy sitting on his porch. "Hey, man, have you seen a cat? A little gray cat about this big?" He walks up and he goes . . . (makes a noise of astonishment) . . . You know, I'm like "What the heck, man!!?" He's got blood pouring out of his pockets. I'm like, "Oh, shit! What happened?" He said, "they shot me." And I said, "who shot you?" He said, "they shot me." . . . Round and round like that for a little bit. And I said, "Man! Don't touch me!!!!"* (Dale demonstrates his fastidious nature, or as Cliff Jewell declares, "Dale doesn't like to get icky.") *'Cause he wanted to touch me. I said, "Don't touch me, man!!!" You know, I said, "You stay here, I'm gonna go get my cell phone," I went to go get my cell phone. The cops pulled up . . . (makes a motion and noise imitating flagging down the police) . . . jumping up and down. Got 'em. Flagged 'em* *over there. They went over there. I gave a full statement. Gave him my card,* I told him as many as he wants. Sam also gave a statement.*

CS: *Okay, you saw the blood?*

DH: *Oh my god! Yeah, I almost puked!!!*

CS: *Yeah?*

DH: *Yeah! Well, I didn't know what it was at first, cause I, you know, he had one big hole right here.* (Dale gestures to his torso.) *And a bunch of thick streams of blood and I'm like, whoa!! He went to touch me! I said, "Hey, don't touch!" And he turned around and I'm like, "Oh, my God!, I-I'm outta here!" you know, I'm . . .* (imitates vomiting) *. . . He had little dots like someone took an ice pick and went pow, pow, pow, pow, pow, pow all over his back. I'd never seen anything like that. I seen it on TV all the time, you know? I never saw it, I was like . . .* (imitates vomiting) *. . . So I ran . . . I went to go get my cell phone and that's when the cops pulled up . . .* (makes sound of tires screeching) *. . . and I'm like . . .* (imitates flagging down the police) *. . . jumpin' up and down! "Hey, over here!" Cause they were on the wrong side of the fence. If you don't mind my asking, did the guy live? Is he ok?*

CS: *He did live.*

DH: *Oh, okay.*

CS: *He's not okay. I mean, who is okay when they get hit with shotgun blasts? You always have scarring for the rest of your life.*

• • •

CS: *We've had electronic surveillances in your apartment.*

DH: *Uh-hum.*

---

*Dale was apparently referring to a business card he may have made for his bartending, photography and/or broadcast enterprises. Or it may or may not be an accurate statement.

SC: *We've picked up some very interesting conversations with Mr. Dieteman and —and including you, okay?*

DH: *'Kay.*

CS: *I don't think you've been completely honest with me about what you've been doing.*

DH: *Okay.*

CS: *I have you saying "We are pioneers, Sam." Would you explain to me why you would say something like that?*

DH: *Just—I don't know—just pioneers, you know, or—I don't know, just—pioneers— we just went somewhere that nobody else has ever done before, so I don't know. Just—just we're pioneers. We're—we act like we're demi-gods and gods. And, and, you know, it's just like a—kind of like joking, you know? I guess other people wouldn't find it very funny. . . .*

CS: *There have been thirty-six random acts of shooting since May of last year, you know that?*

DH: *Dogs, horses, people* (nods head affirmatively). *So you think I'm part of this?*

CS: *What do you think?*

DH: *I think you think I'm part of this. I think you think I'm—me and Sammy are in this car killing everybody since May of '05. That's what I think. You guys are gonna charge me with murder and all this other crap. I'm gonna fucking go to jail and then they're gonna take my house, that's what I think.*

• • •

CS: *You have a history of violence.*

DH: *I'm not, you know, a fucking idiot, you know. Or a homicidal maniac or anything like that.*

CS: *Do you understand why we ask you these questions?*

DH: *Yeah. You've got all kinds of evidence. My car and my guns and I have—I'm a walking weapons arsenal. I have all kinds of guns in the house, you know? I think the only violence I have* *in my past was in ninety two or three, I clunked somebody in a restaurant, you know? So I'm really—I joke about it but I really don't like violence. I mean, like when I saw that other, the older guy who had been shot . . . just about made me throw up all over the place. It was just amazing. I don't get off on stuff like that. I didn't go home and masturbate or any crazy stuff like that, that, that sickos do and stuff like that. I know when you burn something down, people are always talkin' about the sexual gratification. I do not. I do not enjoy violence, because I have a daughter at home I have to look after. I have no reason to go on killing sprees, you know? I—and I understand you don't believe me and that's your job.*

• • •

CS: *My concern is the driving around* [Note: Tuesday night as they were being tailed]. *That to me is a huge red flag.*

DH: *If we did something wrong we would've done it when we were out driving around. We did nothing wrong though. We committed no murders. I committed no murders. Sam committed no murders.*

CS: *That's true. But the flip side is that maybe you guys didn't find a target, either?*

DH: *That's kind of reaching, but, um . . .* (chuckling)

CS: *Is it?*

DH: *Yes, sir, it is because if I was gonna kill somebody I could find somebody walking somewhere out there.*

CS: *How do you know that you could find somebody walking?*

DH: (shaking head negatively) *No sir, I see people walking all the time. All over the place. I mean, people—people don't learn. They just don't listen. People get shot all the time, 'cause they just don't stay home and listen. They just—they're stupid and they just don't listen and there's always somebody drunk and staggering around out there or you know, people just think, "Oh, it ain't gonna happen to me."*

Mesa detective Don Byers has entered the room. He tells Dale of his belief that Dale shot and killed the Mesa girl, Robin Blasnek. He reviews some of their evidence against him, and focuses on the wiretaps.

> DB: . . . *All these conversations—you're gonna hear 'em in court. A jury's gonna hear 'em in court and—and what do you think you're gonna look like?*
>
> DH: *A monster.*
>
> DB: *You're gonna look like a monster!*

• • •

> CS: *I think that what happened was that, unfortunately, in this spree that you and Sam were caught up in? Two people unfortunately died!* I don't think you wanted to kill anybody!! I really don't!! Because if you did I think you would've used something else. I wouldn't think you would be banging away with a .410! You would've been banging away with a 12 gauge! You own a 12 gauge! You have access to a twelve!! You have a 28 gauge! I mean you have access to weapons that could easily, easily kill every single one of these people that I've investigated. You have that access and you didn't do it. Okay? I don't think you meant to kill people! Maybe I'm wrong I don't think you did! I really don't! I think this was all about attention! I think it was all about notoriety! I think that you got caught up in this whirlwind of watching this whole parade! This whole charade! This whole circus that has just swarmed this community! And now it's nationally known! And I think you just got caught up in it and I think it just perpetuated itself one after the other after the other. You have the Baseline Killer! And you have all this media! And you've been following it! And you know that! And I know that you've been following it! I know that! And I know that when*

---

*Note: Clark is still not including the .22-caliber murders from Cliff's files.

the Baseline Killer got a lot of press? When you were getting your shootings? I know that those shootings stepped up! I know that!

DH: (nods head affirmatively) *Yeah . . .*

CS: *I am a nice guy. I am not one of these guys that comes in and starts screaming at people. What good does that do? See, I think you have a conscience. I really do! I don't think you're the person that the media has described here, I really don't! Now, Dieteman, on the other hand, with his past, wouldn't surprise me a bit! It wouldn't surprise me a bit that he is the animal that everybody describes him as. But look at you. You have a daughter—two and a half years old—that you care for all the time because, from what you're telling me, she's deathly sick?*

DH: *Von Gierke's Disease. It's not a very good disease.*

CS: *Right. You take care of her. You're a responsible parent. Something happened here that just came spinning out of control. You and I both know it. The only thing that's left here is to answer why? That's it! That's the only thing that's left!*

DH: *I'm—I'm sorry, sir, you have to go over to Sam and ask him, 'cause I wasn't there for any killings. I did not drive the car for any killings. I did not pull the trigger on anybody. I'm not a murderer. I don't kill people!*

Detective Pete Salazar: *Dale, let me step in right here. My name is Pete Salazar. I'm a detective with Scottsdale Police Department and you just introduced something that's very important. We're already asking Sam, okay? He wants to talk. He wants to cooperate. You've made a couple fatal mistakes. You've introduced information to us that we are the only ones who knew. You introduced the .410. You've introduced that in the idea of using it in the shooting. You've made that mistake. You've told us about the .410.*

DH: *Yeah, I told 'em about everything.*

PS: *We're the only ones who knew that information. You've made that mistake. You've made several errors in this and in our conversations that clearly indicate that you have not provided all the information that you know. In addition to that,* *this is gonna be a problem: we have nothing to take back to the families and you've described yourself, the monster. Is that what you want to be? Or do you want to have an opportunity to show some remorse to the family members who have lost their loved ones?*

DH: *I feel . . . I feel for anybody who loses a loved one, but I didn't take any lives.*

PS: *Well, this is your opportunity. This is your opportunity.*

DH: *Ummm, I've told . . . I'm sorry. You guys are just gonna have to just leave and think whatever you want and tell the families I'm a monster or scum of the earth type of guy.*

PS: *It's not what we think: it's what the evidence can prove . . .*

DH: (nods head affirmatively) *Okay . . .*

PS: *And the evidence can prove that you're responsible for this. Sam is over there laying it all out and this is your last opportunity to tell us what happened. Are you the driver? Were you guys havin'—trying to get a body count? Did you go out on separate nights by yourself? Did you take turns? What were the roles you played in this? How were you keeping score? What was the significance of the map? Why were you keeping details on this? See, I think you guys want some competition. Some sick competition. That's my opinion.*

DH: *Hmmm . . . (inaudible) . . . I'm sorry.*

PS: *I don't want an apology.*

DH: *I mean I'm sorry . . . (inaudible) . . .*

PS: *You don't owe me an apology. You owe the families apologies.*

DH: *Actually, no I don't, sir! I didn't kill anybody. I know what it's like to lose loved ones. It's not . . . it's not a good thing. I lost—*

PS: *All of us do.*

DH: *I lost both of my children that were, in 1994, in a car wreck. I never ever ever want to go through that feeling again*

> *nor would I want anybody else to go through that, so, I know*
> *you don't believe me and you can think I'm full of shit all you*
> *want, but when my kids . . . when both my boys died in 1994,*
> *that forever changed me. The way I look at life and especially*
> *now that I have a daughter, I sure wouldn't be out gunning*
> *people down in the street for no reason to get caught.*

A new detective has entered the room. He is muscular and clean-shaven. He has a deep and resonant voice. His hair is clipped into a very tight crew cut, ending in a widow's peak over his eyes that follow everything with the intensity of a lynx. A detective of thirteen years with Phoenix Police, Darren Udd has been tailing Dale for the last three days and has been listening to the wiretaps all night, as Dale is heard to laugh about killings, reenact them, gloat about the tally and tease Sam for being "chicken."

DH: *So how would he [Sam] know I'm out murdering people?*
I don't even come back and brag to 'im and he doesn't say
anything?

Detective Darren Udd: *You tell me.*

DH: *I don't, I don't know.*

DU: *Maybe he's got a conscience! Maybe Sam over there's got*
a conscience! Because you don't. You are going to jail, you
understand that? Because you are the Serial Shooter!

DH: *No, I'm not.*

DU: *No, you are! Okay? You and Sam are the Serial Shooter!!!*
And quite frankly, I'm amazed that with the notoriety that
you are going to get, 'kay, 'cause guess what? Your face and
Sam's and your brother's even is gonna be plastered nation-
wide* probably internationally, and you are gonna go down
in history!!! Yet you don't want to take any credit for what
you've done!!! Which kinda boggles me because, to be honest

---

*Note: They were; even as Udd was saying this, all networks were covering the press conference in downtown Phoenix.

with you, I have studied some serial cases before and you know the BTK killer?

DH: *Dennis Rader.*

DU: *What a surprise, you knew the name! What, did you ever see him talk about that crime?*

DH: (nods head affirmatively) *Yeah . . .*

DU: *[He speaks] in this very frank monotone. Just like you.*

DH: *He said, "Oh, can I get a cup of coffee? Sure, I'm done with it. Let me write BTK on it, so dah-dah-dah." Yeah, watched 'em all, watched all the specials.*

DU: *Okay, you know more than I do. I'd be willing to bet that.*

DH: *I'm sorry, I don't get where you're going with this?*

DU: *Well, your attitude and your actions are exactly the same as Dennis Rader. You have the nonchalant attitude, but the only thing is that he wanted the notoriety. He wanted his face and name to go down in history. And you don't want that. 'Cuz now you know that you're going to prison.*

DH: (nods head up and down affirmatively)

DU: *Why? Why is that after doing all of this and you guys are the "pioneers"? "RVing"? And that—that's pretty catchy to be honest! I liked it.*

DH: *I never said that.*

DU: *So why don't you want the notoriety?*

DH: *'Cause I didn't do it.*

DU: *You did! You guys are the "pioneers"! You guys outdid the Baseline Rapist, but guess what? You're in here! So, god willing, he'll be in here right behind ya. And you'll still probably beat him as far as the amount of victims. Why don't you want that notoriety? That's what I don't understand.*

DH: *I don't wanna take credit for something I didn't do, especially something that sick, like homicides, and premeditated murder and what-not, you know? I mean Sam's admitting to all those murders, that's good for him and good for you guys,* 'cause that makes it easier, but why he would wanna say I'm in on it, is beyond me, I mean, that don't make any sense.

DU: *Because you were in on it. And you were completely involved in the shootings.*

DH: *I just can't believe you guys think I did all these crimes and I can't—you know? That's amazing to me!*

PS: *Shouldn't be. It's very easy to see that you've done 'em all. If we weren't in the middle of puttin' it all together, I would just lay it all out for you, so you could see it piece by piece by piece by piece. Play the audio tapes of all your conversations and I'd just wanna sit here and see the reaction on your face and it would probably be unfazed. It would be unfazed because you are just a classic sociopath.*

DH: *You can call me all the names you want, but doesn't mean I'm gonna . . .*

PS: *I'm not name-calling! I'm not name-calling.*

DH: *I've been cooperating the whole time and I told you guys everything you wanna know. I don't know why Sam would say all that stuff. It's very upsetting. I was very good to him. Opened up my home to him.*

PS: *How did it feel?*

DH: *What's that? To find out Sam was trying to pin stuff on me? I didn't like that at all!*

PS: *No. No. Watchin' these people go down in anguish and pain?*

DH: *. . . (inaudible) . . . anguish and pain!*

PS: *The slow roll, right up on 'em, and just blast 'em? Were you laughing?*

DU: *Were you?*

DH: *I don't . . .* (shaking head from side to side negatively) *. . .*

DU: *Look up at us, Dale!*

DH: *I wasn't—I wasn't there!*

DU: *Yes, you were!*

DH: *No, I wasn't!*

PS: *Did it arouse you? Was this some sort of perverted fetish?*

DH: *Okay, that's enough! Can I get a lawyer in here if you guys are gonna try this stuff on me?*

DU: *Try what stuff?*

DH: *I—I'm a pervert. Jacking off while shooting people. That's—that's—I mean, come on!*

DU: *Answer his question, Dale. Did you get aroused from the shootings?*

DH: *Ask Sam if it aroused him.*

PS: *He's a broke man. He's remorseful.*

DH: *I'm not gonna be remorseful for somethin' I didn't do. I'm sorry for those people who got hurt and killed. . . . ummm.*

PS: *You've got vivid images. You've seen every one of those victims go down and I can see you enjoyed every minute of it. I'm gonna prove this.*

DH: *No! I wasn't there! I didn't do anything! I don't picture anything because I wasn't there. I wasn't there! I wasn't there! I didn't do anything! I wasn't aroused because I wasn't there!*

DU: *I don't know, you gave quite a reaction to his question.*

DH: *I'm not a pervert! I got a little daughter! I'm not a pervert! I don't like perverts! I don't like prostitutes! I don't like . . .*

DU: *Just because . . .*

DH: *. . . child molestors!*

DU: *. . . you have a daughter doesn't mean you're not a pervert.*

DH: *I know, but that's why it—I don't—*

DU: *You know that, right?*

DH: *I'm not a pervert. I'm . . .*

DU: *What do you classify as a pervert? What's a pervert?*

DH: *Someone who would jack off while they're shooting some-body in the back with a shotgun! I mean come on! That's not right!*

DU: *We didn't say that.*

DH: *Or someone who lights fires with masturbation . . .*

PS: *How do you know they were shot in the back?*

DH: *You guys don't believe me. I understand that. You guys look at me like I'm a psycho-sociopathic monster and I under-stand that and I understand where you're coming from.*

DU: *You understand that because you know it to be true.*

PS: *You know how many university professors are gonna wanna interview you?*

DH: *Uh, zero will get an interview from me. I'm not gonna talk to anyone about that!!*

PS: *You're a textbook . . .*

DU: *Pervert! Look up at us, Dale. You're a pervert, okay? You got off . . .*

DH: *I'm not gonna answer any more questions.*

DU: *Why not?!*

DH: *You guys are being disrespectful. That's why!*

PS: *And we finally found what really gets to you! We found the truth.*

DU: *And that's why you did this. Just to get off, right?*

DH: (no response)

DU: *You don't wanna answer our questions anymore?*

DH: *Not until you guys apologize for calling me a pervert!! I'll be more than happy to answer your questions!*

PS: *You apologize to the family members!!*

(Detectives exit interview room.)

Chapter Twenty-five

No one else believed me yet.

Cliff Jewell

Even before Dale and Sam started talking to Detectives Schwartzkopf, Salazar, Udd and many others, before the day was through, the heads of their agencies as well as the mayor of Phoenix gathered in the great atrium of the Phoenix City Hall and faced the press. The entire nation tuned in.

Several times as reporters asked for details about the suspects, Assistant Phoenix Police Chief Kevin Robinson begged off by saying, "The interviews are still in process." In fact, at that early hour, the interviews had not yet even begun, as police out in Mesa, where the men were in custody, scurried around getting even more search warrant paperwork in place. After the takedown, a Superior Court judge had been roused from his bed in order to review and put his signature on more of the warrants. The wiretaps had been approved hours earlier, under a tangle of emergency statutes requiring only the approval of the county attorney. Mesa officials, who had been in the Serial Shooter business for only two weeks at this point, insisted on more judicial backup. In fact, Dale Hausner's defense team would later make a heroic effort to have the wiretap evidence, where Dale is heard to boast and gloat, congratulate and goad, tossed out based on the use of that rare emergency statute. But after many hearings, including both the compelled testimony of the county attorney himself and the even odder spectacle of one Superior Court judge appearing as a witness before another, the wiretap was declared legal. Prosecutors were glad to win this victory and keep the incriminating conversations in their arsenal, but in order to resolve the question they had actually offered to go to trial without them, saying they were confident they had plenty of other evidence.

Indeed, the confidence of all the officials involved in the arrest and prosecution of Dale Hausner and Sam Dieteman was striking, starting with that early morning press conference on Friday, August 4, 2006, with the entire country listening via all the major networks.

"These are the monsters we've been hunting," announced Phoenix Mayor Phil Gordon. "We have turned the tables on them and these are the guys. The reign of terror is over."

"We know we have the individuals involved," said Assistant Phoenix Police Chief Kevin Robinson.

Assistant Phoenix Police Chief Bill Lewis added, "I assure you these are the right guys. The hunt is over, but the work has just begun."

Indeed, regiments of people—from tow truck drivers who were retrieving Dale's car, and garbage specialists who were taking possession of the Dumpster where Sam had been tackled, to the CSIs who were slipping on booties and gloves to scour the vehicle and waste container, and the attorneys and judges who were plotting out the case with each new scrap of twisted metal, scribbled-on paper or live round discovered—were working hard.

None were busier than Detective Cliff Jewell. Jewell had watched the interviews of Dale and Sam from the monitor in another room. This was a decision made by the head of the Task Force, Clark Schwartzkopf. ATF agents and Mesa and Scottsdale detectives and others interviewed the two suspects—who had dissolved from a seemingly omnipotent and omnipresent villain straight from a graphic horror novel into a pair of scruffy young men—for hours and hours on August 4, but Cliff Jewell was held in reserve all day. He occasionally walked into the interview rooms at strategic moments to perform some small service such as adjusting the camera or bringing in coffee.

So far, none of the detectives who were doing the interrogations had spent much time on the .22 shootings. Scottsdale Detective Pete Salazar had masterfully obtained the elusive confession for Claudia Gutierrez-Cruz's murder. ATF agents had gone in there and pinned down their case for Wal-Mart. Clark Schwartzkopf had spent hours and hours with each half of the Serial Shooter, one cheerful and talkative, the other slumped and terse, but Clark had seemed to confirm his doubt in the .22 series by telling Dale that only "two" people had died, referring only to shotgun victims Claudia Gutierrez-Cruz and Robin Blasnek. Schwartzkopf had appealed for a confession based on Dale's apparently nonlethal intentions, which the detective said were evidenced by his use of the narrow .410 weapon loaded with birdshot.

Cliff Jewell was convinced these two men were also his suspects, but so far he hadn't seen anyone in the interview rooms pursue it.

Neither had Jewell been in on the takedown. He had not entered the weapon-packed apartment; he had not seen the Camry.

"Please let there be a twenty-two shell casing over there, please, please, please," he said to himself silently as the night turned into morning and the sun rose higher and higher, flirting with clouds on this monsoony day, often threatening the rain that Dale and Sam had been heard to complain about two nights before.

Over at the Mesa Police Department evidence bay, stocky Scottsdale Police detective Hugh Lockerby, a young detective with a shaved head who loved a cigar and a joke, had donned booties and gloves and was now opening the right rear passenger door of the Toyota Camry. Lockerby had been at the hospital when the case of Claudia Gutierrez-Cruz turned from one of assault to one of homicide, and he'd worked closely with Pete Salazar ever since, including being one of the four original members of the informal "task force."

Deliberately following chain-of-custody regulations, the car had slowly made its way over from the Windscape Apartments.

While it was being photographed, recorded, given a placard and an ID number and, finally, placed in a Baggie and catalogued, Hugh Lockerby could hardly contain himself. As soon as he could manage it, he reached for his own cell phone and dialed one Cliff Jewell:

"Guess what I just found. In the Camry."

In that moment, Cliff Jewell knew that his and Ron Rock's dedication had paid off. "After ten minutes of listening to Dale, I knew we had the right guys. Then I just needed the twenty-twos. No one else believed me yet. Then Hugh called. I knew I had him."

Tony Mendez, Reggie Remillard, David Estrada and the ghosts and wounds of many, many others who had motivated him since December 29 could be laid at the feet of these men, Dale Hausner and Sam Dieteman. Now Cliff Jewell would see to it they didn't get away; there would be no loopholes, no gaps, no bit of evidence not locked up.

––––––––––––––

Publicity across the nation, from *People* magazine to CNN, from the *Arizona Republic* to the *St. Paul Pioneer Press* to the *New York Times*, filled up the month of August as the country focused on the spectacle of Sam and Dale's capture.

Across the country, people learned that Sam Dieteman was a Minnesotan, who'd had a child at age sixteen and was a union electrician. That he was now divorced and that his mom and stepdad had kicked him out some time before the spree started. That back in Minnesota, Sam had a mile-long tally of misdemeanor and petty arrests, various contacts with police that numbered in the dozens, racked up before Sam even reached his mid-twenties.

They learned that Dale Hausner was a boxing fanatic who inserted himself into the world of professional boxing as much as he could, taking photos ringside and often "selling" them to sports magazines for nothing more than a ticket or a credential to get into the match. That he conducted a radio talk show on the sport, and had a pair of ex-wives who both were afraid of him, according to their divorce proceedings, documented in public records much earlier than the "Year of the Serial Shooter." They also learned about the tragic accident that took Dale's sons Donovan and Jeremiah in Texas when Dale was a very young father of just twenty-one.

It was soon apparent that Sam's family, who mostly maintained the same laconic manner that Sam exhibited, would not be coming forward much to support him visibly, but that Dale had brothers and parents who would become familiar to the press. Dale himself would speak often to the outside world, via the cameras and microphones that sought him out, and through letters to newspapers and TV stations when they didn't.

It was also clear that, although he was physically much smaller, Dale was the leader of the pair.

And, exactly five weeks into this press onslaught, the mayor and the chiefs of police made good on their promise to rid the city of both its serial killers: Mark Goudeau was arrested on suspicion of being the Baseline Rapist, and would be charged with the sex killings of multiple women, some very near the territory of Serial Shooter incidents. The confusing and terrorizing time was over.

Phoenix area law enforcement had nabbed two simultaneously and independently operating serial killers in the space of one year.

It was truly a stunning achievement.

Chapter Twenty-six

The Old-Fashioned Way

By Thanksgiving 2006, Dale and Sam had been cooling their heels in the jail at Fourth Avenue and Madison for four months. Sam had confessed the first day, but he now had a defense attorney who had other ideas about how to proceed through the legal system. Dale had emerged as the dominant personality of the pair, and he was protesting his innocence, through and through. In fact, he couldn't wait to tell as many people at once as he could. The two men had been arrested on a Friday, and by the time the jail hit business hours on Monday, the requests by media to talk to each man had stacked up. Sam resolutely refused, the sheriff's media officers would later testify, but Dale's face lit up and he eagerly signed the release forms. Before noon on Monday, August 7, 2006, he was in front of klieg lights and playing conductor to a full choir of reporters from around the nation. Later, he even hired a publicity agent. But as for talking to cops, he had shut right up, starting the moment Detective Pete Salazar accused him of being "a pervert."

No matter, Cliff Jewell was still doggedly at it. On November 29, 2006, exactly eleven months after his own personal entry into what became known as the Year of the Serial Shooter, Cliff Jewell received a new report that, like everything else, he checked out very thoroughly. His fellow detectives had never been enthusiastic about his theory that both the .22 shootings and the shotgun shootings were connected, nor the idea that all the human and animal shootings were connected as well. But Cliff Jewell had laboriously picked his way through many crimes, and had personally investigated nearly three dozen un-related homicides in 2006 alone. He'd been very careful about what went on his "Related to December 29" list.

The payoff this time would be big.

In this report, a woman named Charisse Kane said she had once known Dale Hausner. But her husband knew him better. And her husband said that Dale had shot up a car last year, a little after Christmas, at a bartending school in Tempe.

Cliff picked up the phone at seven thirty that morning and called Charisse.

The thing was, Charisse told Cliff on that early November morning, her husband was now in jail himself. And she wanted him home. She was expecting his child in a few weeks. She needed him home. She hoped her husband's knowledge of possible Serial Shooter crimes could gain him some kind of a deal with prosecutors. Cliff didn't offer deals; any "deal" would be up to the prosecutor assigned to the woman's husband. But Cliff was very interested in what might have happened at this bartending school. It was his job to pursue it and bring prosecutors into the loop.

Cliff hung up the phone and immediately called someone he knew at Tempe Police. He described the incident and gave an approximate date of within a week or two of Christmas 2005.

He got a hit.

Tempe not only came back with a police report of a car shot at a bartending school, just like Charisse had said, but said it was an unsolved case and they still had the bullets recovered from the vehicle.

The date of the incident?

December 29, 2005.

Charisse's husband, John Kane, had screwed up one time too many. He'd had a number of arrests back in Florida in the nineties for some pretty serious things like larceny and firearms violations. But he had kicked his substance addiction as the millennium approached, and he had a nice wife now and a stable job at ABC Bartending School.

Or so he thought.

Sometime in the summer of 2005, demon rum, not to mention demon cocaine and a few other things, got hold of him again. It was almost bound to happen, surrounded by liquor all day on the job and handling a revolving door of students who were essentially a party crowd. On any given day at least two of them were likely to show up high, he noticed. Come to think of it, immersing himself among people who thought of martinis as a career goal might not have been the best choice for an alcoholic who claimed to be working the 12 steps of Narcotics Anonymous.

John Kane fell off the wagon. He had his reasons, like every addict, but it all amounted to a lot of powerful substances going into his body on a daily basis. He was the kind of addict who could keep up appearances, and neither his wife nor his employer caught on, even though Charisse worked at ABC, too.* Appearances were always important to John Kane, a carefully groomed man who wore his graying, neatly trimmed hair combed straight back, a silver chain around his neck, and black dress slacks, and had the tightly controlled movements of a cat burglar. John Kane was icy, calm and as perfectly poised as he was dressed. Later, at trial, reporters in the press room would make casting calls about who should play him. Robert De Niro would be perfect, all agreed, but someone pointed out that De Niro had aged out of the role. Maybe Tom Sizemore?

In October '05, a few months into John's newest descent into cocaine and Jack Daniel's, a wiry little man with a hunched-over posture, a ready smile, and blue eyes enrolled at the school. The fellow was quite smart and pretty ambitious: he already had a full-time job and did other stuff on the side, like photography and a sort of "vending." Now he wanted to add professional bartender to his résumé.

One of the ways the bartending school made money was to act as a booking broker. When someone, say a wedding planner, needed a bartender for just one night, the school could line up

---

*Charisse's actual position at ABC was unclear. Her husband testified she was the director. Another witness from ABC testified she was a secretary. Kane said that because of his arrest record, she was named director even though it was he who functioned as the actual director.

one of their graduates. The wedding planner paid twenty-five dollars an hour to the bartender. The school then took back ten dollars an hour of the bartender's take for the night.

Fifteen dollars an hour would be a good rate for the new recruit, who was a janitor by day. After spending some time with him during the ABC Bartending sales pitch, John Kane was sure the young man would also make good tips; "he was a likable guy." John wrote the fellow's name, Dale S. Hausner, into the files and made sure there was an "active card" ready for him when he graduated.

It didn't take long for the two men to connect on another level. This "likable guy" let it be known he could obtain high-end liquors and new release movies and CDs for a very sweet price. Dale mentioned something about a friend who worked at a major retailer "overnight" . . . and John Kane knew enough not to ask any more. Soon he was putting in regular orders to Dale for the movies and hooch he wanted. After he graduated from ABC with a brand-spanking-new bartending certificate to hang on the wall, Dale would stop by every week or so with a trunk full of goodies. John Kane was not the only one who did business with him in the parking lot at ABC.

Dale often brought by his adorable baby girl, Mandy. John was an experienced father, but when he reached to cuddle this little one, Dale always admonished him to be extra careful because the child had a feeding tube. She probably wouldn't make it to six years old, he told John. Dale would get angry about the unfairness of it all, how he'd already lost two little ones, how the system wouldn't help someone like him, no, you had to be a fucking minority or from another fucking country to get any help for a sweet little baby like this. Her mother? Don't get him started, she didn't do nuthin'. It was all on Dale's narrow shoulders.

John Kane felt little Mandy needed the money more than ABC did. He waived the ten-dollar-an-hour fee Dale was supposed to deposit after every gig he put in through ABC's job service. Mandy just melted everybody.

Annette Prince needed a new life and she needed some new skills to make good. It was trouble that had brought her to the state of Arizona. She needed to put a lot of space between herself and her past, and those wide stretches of desert were comforting. Stripping pulled in good money, but that's one job you can't do forever, and she was determined to make something new of herself in her new life. She paid the $495 dollar tuition and enrolled at ABC Bartending School in Tempe. Bartending was a good job, one where you could keep your clothes on.

Annette started attending classes at ABC at the very end of 2005. She'd be a graduate by the turn of the New Year. Now that was a good thought: 2006 would be all new and all good. At last.

As Christmas approached, Charisse and John Kane were both thinking about Dale's sweet little blue-eyed girl with the unfortunate feeding tube. Her giggles and smiles were priceless. Whenever Dale brought her to the school, Charisse almost always ended up co-opting the little charmer in her own office while the two men went off to conduct business. John was careful not to let Charisse know just what business the two men were up to. The baby was a great diversion. The couple bought her a large teddy bear for Christmas. What a pleasure to give a soft, funny toy to such a sweet little thing, one who wasn't expected to live past first grade.

On the day after Christmas 2005, a Monday, ABC Bartending School was open for business—but when little Mandy and her daddy showed up at the school, John Kane was not full of Christmas cheer. He was in a downright foul mood. His wife had had an unpleasant surprise earlier in the day.

A female student, a girl named Melissa, had marched into Charisse's office with a complaint about one of the instructors. Melissa had marched into the school director's office with a complaint about sexual harassment from this guy, John Kane, who taught her class. Melissa hadn't noticed that the school director's name was also Kane.

By the time Dale and Mandy showed up around 6 p.m. that Monday, John felt harassed himself, by his wife's confrontation with him and that girl's dirty rotten stirring up of trouble for what he felt was no reason.

Dale handed off Amanda as usual to Charisse, who disappeared with the child into her office. Behind closed doors in John's office, the story came tumbling out.

"Did you do it?" Dale wanted to know.

"Hell, no," John assured him. "I was probably a little over-friendly, but I didn't say what she said I said!"

"All right then," Dale said, "don't worry. I'll take care of it."

John didn't ask him what he meant by that, but he did point out the girl and her car to his movie and booze supplier. He even gave him her home address.

"You won't know when," said Dale, "but afterward, you'll know." There was that big smile of his, the one that made him so likable, and a bit of a wink this time.

———————

As he drove out to Tempe on the morning of November 29, 2006, Cliff Jewell thought about the legal system. "Case agent" meant he was officially responsible for seeing his cases—Timmy Tordai, Marco Carillo and Jose Ortiz— all the way through trial. He'd attend court every day. He'd shepherd much of the evidence in and out of the courtroom, whispering to prosecutors when he thought he could help, handing them a plastic evidence Baggie when they reached for it. Cliff Jewell would dearly love to have as much forensic evidence as possible against this person who had laid dead people as well as dead horses and dead dogs at his feet for a year. He wanted very much to see what evidence Tempe had.

He looked over their file when he arrived at the Tempe Police Department.

When he was done, Cliff Jewell took custody of the bullets retrieved from the shot-up car and made a beeline back to 620. He hand-delivered the bullets to the ballistics lab, without stopping to do the paperwork first. They were .22s, all right.

Soon arrangements were made for John Kane and his attorney to meet with Cliff Jewell. Clark Schwartzkopf also attended. The interview took place on December 6, 2006. John Kane himself was in custody on drug and weapons charges. In black-and-white stripes, he was brought to 620, where Ciff Jewell plied him with a Big Mac and a Coke, a special treat for one living on jail fare. He wanted John Kane to be good and ready to talk.

Facing thirteen years in prison if he failed to cut some kind of deal, John had done a lot of weeping* on the phone to his

———————

*Taped conversations played in court.

wife from jail. He was sorry he had screwed up. He would do whatever it took to come home. She had been so good to him, even trying to make his life as comfortable as possible there behind bars. Charisse even sent him a subscription to the Sunday paper.

And it was in one of those Sunday papers that John had found what he hoped would be his ticket out in time to enjoy at least part of his coming baby's childhood.

Jail is a controlled environment, of course. The TV was limited to approved programming such as *Family Feud* and *Dukes of Hazzard*. There was no news. Not that John was into the news anyway. When his Sunday paper came, he headed for the sports page and the comics. The paper was a desirable item inside those grim walls and it got divvied up pretty quickly upon its arrival; he usually didn't see the rest of it. But at the end of November, having been an inmate since early summer, John Kane noticed a front page on the floor of his cell. He leaned over to pick it up because he was amazed to see a front page photo of his ol' pal, the daddy of little Mandy, the vendor with the trunkful of goodies, one Dale Hausner.

He read the article.

John Kane was stunned. He had not heard of the Serial Shooter before. But he remembered the night last Christmas season when Dale Hausner had scared him.

He called his lawyer. His lawyer made several calls but couldn't seem to get anyone interested.

But then some paperwork made its way in front of Cliff Jewell, on November 29. Jewell immediately called Charisse, drove out to Tempe, and then back in Phoenix slapped a bag of bullets on the counter in the crime lab.

And now here they all were on December 6, 2006.

Ready to talk, ready to listen.

———————

A few days after Charisse and John had tangled in 2005 over a sexual harassment complaint made against him at the bartending school and John had unloaded on the visiting Dale Hausner, the couple were at home for the evening when John's phone rang. He answered and had a strange, short conversation with Dale.

"Where are you?"

"At home."

"Anyone with you?"

"Charisse is here."

"Good. You're covered."

Dial tone.

John didn't have any idea what the guy meant. He just shook his head and went back to watching the Thursday night must-see TV lineup with Charisse.

———————

On this last Thursday of the year, Annette Prince was looking forward to starting the New Year fresh and safe. Above all, safe. Everyone here was new. No one wished her harm. She was almost through with the bartending classes and 2006 would be all good.

At the end of the night she walked out of the classroom—shaped like an actual bar, with a U counter, students on the patron's side, instructor on the interior—and headed to her car. The gold Chevy Cavalier was parked with its tail toward the building and the hood facing out toward a major thoroughfare.

When she got close, Annette felt sick. It couldn't be true. It just couldn't be. But it was true. The blood drained out of her face and she ran back inside the building.

———————

John Kane received another phone call that Thursday night, a couple of hours after Dale's odd call. This call was from a colleague at ABC. There'd been an incident at the school. A shooting. No one was hurt. But everyone was shaken up. One of the student's cars, Annette Prince's, had taken at least five bullets through the windshield.

Now it was time for John Kane's blood to drain from his face.

He said nothing to Charisse.

———————

In the morning, Dale swung by ABC. He had his giggling baby girl with him. Charisse scooped her up.

John grabbed Dale and shut the door behind the two men, alone in John's office.

"What the fuck did you do?" demanded the bartender.

"Oh, a little birdie told me you had an incident last night," Dale said, chuckling.

"That was you?"

"Shh, they'll hear you." The two men put the stereo on. The smile got bigger. "My little twenty-two."

John Kane resumed. "Are you fucking crazy? Someone could have been hurt."

"Well, that's what she gets, a lying bitch deserves what she gets."

"Dale, they could've seen you."

"No one's seen me yet."

John was taken aback by that comment. Yet? How many times had his "friend" done something like this? He left the question unspoken. His mind was racing and he thought it best not to ask or know.

But John had a surprise for the person in his office who seemed to be enjoying a private triumph: "You got the wrong car."

Now Dale seemed perturbed. "What the fuck?"

But John told him he was grateful for the mistake, "Because if you would've gotten the right car there was a girl sittin' in that car waitin' on the bitch that lied about me and if you would've shot the right car you would've hurt her."

"Well," Dale said, "that's what she would get for being friends with a lying bitch." John was shocked.

John Kane considered that he didn't know this guy too well really. When he'd been free with the information on Melissa's car and address, he'd expected maybe a tire letting—he'd be okay with that, as mad as he was and as high as he usually was. But this, this was crazy. If Dale was willing to be this brutal to someone he didn't even know, how would he react to someone he considered to have betrayed him? Instead of being a likable, friendly guy, a devoted daddy, a helpful amigo, Dale Hausner now seemed unpredictable and even scary. Considering John Kane's own career, that was saying rather a lot.

One thing John Kane didn't need in his life was any more trouble, especially the kind that brought police poking around. He decided it was time to change the subject. He pulled out his wallet and paid for items from Dale's trunk.

He did not place a new order.

And he never said a word to Charisse.

Cliff Jewell was extremely interested in this story. He had five .22-caliber bullets in his evidence cabinet, retrieved a few days ago from Tempe Police. That caliber was not public information. And the date December 29 was extremely intriguing.

Two weeks after this little chat with John Kane, Cliff Jewell got forensics back on the five bullets he had submitted from Tempe. There was a direct match to the shell casing that had been retrieved from the Timmy Tordai shooting.

Now Cliff Jewell wanted to see the rest of that Chevy Cavalier. He tried to locate Annette Prince, but it was unusually difficult. When he finally found a current phone number for her, she was surprisingly uncooperative. What could be the matter? He was bearing good news, he was solving her crime. He hung up the phone very puzzled.

The next morning Phoenix Police detective Clifton Jewell picked up the ringing phone on his desk to find himself talking to federal officers. What did he want with Annette Prince? they wanted to know.

"She's a victim of a property crime that is linked to a series of homicides I have and I want to solve her case and take a look at her car. Exactly what do *you* want with Annette Prince, if I may ask?" he said to the feds.

It was one of those bizarre moments impossible to see coming.

Turned out, Annette Prince—who'd never had anything to do with John Kane or Dale Hausner—was in the Federal Witness Protection Program. She was fleeing another very violent group of people, and when she found her car shot up on December 29, 2005, she feared for her life for very, very good reason.

And so did her federal agents. They immediately moved her out of Phoenix and out of Arizona altogether.

It was a shock to everyone involved. Cliff Jewell was brought into the feds' secret little world. He flew out to Annette's new locale and examined the car with more vigor than it had received yet. He found two more bullet fragments and bundled them back up to Phoenix.

The forensics from the ABC Bartending School incident provided strong evidence in the case against Dale Hausner. Dale claimed that Sam Dieteman was the Serial Shooter, as confessed, but that he achieved this crime spree by secretly taking Dale's car without Dale's knowledge. If that theory were true, it would not explain how bullet fragments matching the ABC Bartending School incident ended up inside the Camry. By all accounts, Dale and Sam did not even know each other yet on that night. Sam Dieteman never attended ABC. John Kane never met Sam Dieteman.

The testimony of John Kane, if believed, fleshed out the circumstances of why this shooting occurred, why this car was targeted and what Dale's thoughts and attitudes were. It would also be the first known shooting of that bloody, bloody December 29.

After the incident where, according to John Kane, Dale admitted to using his "little twenty-two"* to send John's tormentor a message, John let Dale "drop off the radar." He himself lost his ABC job just a few days after this. He only saw Dale once more outside a courtroom.

It was well into 2006 then, in the springtime, a good three or four months since the day the two men had turned up the stereo to cover their voices, and before either one of them was arrested for anything. The Year of the Serial Shooter was in full swing. John Kane had gone to the grocery store and, of all things, run into Dale Hausner in the parking lot.

"So, what've you been up to?" he greeted the redhead.

The answer came with that familiar grin: "Just having fun the old-fashioned way."

---

*On the witness stand later, Dale himself used this phrase in describing his weapon.

Chapter Twenty-seven

Likely, Highly Likely, Identification

The .22-caliber bullets from the cases steadfastly pursued by Cliff Jewell, in collaboration with Ron Rock, shared some distinctive characteristics. Ballistics is a "grading" science where the more characteristics that match, the higher the grade of certainty.

When ballistics experts examine a bullet or shell casing from a crime scene, the first thing they look for are the easy or general characteristics such as caliber. Among these gross characteristics are the "lands and grooves," markings left on the bullet by the barrel of the weapon.

Inside the barrel of a rifle, manufacturers design alternating lands and grooves—lands are simply the flat part between the grooves. These grooves provide a twist to the bullet as it accelerates through the barrel, much like a quarterback throwing a football. The twist is believed to increase the accuracy of the projectile. The twist can be oriented to the left or to the right, depending on the manufacturer's theory about which direction would best serve that particular weapon. The number of grooves and the spacing between them are also decisions made by the manufacturer separately on each model it produces. Therefore, the direction of the twist and the number and spacing of the grooves vary from model to model and brand to brand, but six is a common number of lands and grooves. The striations left on the bullets are visible to the naked eye.

In the .22-caliber shootings that Cliff Jewell had been grouping together, ballistics reports—some of which took almost a year from the time the cases started—found all of the bullets to have certain distinct matching characteristics that could be seen with the naked eye. Being a certified firearm instructor, Detective Jewell could see these characteristics and realize their importance when he retrieved bullets himself, from dark sheds and gutters or desk drawers where they'd been saved. They all had an unusual number of lands and grooves: sixteen. This gives a distinctive appearance to the striations, which are so closely placed together they are considered "microgrooves." They all had a right twist, and they all came from what is called a long rifle cartridge.

These shared characteristics in all the bullets and shells found from the cases in Cliff Jewell's files were very suggestive. The unusual number of lands and grooves shared across so many crime scenes was especially disturbing.

At the Phoenix Crime Lab, ballistics expert Phillip Wolslagel put the bullets and shells under a microscope. He testified that after being able to group all the bullets and shells together by general characteristics, he moved on to more specific characteristics. These would be more unique identifiers, such as a specific defect in the barrel of a particular weapon that left a mark on the bullet or shell. The more of these identifiers present, the stronger the case. The process begins by eliminating weapons, creating an ever smaller universe of possibilities. When all the bullets turned out to be .22-caliber, the lab could eliminate all non-.22-caliber weapons. It could further eliminate all .22-caliber weapons that had a left twist instead of a right one. And so on. Sometimes the more subtle types of identifiers might not be present in the evidence being examined, not because a potentially specific weapon did not fire the bullet, but because the bullet is too damaged to retain the mark. For instance, if the mark is expected to be found on the nose of the bullet; a bullet that has smashed against a concrete wall after it passed through the victim may no longer have any nose at all. In fact, lead .22-caliber bullets are designed to disintegrate upon impact. Frequently all that is left are pencil tip size fragments. The more intact the bullet or shell is, the more definitively the examiner can determine which weapon fired it.

Wolslagel used a tiered system of increasingly more matched characteristics. Grouping all the .22-calibers together with the right twist, the long rifle and the sixteen microgrooves was the first or lowest level.

The next step was to match even more characteristics. In this manner, some bullets could be paired or grouped. While far from being a perfect match, the expert determines that these groups or pairs "cannot be excluded as having been fired from the same gun." In this category, Wolslagel put the following bullets:

- A bullet from the shooting scene of the two black dogs, Peyton and Martin, in east Phoenix—where Cliff Jewell had entered a spider-ridden shed to look for it—was paired to a bullet from the murder of Marco Carillo, whose body was found in downtown Phoenix. All three crimes occurred on December 29, 2005.

- The two bullets recovered from the body of Marco Carillo were paired to the bullet recovered from the body of Jose Ortiz a block north the same night, as well as to a bullet recovered from the body of David Estrada, who had been killed six months earlier in a different town.

- Two bullets recovered from the little mixed breed dog, Irving—shot right in front of the thirteen-year-old David Cecena—were paired to the purebred Anatolian shepherd dog, Shep, shot the same night. Both of these dogs were shot on the same night that Nathaniel Shoffner, who died defending a stray dog, was murdered with a shotgun.

- A bullet recovered from the body of candle bearer Tony Mendez, murdered moments after biking ahead of his friend Ricky Kemp on May 17, 2005, was paired to the two bullets recovered from the body of Marco Carillo.

- A bullet fragment recovered from Reginald Remillard's spine, just below the neck, was paired to both bullets recovered from Marco Carillo.

The next level Wolslagel used was "likely." By this he meant the bullets from two different crime scenes shared enough unique characteristics that it was more likely than not that they were fired from the same weapon. In this category, Wolslagel placed:

- The shell casing found at the scene of Timmy Tordai's shooting from December 29, 2005, considered a likely match to a shell found in Dale Hausner's Camry under the plastic molding between the carpet and door of the right rear passenger side.

- Finding the shell in the cabin of the vehicle also suggested that it had been expelled from a weapon that had been fired from inside the car. This would be true of all the shells found inside the Camry. There were seven of them. The Phoenix Crime Lab did not test all seven, considering a few positive "samples" sufficient.

The next highest grade Wolslagel used when even more characteristics matched was "highly likely." This meant that it would be unusual, but not impossible, that bullets or shells sharing so many characteristics were not fired from the same weapon. Almost all weapons but one could be excluded. It would be extraordinary to find two weapons with these many matching characteristics. Bullets and shells that fit into this category were:

- Several shells and fragments found in Dale Hausner's Camry underneath the right rear seat matched to the shell found at the Timmy Tordai shooting.

- A shell or fragment found in the Hausner trunk matched to one found under its left rear seat.

- The shell from the Tordai scene matched to at least four of the shells and fragments recovered from the car shot at the ABC Bartending School.

- The shell from the Tordai scene matched to one recovered from the fatal shooting of shepherd mix dog Peanut, as well as to a shell recovered at the scene of the fatal shooting of the horse Sara Moon, shot exactly six months earlier and many miles away in rural Tolleson. Sara Moon had died on the same summer night as David Estrada had, also in Tolleson.

- A casing from the December 29, 2005, shooting of Peanut in east Phoenix matched to a casing from the July 20, 2005, shooting of the Akita Whiskey in the westside town of Avondale.

———————

The highest possible category used by Wolslagel is "identification." In this category, over a dozen characteristics match perfectly, and the expert considers it impossible that the samples were not fired from the same weapon. All other weapons have been definitively excluded.

In this category, Wolslagel placed the following:

- A shell from the Camry found under the right rear seat matched to the shell found at the Timmy Tordai scene of December 29, 2005.

- A shell from the Camry found under the left rear seat matched to a shell from the fatal shooting of Whiskey on July 20, 2005.

- The shell from the Tordai scene matched to two shells from the ABC Bartending School incident.

- The shell from the Tordai scene matched to a shell found at the scene of the fatal shooting of Peanut.

———————

At trial, Dale's defense team introduced their own ballistics expert. Jim Serpa, a private forensic consultant who had retired from the Maricopa County Sheriff's Office, disputed the categories. But under cross-examination by Vince Imbordino, Serpa said he actually had no quarrel with Mr. Wolslagel's work on the above described bullets and shells and fragments. He said he not only worked with Wolslagel often but also relied on his work. The only dispute was over semantics. Serpa also confirmed to the court that the rifles Dale had owned in Texas, which had never been recovered, were known to have sixteen lands and grooves with a right twist. Paperwork required by federal law during the purchase of the weapons from a Texas pawn shop had recorded exactly which models Dale had owned.

Dale had claimed that the Texas weapons never left that state. He stated he had sold them to a neighbor whose name he could not recall. Being a private sale, no paperwork was generated. A third .22-caliber rifle had been purchased from a pawn shop in Phoenix the spring of 2005, but Dale testified it had never functioned, so he'd gotten his brother Jeff to saw it in half. Then, Dale claimed, he threw one half into a Dumpster near Jeff's apartment and the other into a Dumpster near his own. He did this, he said, because he did not want kids finding an intact firearm and possibly getting hurt.

But there is another theory as to what became of at least one of the .22 rifles. Sam Dieteman had spent a lot of time drunk or high on meth, and after the killing of Claudia Gutierrez-Cruz, he used the drugs actively trying to forget. The more sober he got in jail, though, the more his memories came back—in a piecemeal fashion over a long period of time. It frustrated authorities that he often did not remember things when directly asked but months later would notify them he had suddenly recalled a specific incident or fact. Although they would have preferred to hear everything well before Dale went to trial, they continued to be grateful for any tidbits he could provide no matter when. When Dale's trial was nearly over, Sam told authorities behind the scenes that he now recalled the day a .22-caliber rifle was cut in half by the Hausner brothers. Sam told Detective Cliff Jewell that he and Jeff had been hanging drywall at the house of a Hausner family friend when Dale had stopped by as they were working. Sam remembered the brothers then destroying a rifle together. He had the impression that the two parts had been either buried in the backyard or had been slipped inside the walls Sam and Jeff were working on. Sam drew a map to the house for the detective, who followed up and confirmed the address and who the occupant had been at the relevant time. But prosecutors felt it was insufficient for a search warrant. Cliff Jewell has driven past the house but has never been able to enter and search for the .22-caliber rifle Dale and Jeff may have hidden in its walls or beneath its backyard soil.

December 29, 2005, was the night that Phoenix detective Cliff Jewell first caught the trail of a serial killer. It was Cliff Jewell who paid attention when a frustrated detective from a tiny farm community told him about the murder of David Estrada and the shootings of horses Sara Moon, Apache, and Little Man, as well as that of Whiskey, the Akita. It was Cliff Jewell who prompted the Phoenix PD to hold its first "Serial Shooter" press conference on January 27, 2006. It was Cliff Jewell who ferreted out the Glendale shootings of two other dogs and took over their cases. It was Cliff Jewell who anticipated the killer's change of weapon and recognized the shotgun killing of Claudia Gutierrez-Cruz for what it was. It was Cliff Jewell who called the profilers at Quantico and escorted them around the crime scenes. It was Cliff Jewell who doggedly insisted that the .22 shootings were connected to the shotgun shootings and the human targets were connected to the pets. And it was Cliff Jewell who paid attention to Charisse Kane and who flew out of state to pry twisted fragments of lead out of a car that was deeply shrouded in the Federal Witness Protection Program.

Sam Dieteman's boastings to Ron Horton about a shotgun not leaving a lot of forensic detail is true. While there is a great deal of evidence linking the crime scenes to Dale Hausner's possession of certain types of shotguns, there is much less ballistic detail that would finger a very specific and unique shotgun.

But the .22-caliber rifle that left its singular imprint on bullets associated with Timmy Tordai, Sara Moon, Whiskey, Peanut and the ABC Bartending School can also be placed with deadly certainty inside Dale Hausner's silver Camry.

It is a long list of victims of .22s whose bullets interlock in the ballistics report. Although the level of certainty varied, it seemed impossible that so many crime scenes—as well as Dale's Camry and his Texas paperwork—could be linked together by mere coincidence.

It was Cliff Jewell, with his quest for .22s, who slammed the cell door good and shut on the Serial Shooter.

Chapter Twenty-eight

Nobody knows what's inside me.

Jeff Hausner

For two years, from 2006 to 2008, as Dale's trial approached, Phoenicians came to think of the Serial Shooter as Dale Hausner and his virtual cat's-paw, the hulking Sam Dieteman. In the early weeks right after the arrest, there were reports of the possible involvement of one of Dale's brothers, but the talk died down and the name Jeff Hausner got much less play, and some reports even cleared him of involvement.

Jeff Hausner is six years older than Dale. Like Dale, he has two ex-wives. Like Dale, he has children, two daughters and a son and stepdaughter. There is a strong family resemblance between these two brothers, with the exception that Jeff is a tall and powerful man, while Dale is only around five-eight or less and has a hunched and insubstantial build. Jeff was in the same line of work, janitorial, but without Dale's side activities.

During the Wal-Mart investigation, Jeff Hausner had been briefly surveilled by GPS and discarded as a suspect after about a week. He was discarded because he was not seen to be doing anything suspicious related to the Wal-Mart fires, and City of Glendale surveillance resources were limited. How he came to be surveilled at all is unclear. His name may have come up in interviews conducted with informants, but the Glendale reports have been heavily redacted. Jeff has never been charged in the Wal-Mart fires and there is no evidence putting him there. The video from inside the stores and out in their parking lots tells the story quite well of what happened, and it is Sam on that tape and Dale on that tape, without question.

But after his arrest out by the Dumpster that night, Sam Dieteman, the man who had "to get drunk to get to sleep," had a lot to say. He said it sporadically over the next two years. And one of the things he said was that he had been present one night when Jeff Hausner stabbed a man who asked him for change.

Detective Clark Schwartzkopf researched the details that Sam provided and found a man named Raymond McQueen who was "ecstatic that anyone showed up and cared" about his case. McQueen indeed had spent a month in a hospital after he'd approached a man in the parking lot of a convenience store and asked for a little handout. The incident took place on Friday, April 14, 2006—three weeks after Tim Boviall was shot while he was biking and two weeks before Claudia Gutierrez-Cruz and Kibili Tambadu were shot while walking

The man who'd stabbed him, Raymond told Detective Schwartzkopf, had said, "Sure, just a minute," and turned around, making gestures toward his pants as if to retrieve pocket change. Instead, a knife had appeared in a swift motion that ended deeply in Raymond's belly.

There were other people around, including Raymond's own girlfriend, so help was summoned quickly. The knifer had darted away into a car, which immediately fled the scene.

The story matched exactly what Clark Schwartzkopf had heard from Sam Dieteman.

Sam had been in that car, he'd admitted to the detective, and Dale was driving it.

The story was similar to something else. On the wiretaps, Dale and Sam could be heard talking about a .38-caliber revolver. Sam wished he had one. He talked about how he'd use it.

The two men then proceed to role-play.

Dale portrays a panhandler. He approaches Sam and asks him for money.

Sam turns around, in a gesture simulating reaching for

money, and instead returns to a straight posture with an imaginary pistol in his hand and "blows" away Dale, who acts out being shot.

———————

Raymond McQueen lost a gallon of blood. The wicked jackknife that flicked open while Jeff Hausner briefly turned his back to McQueen caused "serious injuries and hemorrhagic shock," according to court filings. The entrance wound measured four centimeters. The pain would last for years, possibly indefinitely. The victim believed "that the defendant intended to kill him, but he reported that the defendant's companion, who had been identified as Sam Dieteman, did not take part in the crime."

———————

On March 13, 2007, Jeff Hausner pled guilty to the crime of stabbing panhandler Raymond McQueen. But he wasn't sure how everything had gone so wrong. After he was in custody and made his plea deal, he reported that he had first encountered the victim inside the convenience store moments earlier. His version of the incident is recorded in the pre-sentence report submitted to the court by adult probation officer Paddy McDonagh: "The victim seemingly 'slammed' into the defendant as he walked by him, and the defendant apologized for the incident in order to appease the victim, who was verbally aggressive. Once outside the store, the victim requested the defendant's spare change, but as the defendant looked for some money, he perceived that the victim began approaching him in an aggressive manner. The defendant subsequently observed what he believed was a knife in the victim's possession, and he responded by making a sudden move toward the victim."

In fact, Jeff Hausner told authorities, not only had he not intended to stab Raymond McQueen, he hadn't even realized that he had. He said he left the scene only to avoid the gathering crowd.

By way of remorse, Jeff Hausner said "he overreacted to this situation, and he feels dismay that he seriously injured the victim. The defendant never intended to harm him, and, despite what he reportedly has read in the press, the defendant states he has never harbored feelings of ill will toward homeless people. In reality, the defendant states that he often reached out to help others in need, and the behavior he displayed during the present offense is uncharacteristic of him."

Jeff Hausner repeated as often as he could that he meant no harm to the panhandler. But those listening to him had a lot of other facts in front of them. Adult probation officer Paddy Mc-Donagh wryly observed on the last page of the pre-sentence report, "Given the extent of the victim's internal injuries, the defendant's statements seem difficult to believe."

Still, Jeff had many fans who did believe him, and they wrote to the court, asking for mercy. Many were relatives.

Jeff Hausner had lived with companion Celeste Vance, the leaseholder on the Elm Street apartment adjacent to the site of the shooting of Viet Nam veteran James Hodge, for five years. She wrote, in wobbly handwriting indicative of her physical disability and chronic pain, "I have known Jeff Hausner for 20 years. In all the years I've known him I have never known him to display any violent tendencies." During the time he'd lived with her, he had "taken in" four homeless people. "He has also taken in stray animals who have needed a home. These are not the actions of someone who is violent."

She wrote this letter even though the minute Jeff Hausner had become embroiled in the Serial Shooter case after the arrest of Dale and Sam, her lover had packed up and returned to his ex-wife Brenda Hausner.

Brenda was apparently very glad to have her ex-husband Jeff back. She wrote one of the longest letters to the court. At the time of her divorce from him a decade earlier, Brenda had filed that her income was from public assistance (and that it exceeded Jeff's income), but she told the court she was now a bookkeeper. She said that their now seventeen-year-old daughter Jenny* was "shaping up all in all to be a very kind and wonderful human being— We are all very proud of her." Brenda assured the court that Jeff was a good human being, too. "In all the years I have known Jeff I have never seen are [sic] heard of him being violent to any of his fellow man. He has always been a good neighbor and friend and there to help in times of need. He has always showed compassion to the Homeless in ways like offering food, money, clothing and even shelter.

---

*Denotes pseudonym.

"Jenny and I have been praying that Jeff will be able to be home to see her graduate and not to be out of her life for to [sic] long. He is very much needed and loved."

Yet other family members confidentially told detectives that over the course of their twenty-year association, Jeff had permanently disfigured Brenda with beatings.

Jeff's brothers also stood by him. Kristopher Hausner, older than Jeff but developmentally disabled, wrote "Jeff is a very good person. He has never ben [sic] a violent person. He has helped a lot of people. For years he has helped a lot of homeless people. He has even taking [sic] them in too [sic] live with them. The End."

Oldest brother Gregory wrote, "Jeff Hausner is not a mean man in any way shape or form. I am shocked that he is charged with this. He is a kind human being who has helped people. He has helped homeless people by allowing them to live with him." Gregory went on to bemoan everything his brother was missing while in jail. "I am pleading with you to please give him time served with probation. This way he can get his life back. I am a believer in second chances and this would help him out greatly."

Fourth of the brothers, janitor-cum-comedian Randy, spoke directly with the court, telling them Jeff "has never displayed this type of behavior before." Randy also provided the now familiar litany of Jeff's graces toward people in need. He echoed Gregory's plea for "a second chance."

On March 5, 2007, at the age of seventy-two, Eugene Hausner wrote to the court: "I am Jeff's father and I consider him to be a person who likes to help people. He is not a violent person and always been a help to us."

He put "Jeff's dad" above his signature.

Rosemarie also wrote on behalf of her middle child: "I am Jeffrey's mother. Jeff has always helped many people. He is not a violent person. From his early teens he has helped many homeless people. He has taken in homeless people and helped them until they were on there [sic] own. He's a very good person."

Jenny, Jeff's seventeen-year-old daughter, begged the court to have her father out of jail in time for him to see her graduate. "I just recently lost my stepfather in July of '06. Now it seems I am losing my father as well." She also told the court, "My father has never shown any violence toward anyone, unless they threatened him or someone he loves."

There was no letter from Dale.

Jenny would not get her wish. At his sentencing hearing in April 2007, Jeff told Judge Klein that he was angry about the pre-sentence report written by a probation officer.

"He spends fifteen minutes with me and he knows me? I don't think so. Nobody knows what's inside me."

He was also angry with Detective Schwartzkopf.

"He doesn't know my remorse," Jeff complained to the court.

"You're right," Judge Klein responded. "No one knows what's inside you." But the judge held up the pre-sentence report in his hand and said, "You say you didn't know you had stabbed the victim. But if you had stayed, you would have known. The only reason Ray McQueen didn't die is a random inch, not anything that you did to prevent it."

In contrast to the letters of admiration from Jeff Hausner's relatives and friends and lovers, Detective Clark Schwartzkopf entered this letter into the file on the stabbing of panhandler Raymond McQueen:

> This letter is being written to be included in the pre-sentence report filed with the court for informational purposes on the defendant in this case, Jeffrey Hausner.
>
> As the lead investigator in this particular case, I would like the court to know that on two separate occasions I have met with the victim in this case. Besides being ecstatic that someone actually took an interest in his case, he related that he is 100% sure that the defendant in this case was attempting to kill him. The victim's crime that day was asking the wrong person for some spare change. For that, he received a knife in the stomach and a month long stay in the hospital. A brutal attack committed by a man with little or no conscience.
>
> This crime has been linked to another valley series of crimes reported by the media as the 'serial shooter.' Although a knife was used instead of a gun, this crime was linked because of the presence of the defendant's brother, Dale, and his roommate Samuel Dieteman. Jeff Hausner was a part of the ongoing criminal enterprise being perpetrated by these individuals.

Jeff Hausner has repeatedly been interviewed and refused to discuss his involvement in not only this crime, but all crimes associated with the series. Not once has he shown any remorse for his actions or knowledge of the pain he or his cohorts has [sic] inflicted. The cold callousness of his actions in this case show that he belongs in prison with the other dregs of society who have no respect for the rule of law. The fact that he picked a homeless, defenseless individual to purposely attack reflects a mindset associated with the other attacks in this series of crimes.

The Phoenix Police Department and the victim have no issues with the plea agreement reached in this case. However, as lead investigator and on behalf of the victim, I ask the state to impose the maximum sentence allowed by law as the penalty for the crime committed by Jeffrey Hausner. Maybe then the defendant will fully understand the pain he has inflicted and the damage he has caused to this victim and the community.

———————

Although Jeff had been staying in the same downtown Phoenix jail with his baby brother for months, the two had never been allowed to see each other. They remained in separate units. Jeff was sentenced to seven-and-a-half years for stabbing Ray McQueen. He would spend them in Florence, in the prison complex of that historic frontier town that produced generations of law enforcement professionals, some of them named Salazar. There would be no hugging his daughter in her cap and gown that spring.

Back in November 2006, when Dale had been in jail for months and Jeff was just crossing the same threshold after his own arrest, Jeff had told reporters he hadn't done anything wrong and "neither did Dale. We're both innocent."

After pleading guilty, Jeff couldn't claim innocence any longer, but he did not want to be associated with the Serial Shooter crimes. His lawyer, Candace Shoemaker, said that her client was merely "wrapped into" everything else.

But by all accounts, Sam and Dale never met until 2006. Sam has not had a car in years, not in the memory of any of his friends or relatives. And no one has ever found any evidence to suggest that Sam ever possessed a .22-caliber weapon of any kind.

Sam didn't even know Jeff, let alone Dale, until the fall of

2005, shortly before he decided he "didn't deserve" to bunk at Ron Horton's anymore. By that time, Tony Mendez, Reggie Remillard and David Estrada had all already died from .22-caliber bullets, their lungs flooding with blood, their panic rising as the struggle to breathe was lost.

The Burger King building had been shot at with a .22. The three horses Sara Moon, who had drowned in her own blood, Little Man, who had lain down and gurgled out his last breath in the pasture, and Apache, whose shots caused him agony and changed his temperament forever, were all shot with .22s. Buddy the burro had hung his head in misery, a small-caliber bit of lead and brass embedded in his donkey skull forever. Whiskey the smiling Akita died riddled with .22-caliber bullets.

All of these things and many more happened before Sam Dieteman met anyone at all named Hausner.

Sam told detectives that as he entered the Hausner brothers' world of professional shoplifting, his skill at the petty crime earned him their trust and the brothers began to brag to him about the far worse crimes they had committed together. Sam was not present for these crimes, he said, and there is no evidence or claim that Sam had met the Hausners at the time these crimes occurred; he relayed the stories to police secondhand, as he remembered them from the festive boasting of the Hausner brothers.

One of these stories involved a black man getting blasted front-on with a shotgun after trying to intervene in the attempted shooting of a dog. As Sam heard the story, the black man had beer cans with him and was belligerent to the brothers, whom he approached on foot as they sat in a car. When the man ordered them not to shoot the dog, it was Dale who responded and it was Dale who aimed the .22 at him and who grew frustrated because it jammed. It was Jeff who argued that a .410 wasn't lethal enough to kill the man, and killing is what they wanted. It was Jeff who handed Dale the .410 anyway, to see how much damage it would do.

When detectives looked up this previously unknown case, they found Nathaniel Shoffner, they found the beer cans in evidence, they even found photos of a dog scavenging the crime scene. And, yes, the shotgun could and did kill.

As of this writing, Dale Hausner has been charged with this crime.

Jeff Hausner has not.

Detectives continued to encourage Sam Dieteman to talk. Another story came out of him, one which did not involve a gun. This story described yet another incident they'd been unaware of. But when they went looking, they found a record of something that matched.

On May 17, 2006, thirty-four-year-old Timothy Davenport set out for a late night walk to his friend Dave's house. They both lived on the Westside of Phoenix. Timothy, a man with a handlebar mustache, Elvis sideburns and a gentle voice, was walking down Seventy-third Avenue, southbound, when he decided to cut across a church parking lot that would take him to Camelback Road in the westerly direction he was seeking. There wasn't much traffic, so he noticed the small-model silver car going eastbound on Camelback Road. He watched it turn northbound to a point behind him on Seventy-third Avenue. He thought it was a little odd that the car stopped, let out a passenger, then did a U-turn. The passenger headed toward him on foot from behind. The car reached a point in front of him then did another U-turn. The silver car entered the parking lot and rolled right up to him. The driver had the window rolled down and the man at the wheel beckoned him, saying, "We're just stopping to see if you're okay?"

Timothy, a healthy working man, well-dressed and with no appearance of need, was surprised. *See if I'm okay?* he thought. He looked at the driver in puzzlement for five or six seconds. He started to say the words "Why wouldn't I be okay?" when his speech was stopped by a horrible sensation of pain and wetness in his shoulder blade.

A couple more knife plunges and Timothy Davenport stopped wondering. "I turned around to see what was going on, that's when I got slashed in the face."

Timothy started running, and "I never looked back." He kept running until he reached his friend Dave's house. Dave immediately drove him to the nearest hospital.

He remembers being air evaced, but then "someone asked me to count backwards from ten and I don't remember anything after that." When he came to, he was in a hospital. He remained there for a full week.

Timothy needed eight pints of blood. He had three stab

wounds in his shoulder blade, one in his ribs and one across the left side of his face. He also had a punctured lung.

He had never seen the person who attacked him. The church had no lights on. The parking lot was dark. The knifer had been a shadowy male figure padding through the dark and always at Timothy's back.

As for the driver, Timothy had only seen the man's face for a handful of seconds, "but it was enough to remember it for the rest of my life."

Timothy Davenport's own face would also carry that slash mark for the rest of his life.

Two years later, on May 9, 2008, Timothy received a visit from one Detective Cliff Jewell of the Phoenix Police Department. Timothy was surprised to see an investigator so long after that terrible night when his punctured lung had miraculously not prevented him from fleeing his attackers and running all the way to a friend's house. Timothy thought there was no hope of prosecution at this late date. But Cliff Jewell showed him a photo lineup.

The faces of six men with similar features were arrayed in front of him, in black and white, and all clean-shaven.

Even so, Timothy was "one hundred percent sure" when he pointed to the face in position number four: "He was the one that drove the car and distracted me while the other guy stabbed me."

Timothy could not identify anyone else, including a lineup that, unbeknownst to him, included a photo of Jeff Hausner.

What he did not do was tell Cliff Jewell that there had been a third man there. Because he hadn't seen one.

But Sam Dieteman, detectives now believed, had been sitting in the backseat of the Camry when Dale pulled up to Timothy. It was Sam who had told them of this incident and led them to the gentle man with the slash scar across his cheek. They were inclined to believe Sam when he said he was there. The Camry had tinted windows and the parking lot was unlit in the dark of night. It was easy to explain how Timothy had not noticed him.

A few days later, Clark Schwartzkopf also visited Timothy Davenport, who again ID'd Dale, but not Jeff Hausner.

In July of 2008, with his trial on dozens of other charges just weeks away, Dale Hausner was also charged with the stab attack on Timothy Davenport. Prosecutors soon thereafter also charged

Jeff with this crime.* In August 2008, many in the Hausner clan, including Jeff's ex-wife Brenda, brother Randy, mother Rosemarie and others, gathered in court to hear Jeff testify in a hearing related to Dale's case, but they were disappointed when it was announced that due to prison transportation constraints Jeff would not be appearing after all.

A few weeks later, Jeff did make the ride in from Florence and appeared in court to be sentenced for the crime of stabbing Raymond McQueen, to which he had already pleaded guilty. He had been studying scripture. He had a certificate of completion for a course of Bible study. He had letters of recommendation from prison pastors. At the time of his own sentencing, he had told the judge he planned to "join a real good church" when he got out. The judge at that sentencing had noted Jeff's "strong family support" and lack of felony priors and sentenced him to only half of what he could have invoked, seven-and-a-half out of a possible fifteen years.

Seventeen months later, when Jeff took the stand in baby brother Dale's proceedings, he invoked his Fifth Amendment right not to incriminate himself and said nothing more.

———————————

It has never been widely reported—and, in fact, the opposite has frequently been reported—but investigators considered Jeff Hausner to be a far worse specimen than Sam Dieteman. Because of their dual arrest and the global publicity their faces received over the next two years, always appearing together, Dale Hausner and Sam Dieteman will forever be considered "the Serial Shooter" in the minds of most. But many of the crimes occurred before Sam Dieteman ever met the Hausner boys. Investigators believe that "the Serial Shooter" was actually a shifting trio, in which Sam played the smallest role, and he has certainly been the only one to confess or show remorse.

In 2008, Sam Dieteman took the witness stand. "I wish I had never met Jeff," he said.

———————————

*Jeff was convicted of the stabbing in May 2009.

Chapter Twenty-nine

You have a bunch of idiots together doing somethin' funny.

Sam Dieteman

One day, after three long weeks of coma, his belly half blown away, doctors told Mrs. Patrick it was time to give a tracheotomy to her son, the last awful step toward a point of no return. "One more day," she told them, her heart heavy and exhausted, "give him one more day."

She knew Paul had a slightly claustrophobic nature and the tracheotomy would be an unbearable psychological burden, even if he supposedly couldn't feel it.

On that next day she sat by his bed, staring at the tubes, staring at the ventilator. The machine marked each breath with a rhythmic green blip. But now she noticed an extra dot coming on-screen, out of sync, offbeat from the others. She stared at it and tried to understand. It reappeared. She called in the nurse and asked what it meant.

"That's him trying to breathe on his own," the nurse answered joyfully.

It was a true Hollywood moment, the patient returning to life on the extra day a mother's vigilance had bought him.

Paul's journey back would be long and difficult, but he made it. The outside of his abdomen shows a large circular scar, where the 12-gauge blast entered him. Surgeons placed a plastic sheet underneath it and periodically removed it and replaced it with a smaller sheet, then an even smaller one, shrinking the scar tissue. They also did a lot to his internal organs.

Paul has been able to tell his family why the mention of Colleen's visit agitated him so. "If Colleen's coming," he had recognized, "it must be bad." Deep, deep in his sleep, Paul did not want to know his prospects were so dire.

Colleen did come to visit, thinking she was just days ahead of a funeral. Instead, her brother slowly came back to the real world. He had a new purpose as he discovered how life would be changed for him. He called it his "beautiful duty." Paul promised to "put a human face" on the victims. At trial, the jury endured many hours of dry testimony regarding invoice numbers, chain of custody, the minutiae of ballistics science. Paul made a promise to attend every day, to remind the jurors that behind every cold detail was a human heart, a broken body, a stream of tears, a cold gravestone.

Mrs. Patrick came to trial with him. Paul laughed off his coma. "It didn't bother me, I slept through the whole thing. She's the one who suffered." They rode matching scooters down Central Avenue and parked the little vehicles in the first row of the gallery of the fourth-floor courtroom.

Every day.

"I promised the other victims," Paul reiterated. "It's my beautiful duty."

Dale Hausner's physical appearance changed significantly from the night he first came to world attention. The changes began almost immediately. On Friday, August 4, 2006, the world awoke to images of a red-haired man with a face full of red whiskers from chin to cheek. Dale's face and neck had a pronounced pink tone, and his bare chest revealed the starkly pale complexion of the naturally fair. He was a small man and not at all overweight, but he had a slightly protruding belly and his face was filled out. His hair was combed straight back, with a bit of a pompadour.

By Monday, August 7, when Dale Hausner held his press conference, he was completely clean-shaven and the pompadour was gone, though his face was still pink and full.

Dale was not happy in prison. He leaned on his next oldest brother, Randy, a great deal. Randy was the one who usually spoke for the family, and it was Randy who hired the publicity agent on Dale's behalf. On the day that Dale was arrested, Randy told reporters, "He's my brother and this whole thing is devastating to my family. I've been getting sick all day about it."

Randy's long-term efforts to help his brothers over the next few years as the legal system lurched slowly forward could be seen in his frequent attendance at the many court hearings. As a City of Phoenix employee, a janitor, Randy's many appearances in the gallery had to be fit around his full-time job. Like Dale, Randy had many side activities. While Dale had hovered about the local boxing scene, Randy's interest was in the venues of local comedy, where he found he was better at booking and promoting other comics than performing stand-up. He worked hard at this side business. He also was very active in organizing singles activities, especially through his church. Finding two of your brothers under scrutiny as potential serial killers is not an experience anyone prepares for. In the months following Dale's arrest and then Jeff's, Randy found himself pulled on stage by a friend in the comedy business. He confronted his situation by making a widely reported joke: considering all that had happened, he told the crowd sipping martinis, he was thinking about changing his name to something less controversial, "like, say, Manson."

Randy created his own comedy venue, setting up a monthly comedy night at his church's rec center. It blended well with his organizing singles activities, although the comedy night was billed as "family entertainment." Randy promoted his image as "the clean comic." Indeed, a visit to the Mountain View Community Church rec center comedy night in 2008 showed a full house of at least two hundred people, from families with young children, to groups of twenty- and thirtysomethings sitting together, to retired couples and seniors. Randy seemed well loved, receiving enthusiastic applause, even though he did not perform. Also in the crowd that night was Rosemarie, who was clearly helping manage the event, and other family members. The close-knit nature of the Hausner family was on full display.

But Dale was missing it all. At his first public appearance, the jailhouse press conference on August 7, 2006, he had appeared calm, relaxed and supremely confident. But by the fall, Dale was saying things like "I'm thirty-three years old and my life is over."

And by December 2006, it nearly was.

At 3:45 a.m. on December 7, 2006, a jail guard found Dale unresponsive in his cell and covered in vomit. A letter was found in the cell. It was addressed to Randy. The letter gave instructions to his brother on how he wanted his affairs handled.

Dale did not die that day. Through the swift actions of the guard, he received medical attention in a timely manner. Dale later admitted he was trying to kill himself and had been hoarding over-the-counter drugs such as antihistamines, decongestants and pain relievers for six weeks. He had concealed the cache in a packet of M&M's, which had escaped the notice of the guards who performed the daily searches in his high-security cell. Dale claimed the number of pills he had concealed and then swallowed was 260.

Dale was moved to a psychiatric unit for a time. He made a full recovery.

But by the time he went to trial two years later, in September of 2008, Dale no longer looked pink and full. His hair now looked a dirty blond at best.* His skin was sallow. And after two years in jail plus a suicide attempt, Dale had lost somewhere upward of twenty pounds. His waist was trim and his chest sunken and his face, robbed of flesh, showed more pronounced than ever the pugnacious family stamp, with the jutting chin, receding mouth, and overall pinched quality.

Dale had remained clean-shaven† since that first Monday when he appeared at his jailhouse press conference, and the

---

*Linda Swaney testified that Dale dyed his hair red during the weeks previous to his arrest, but Dale denied it. Marianne Lescher also testified to Dale dyeing his hair red. To many observers, he appeared to have red hair in his photos at the time of his arrest. Other witnesses also testified to Dale's red hair. Jenny Hausner testified that her uncle had a history of hair dyeing, including a stint as a blond around 2003.

† Dale had had a full beard and mustache the previous Friday when he was arrested.

pompadour seemed gone forever, too. Police officers from all over the Task Force had a theory that Dale probably missed that pompadour very much.

During his first interview with Detective Clark Schwartzkopf on August 4, Dale had talked about the serial killer Charles Starkweather. He told the detective that he'd watched a movie about him and felt an affinity for the killer, because "Nebraska, which is, you know, my home town." At Detective Schwartzkopf's prodding, Dale went on to say, "It's—it's—it's very fascinating. It deals with the morbid side of people, like the bogeyman or something like that. And you can't go anywhere without hearing about it. I'm sure you get sick of hearing about it, being a police officer. But you can't go to a bar, you can't go anywhere, my work, people are always, I find it in the garbage cans, people are always reading about the Serial Killer, it's everywhere."

When the detective asked whether he knew a lot about serial killers, Dale hedged, saying again that he knew about Starkweather because of the Nebraska connection.

"I don't study them with a passion or anything," Dale insisted, adding, "I like boxing, too, so I don't know if that has anything to do . . . I kinda like the rough stuff. Even though I'm not a rough guy or anything, but . . . I just find it interesting how we love to sit down with some fool like Jeffrey Dahmer or something and just ask him why in the hell would you wanna eat all those people, and—the BTK killer? I mean he's killed eleven people for no absolute reason. There's just no reason for that. And to just ask him—chained up, of course—what the hell were you thinking? What the hell goes . . . why are you normal one second? What makes you click over to be a maniac the next? I just don't get that. I have never understood that. And to me, it's, it's, it's fascinating in a morbid way. I've saved all the clippings from the BTK, excuse me, from the Serial Killer and from the Serial Sniper and I got 'em at home in scrap books."

One of the things that all of the police officers involved in the crimes from 2005 and 2006 attributed to the Serial Shooter noticed was that the weapons involved were slightly unusual. What they would consider to be a run-of-the-mill assault or homicide, they say, would involve a handgun, a .380, a .38 or a 9mm.

A .410 is a narrow-gauge shotgun. Police say they don't see it often in assaults. A .22 rifle is also not favored by the typical violent criminal in Maricopa County. And neither is a 12-gauge, which is what Paul Patrick was shot with on June 8, 2006, and Michael Cordrey a month later, on July 11.

After listening to Dale talk and taking note of his little pompadour, many of the officers involved in the Task Force found that peculiar array of weapons to suddenly make sense. Charles Starkweather had used three weapons in his 1950s Nebraska crime spree: a .22, a .410 and a 12-gauge.

When they looked up the old Nebraska case and found photos, they found that Starkweather had also combed his hair into a small pompadour. His face was strikingly similar to Dale's. Starkweather had red hair. Dale dyed his red. The more they looked at the Starkweather case, the more similarities they found. The Phoenix area law officers felt that their suspect was emulating someone he admired. A flier comparing Hausner and Starkweather circulated around 620 and many of the other agencies.

By the time he went to trial, both the red color in the hair and the pompadour style had disappeared from the man sitting at the defense table. There were those at the prosecution's table who believed he missed them very, very much.

Dale Hausner kept Detective Clark Schwartzkopf very busy. On the wiretaps, Dale was heard to pout that the police were not giving him credit for "that fucking guy I shot at Twenty-seventh Avenue . . . in the yard." Clark hunkered down trying to give the man the credit he craved. After a grid search of potentially matching crimes, the detective found the sad case of David Perez, who had been talking on his cell phone in front of his house on July 7, 2006, when he took an inexplicable shotgun blast through the neck. The phone was knocked out of his hand, destroyed. A neighbor rushed over to apply pressure to the man's neck and use his own phone to call 911. David Perez survived the attack. He said that the shot came as a drive-by, from a blue sedan. Clark assigned Dale the credit he was seeking by making the Perez case counts 73 and 74 against him—attempted first-degree murder and drive-by shooting.

Dale appeared in court every day in civilian dress, an important point to his defense attorneys, who argued hard for his right to do so. He didn't wear a suit, just solid-colored button-down shirts and slacks with a belt. In casual Arizona, where witnesses have taken the stand in shorts and flip-flops, this was not seen as underdressed, even given the seriousness of the proceedings. Dale was fidgety in court, often rapidly bouncing his knee, a jiggling that usually engaged his whole chair, especially when the testimony focused on his car or the ballistics or the reports documenting his ownership of .22-caliber rifles.

Testimony on the suffering of victims or the grief of families didn't seem to trigger a reaction.

Out of the presence of the jury, during breaks, he sometimes stood and stretched. During those moments, it was possible to note the electronic security belt around his waist, worn under his shirt, and the other security device he was wearing, a leg brace.

One day, early in the trial, the courtroom went black. Dale's oldest brother, Gregory, an agile and able-bodied man, was seated in the back row. The lights did not flicker back on immediately. The darkness, in a windowless government room, was deep and total. It was not possible to see the defendant or any movements he might be making. Nor was it possible to see his brother.

All was silent.

A guard pulled out a flashlight and searched, but did not find, the defendant in the beam. A flashlight appeared from far across the room, some thirty or forty feet away from the defendant, from the hallway that led to the series of rooms used to transport the inmate, but this light couldn't find him either. Since trial began, Dale had been allowed to traverse this territory alone so that he entered the courtroom with the appearance of a free man. Even the pool TV camera in the back of the gallery turned on a light and began roaming in search of the man on trial. In this deep, black, unexpected darkness the whereabouts of the diminutive defendant suddenly seemed uncertain, and the man believed to be responsible for the deaths and maimings of dozens seemed remarkably untethered.

Paul Patrick, sitting in the first row of the gallery, let out a yelp. His mother, sitting three feet nearer the defendant, said she felt the sudden eerie terror, as well.

"My heart stopped. You suddenly realize how vulnerable you are. I mean," her eyes fluttered, "he's right there."

The silence was broken at last by Dale's own voice.

"Here I am," he called out.

The guard's flashlight took a moment to orient toward the voice and then Dale was lit up, standing, waving toward his captor.

The room lights came on a while after that, and Judge Roland Steinle made a joke about the county not paying its electric bill.

The jury laughed and testimony resumed.

By the time it was over, the blackout seemed quite random, after all, and the only thing Dale Hausner had done was demonstrate to the jury his incessant helpfulness.

Dale Hausner continued to deny any involvement in the Serial Shooter crimes. During his first interrogation on August 4, 2006, detectives began to show him clips of video from the other room, where Sam Dieteman was already confessing. At first, Dale pointed out that Sam never mentioned him by name, simply making references to "we" and "him." Detectives returned to Dale's interview room a half hour later with a new clip. When they popped it in and hit play, Dale could see his roommate clearly saying "Dale" and confessing to the crimes he said they had committed together.

After unhappily watching that video, Dale was willing to agree that the man sleeping on an air mattress in his front room for the last several weeks might actually be the infamous Serial Shooter. He could see for himself that he was claiming to be. Perhaps falsely, Dale suggested. If the confession was true, he told both officers and reporters, then it could only be because the keys to the Camry were kept near the front door of Dale's apartment. He said he slept in a back bedroom with Mandy. He could go to bed and Sam would have unfettered access to both the Camry keys and the front door. He theorized that Sam must have taken his car keys and gone out committing the Serial Shooter crimes in Dale's Camry without his knowledge. Dale told the officers he'd be good and angry if his car had been used in this way.

But Sam's August 4 confession contained many details, including accurately inventorying which victims had been shot with a .410 and which ones had been attacked with a 12-gauge, guns that belonged to Dale. This was ballistic information that had never been made public. Sam also had the accurate backstory that the 12-gauge had been a gift to Dale from his father.

Sam even announced to detectives that "Dale said he used to use a twenty-two." The .22, so diligently pursued by Cliff Jewell, was hardly public information, either. It wasn't even much disseminated among the Task Force. True, it had been mistakenly used in *America's Most Wanted*'s B-roll video, but Cliff was always convinced that the person paying the most close attention to that tiny clip would've been the killer himself. The *AMW* mistake had not been repeated widely in the media, and Cliff had asked the show for a retraction.

Sam relayed that Dale used latex gloves to handle the guns and ammunition. Not only was a box of latex gloves found among Dale's possessions, but a used latex glove in the Camry had both gunshot residue and DNA—Dale's. One of the more piercing statements that Sam made about himself was that "when my kids came to visit, last month," he had turned on the TV and watched news of the Serial Shooter case at "my mom's place, where they were staying."

After this sweeping confession, and when the shock of the takedown had worn off, Sam Dieteman was assigned a defense attorney, Maria Schaffer. She took his case in a new direction. She had her client plead "not guilty," in spite of his admissions. She joined many defense motions asking for a change of venue, the suppression of the wiretaps, and so forth. A trial date was set for Sam in spring of 2008.

But Sam's trial never got started.

In April 2008, Sam Dieteman ended his attempts at exoneration. He pleaded guilty to the murder that Pete Salazar had worked so hard to get him to admit to, the one where he was only five feet away when he blasted Claudia Gutierrez-Cruz, leaving her paralyzed and dragging herself by her arms to get help, with the large shotgun cup forced all the way inside her. He also pleaded guilty to being an accessory to murder for being in the passenger seat of the car when Dale allegedly took aim at Robin Blasnek, her cell phone in hand, and left her in much the same condition, also bringing her young life to an end. "I did nothing to stop it," Sam testified. "I'm guilty."

In exchange for these two guilty pleas, charges against him for several of the other Serial Shooter crimes were dropped.

Charges were dropped, but Sam Dieteman's plea "deal" did not include any promises for his sentencing. Life or death for Samuel Dieteman would be decided by a jury, not a prosecutor.

He testified against Dale Hausner, but he still faced the death penalty himself. As Sam wrote to the *Arizona Republic*, "I am in no way trying to play 'Mr. Innocent,' as Dale Hausner is. I have taken responsibility for my crimes, I signed a plea agreement to where I am still going to 'Death Row,' the only benefits I get out of that deal are avoiding an unnecessary trial and being able to help put Hausner away."

Dale and Sam have never had a moment alone together since the first step Sammy took out of Apartment number 1083 late on the night of August 3, 2006. However, on occasion, they have appeared in the same courtroom at the same time. During these pretrial hearings, both dressed in black-and-white jail stripes and shackles, Dale* was at the defense table and Sam was kept away from him, usually in the empty jury box.

The sheriff's deputies assigned to sit near Sam were always big, muscular men, while those near Dale were often much slighter and older. Sam's physical presence was so imposing— and Dale's so negligible—it was easy to forget that it was Dale who, if the charges were correct, was the dangerous one.

Their distinct personalities played out in sharp relief during these joint appearances. Dale engaged with people—his attorneys, the guards, the bailiff—reaching out to shake hands with court personnel sitting near him. Sam, on the other hand, waited for people to approach him, and only his lawyers did.

As for their interaction with each other, there was absolutely none. No angry stares, no side glances, no gestures or grimaces. They never even looked at each other. There was no acknowledgment that the two men ever even knew each other, that they once killed together and that during these hearings the one was trying to put the other on Death Row.

Sam Dieteman wasn't fighting the death penalty. "If I were on my own jury, I would vote yes, give me the death penalty. I deserve to die for what I've done," he testified. "Sometimes I lie in my cell all day and think nothing but 'hurry up and give me the needle.' Other days, I wonder if there is some good that I could still do. I do have children . . . ," he said, his voice trailing off.

---

*Dale's right to wear civilian clothes applied only when the jury was present.

Chapter Thirty

I just love shooting people in the back.

Dale Hausner

Dale's defense attorney, Ken Everett, did not believe Sam Dieteman's morose speeches. During opening arguments at Dale's trial, he told the jury that "Killer Sam" was trying to save his own life by framing Dale.

As this book goes to print, Dale Hausner faces eighty-seven counts ranging from arson to animal cruelty to first-degree murder. His mother and his brothers attended trial as often as they could. Early in the trial, his father, Eugene, passed away of a heart condition. His mother returned to her seat on the hard benches, rubbing her neck during testimony and receiving Dale's quick wink when he entered the courtroom, a few weeks after laying her husband to rest. Dale and Rosemarie were not allowed to speak to each other, but she sat a few feet behind him. He knew she was there.

None of Dale's girlfriends or ex-wives came to his hearings or his trial, though most of them were on the witness list. Marianne Lescher, the school principal and nationally respected curriculum specialist, fought her subpoena desperately. That subpoena was issued by the defense.

Linda Swaney, the mother of the little girl who was tucked away in Dale's apartment amid shotguns and ice picks the night he found himself surrounded by a shouting, glaring SWAT team, cooperated with police instantly. That very night, Linda Swaney turned over everything Dale had ever left at her house. She told the police that she'd had her locks changed recently to keep him out. She told them about the order of protection she had tried to get against Dale Hausner, and she told them how she did not want him near their daughter. Officers also learned that Mandy's diagnosis was much more optimistic than Dale usually portrayed. Von Gierke's disease is very serious, but with proper care, Mandy could expect to enjoy a full adulthood. Although Dale ostentatiously demanded attention for the child's feeding tube from people like John Kane, court filings from Linda describe several incidents in which Dale failed to keep the girl's blood sugar up, as the disease demands, by taking naps for hours and otherwise neglecting her. On the witness stand, Linda was asked what defense attorney Ken Everett appeared to consider a simple statement rather than a real question, "Dale loved little Mandy, didn't he." The courtroom went tense as Linda remained silent. After several agonizing moments, she said, "That's not easy to answer." Across the room, Dale lifted his head. He had kept it cradled in his arms on the table throughout most of her testimony. He exclaimed "Shit!" loud enough for the whole room to hear. "I think he wanted everyone to think he loved her," Linda finished. "That's fucking bullshit!" Dale said again.

Dale's attorneys fought hard for him, and he worked vigorously alongside them. He paid close attention in trial, often whispering to his attorneys, passing them notes and reviewing files. He muttered to himself in reaction to testimony and made wrist flicking gestures as if to say, "See! Not me," or gave a thumbs-up, with the word "yes!" at his lips. Sometimes he joked, keeping an eye on the media sitting behind him, more than once trying to establish eye contact and engage a smile, even making quips he hoped would end up in print.

One of the most devastating witnesses for the prosecution provoked a remarkable reaction from the defendant. Ashley Armenta, alert to her surroundings and well versed in vehicle models, had given the car behind her a good hard look on that summer night, after storming out of the family minivan because of an argument with her husband. Moments after staring at the strange silver car, she was shot. In court, she described the sedan stopped at a corner behind her to a tee. How sure was she that it was a Toyota Camry, model year 1997–1999? With tinted windows? "As sure as it's possible to be sure." She positively ID'd a photo of Dale Hausner's car from the witness stand. She was clear and calm. The rapport between herself and her husband showed a couple who had weathered a horrible ordeal together and were strongly in tune with each other and shared great fondness, their quarrel long since turned into a private marital joke.

Jurors wanted to know about continuing pain from the pellets left in her body. "The one in my temple, yes," she said, cheerfully.

Paul Patrick and his mother sat at an angle where the front of Dale's face was usually visible to them. He wasn't much interested in her pain, they reported. But the Patricks said that during Ashley's confident and accurate description of his vehicle, both from memory and her later ID of the photo, tears were streaming down Dale's face, from both eyes. "At the end of it, he reached for the tissues and was dabbing his face," Mrs. Patrick said. "He was crying and crying."

"He didn't like that testimony, at all," her son Paul joined in. He lifted his fingers to his face to demonstrate the tear tracks he observed at the defense table. "But as soon as the car testimony stopped," Paul snapped his fingers, "he was done crying, back to his old self."

During his many statements to police, Sam Dieteman admitted that he was the one to pull the trigger on Ashley Armenta, and Ashley's own memories of the night were consistent with a passenger-side attack. Sam claimed that he "aimed high, trying to miss." Ashley's wounds, indeed, were less devastating than many others', and they were high. Sam also claimed that Dale had at times scolded him for failing to get a good shot, a killing one, because the nonfatal cases "will get us caught."

It was, indeed, a nonfatal shot that had led to some very incriminating testimony and had the usually confident Dale Hausner streaming tears and reaching for tissue.

During the investigation, the suspect vehicle was most often described by witnesses as silver or blue. At trial, people who climbed into the witness box not only described it as blue or silver but also white, metallic, green and even purple. The mystery of the car's color was solved when photos were introduced showing the Camry in different types of light: soft incandescent light, bright fluorescent light, daylight, etc. In each one, the Camry appeared a different color. It had a metallic mix paint containing tiny chips of different colors. The color that became prominent would depend on which chips were catching most light.

Trial was a sad spectacle of crime scene photos, blood trails, autopsy reports and trauma surgeons.

Rebecca Estrada sat stoically when the big screen lit up with a three-foot image of her son David's body sprawled violently across a Tolleson sidewalk. But four or five seconds later, she crumpled, her hands flying to her face, her body shivering with silent sobs. Paul Patrick handed her a box of tissues.

Deborah Haddock took the witness stand and described walking out into the pasture to find her mother's pony, Little Man, lying dead in the tall grass, his tawny coat riddled with rivulets of dried blood. When pressed for certain details, she went blank, finally answering, "There's a lot I try to forget."

But the trial brought its moments of strange comfort. James Hernandez testified about seeing Viet Nam vet Reggie Remillard get shot at a bus stop. He described his own call to 911 and his efforts to encourage the dying man to "hang in there, hang in there." When Hernandez climbed down from the witness stand and passed out of the courtroom, a woman stood up from the gallery and followed him. In the hallway, past the courtroom doors, she grabbed the young man and enfolded him in a bear hug. She was one of Reggie's sisters. "We couldn't find you," she cried into his neck. "Thank you so much for what you did, we wanted to thank you, we couldn't find you."

Innocent people across the country have even benefited from what happened in Phoenix and how the community stepped forward to work together in unprecedented ways. John Jacobs, from Clear Channel Outdoor, did not stop with his initial engineering of a valuable donation of billboard space to the city's efforts to catch two serial killers. When suspects in both the Serial Shooter case and the Baseline Rapist case were in custody, Jacobs worked tirelessly to expand the program nationwide. Clear Channel now has agreements with the FBI, *America's Most Wanted* and municipalities from coast to coast to provide emergency billboard space as needed. With the development of digital billboards, this information can be updated instantaneously. If a crime occurs in the morning and officers are looking for specific information such as a vehicle with a description, it can be posted for the morning rush hour. If a suspect license plate number is developed later in the day, commuters will see it on the same billboard as they drive off for their appointments or lunch. Clear Channel Outdoor operates 144,000 advertising displays across the country, including in Times Square in New York City. Anywhere you see these signs highlighting a local crime, thank the man who tried to do his part, John Jacobs.

John Jacobs did see the targets of his billboards get taken into custody. But he did not see justice play out its full story. On September 22, 2008, John Jacobs succumbed to a debilitating illness. He was only forty-eight years old.

Every one of the acts of the Serial Shooter caused lasting changes. Paul Patrick did wake up from his coma. But his life as a provider, slinging boxes and driving forklifts, was over. He had nightmares every night. His dog Misty's job became to scramble to the top of his chest, where it didn't hurt as much, avoiding his abdomen, which she somehow knew was too fragile to bear her, and lick Paul's face, reel him back in from his subconscious, the little REM movie of the night of June 8, 2006. He hobbled painfully when he walked and rode his scooter to go anywhere farther than across a room. Misty hopped on and rode the running board. Paul laughed at his scooter and the canine hitchhiker and said, "My shoes last forever!" With so much of his intestinal tract missing, Paul had difficulty absorbing nutrition and experienced health problems associated with that. He still had eighty pellets inside his torso. He feared lead poisoning over the long term. In his one-room apartment he kept bits of his former life on the walls, to remind him of how good life used to be. Loud noises cause him to sweat and shake. "Sometimes," he said of the miracle that he did not die, "I wonder just how lucky I was."

Kibili Tambadu still had numb fingers and pellets that he will carry for life. While he was recovering from his painful and bloody injuries, he was fired from his job at Burger King. This downward spiral brought on financial difficulties that led to an argument over money with a girlfriend in 2008. She threw him out of the apartment, but his terror of the nighttime, the dark streets, the lurking random surprise, drove him to a break a window to get back in. As his defense attorney wrote, "considering what happened to him the last time he walked home at night," his actions have a certain understandable context.

Burger King contains many ideals in its vision statement about "investing in its people," "supporting our communities," "developing and retaining diverse employees," and "maintain[ing] an ever-expanding tradition of good corporate citizenship with a commitment to the communities in which we do business." When corporate headquarters in Florida was contacted about one of its own employees being a victim of the Serial Shooter (a case that had first directly affected one of its own restaurants) Burger King initially showed some interest in pursuing relief for the young man through its corporate resources.* But after September of 2008, no phone call, e-mail or letter to Burger King was ever returned. It is hard to understand how the case of Kibili Tambadu, a young man universally admired and praised by teachers and everyone else he ever met, can square with Burger King's stated corporate ideals.

———————

Ron Horton, after absenting himself from his large extended family for their own safety, began to repatriate himself. About a year after the arrest of Sam Dieteman and Dale Hausner, Ron came forward, and for the first time, the people of the community that had been terrorized by the Year of the Serial Shooter learned who the informant was who had lured out the suspects and put the Task Force on their tail. He received a wave of publicity, including a spread in *Reader's Digest*. Much of what was published strayed from the truth. He never managed the legendary music venue the Mason Jar, for instance, as has been widely reported. He did receive a payout from the reward money of-

———————

*Burger King has foundations and institutions through which it "invests" in its employees and communities. Burger King seeks and receives positive publicity for its efforts through these foundations and for its Diversity Action Council.

fered on the Clear Channel billboards. "But he was never the same," his sisters say. Ron's battle with his conscience, over betraying a friend, never ended. Some of his biker friends wouldn't let him forget the code he had broken. He gave most of the reward money away. Sisters Rennee and Cindi remember him coming to the big family party of Christmas 2007. "He had long sleeves on," they both say in hushed tones. "He wouldn't let anybody see it, that thing on his arm."

The "thing" on his arm was a staph infection called MRSA. "He was laughing and bringing Christmas presents and all that," they say. "He didn't let us know how serious it was."

Three weeks later, Ron Horton was dead.

His three boys were placed in foster care. The paternal relatives stayed in contact with the boys as much as they could, but they only had claim to the one son who was biologically Ron's. The mother of all three boys had not been able to get her life together enough to shepherd them through the system either toward herself or toward the Horton clan. The record is clear: Ron Horton loved these kids, and he left them a legacy of bravery and integrity. It is hoped that as they come of age, they can each realize and appreciate this legacy and they can accept the humble thanks of a community. The man's grief over the murder of Robin Blasnek and his dawning astonishment at the killing of Claudia Gutierrez-Cruz awakened his sense of connection to a larger world. No one knows how many lives Ron Horton saved by his actions. The boys he loved so much can look up to him as they become adults and become a part of that world in their own right.

Ricardo Lopez, young father and dog lover, had an open front yard before December 29, 2005. After Peanut was shot, he put in a fence around the front yard, all the way across the driveway, and kept it secure with a padlock.

Issac Crudup changed out his cyclone fence for a high cinder-block wall.

Horse owners in Tolsun Farms have erected expensive new structures; many of the horses no longer enjoy the free roaming pastures they did before 2005, and many have been moved out of county, far away from the daily pettings and treats received when they lived in their person's backyard.

Federal witness Annette Prince pulled up stakes yet again and will probably never stop looking over her shoulder.

Chiropractor Goudarz Vassigh had treated most members of the Hausner family. He couldn't understand why the Hausner boys would target him and he still hoped it wasn't true. Goudarz's most frequent patients were Dale's parents, Rosemarie and Eugene. Eugene performed handyman chores at the chiropractor's office, and Goudarz has particular admiration for the disabled second son, Kristopher, whom he remembers as someone who worked very hard. Goudarz was shocked the morning that he found himself staring at a television screen with Eugene and Rosemarie's youngest son on all channels. "I immediately picked up the phone and called them. I just said if there was anything I could do for them, to please let me know. I wished them well. It was a terrible day," he said in his soft Persian lilt.

These are just a few pieces of the aftermath. Of the shotgun victims who survived, every single one still carried tiny lead pellets in his or her body. Sometimes these pellets would make their way to the surface, and the victim received them through a fresh wound, one that is appearing in reverse order, from inside out. As time passes, the pellets travel inside the body, rubbing up against nerves, getting infected, pressing on organs, causing pain and disorders. Paul Patrick, with his series of major surgeries to restore some intestinal function, had an early scare when an inattentive radiological team rolled him into an MRI machine. When he realized where the gurney had traveled, he frantically called out to halt the procedure. Some people are afraid of MRIs for reasons of claustrophobia, so it took some moments for the technicians to comprehend the true reason for his panic. "An MRI is a huge magnet," Paul said, shaking his head. "I would have been a human blender."

All of the victims had their moments when they realized, yet again, how life had changed. These few examples should give a glimpse of the extent to which one flick of the trigger will reverberate forever.

There may be even more charges laid against Dale and Jeff Hausner and Sam Dieteman for years to come. Detectives Cliff Jewell and Ron Rock, and so many others, are still digging through at least six thousand cases, looking at them through the

lens of the Hausner brothers and Sam Dieteman. The case of
Timothy Davenport, stabbed from behind, came to light during
the writing of this book and was charged to Dale in time for it to
be included in his initial trial. During trial, Cliff Jewell was
paged by surgeons to attend the dangerous surgery suddenly
needed to remove the bullet from Tim Boviall, whom Jewell had
once entertained at a Taco Bell. The bullet had moved too close
to Boviall's spine, and surgeons now felt it was more dangerous
to leave it in than to remove it. Jewell missed testimony in downtown Phoenix while he was inside the surgical theater, ready to
receive the bullet into evidence, verifying chain of custody.

As of September 3, 2008, when Dale Hausner first donned
street clothes and entered the capacious fourth-floor courtroom
for trial, he was facing eighty-seven charges which included
eight homicides, nineteen assaults, and attacks on three horses
and eight dogs, plus two arsons. Each incident had resulted in
several charges. For example, the May 30, 2006, shooting of
James Hodge showed up as counts 41, 42 and 43: attempted
first-degree murder, aggravated assualt and drive-by shooting.
This long list did not include the shootings of Tim Boviall, or
Buddy the burro, or the chiropractor Goudarz Vassigh's office,
or Ray McQueen (knifed by Jeff Hausner), or several others
believed to belong to the Serial Shooter. The decision to prosecute rests on many things, and these cases, perhaps even un-
told others, were not ready for trial in late 2008. Indeed, some
of the eighty-seven charges were vague, like count 33, which
states simply "conspiracy to commit first degree murder occur-
ring on or between April of 2006 and August 4, 2006, within
Maricopa County."

With so many charges of serious violent crimes laid at Dale
Hausner's door already, it seems likely he will be very familiar
with a jail cell for many years.

It is also likely that Sam Dieteman will never walk our streets
again. His sentencing will wait until after Dale's trial. His own
fate depended largely on his testimony against his former roommate and friend. During that testimony, which occurred in January and February of 2009, he said, "There's no way I'll ever get
out of prison. I wanted to plead guilty since I got arrested—to
everything that I did, for everything that I was there for. Basically, I wasn't allowed to plead guilty for months and months."
Sam's attorney, Maria Schaffer, fought hard to get him a plea

agreement instead, something he bickered with her about.*

Dale's defense attorney, Ken Everett, attacked the deal as cheapening Sam's veracity. "What did you want to plead guilty to?" Mr. Everett asked in accusatory tones, laying ugly crimes at Sam's feet, making sure the jury was reminded of heinous acts. "The whole conglomeration of everything that me and your client had done since May 2, 2006," Sam responded from the stand.

Up there in the witness box, Sam was clad in ominous black-and-white prison stripes and red flip-flops (to deter escape), he had shackles around his ankles and there was a SWAT team visibly present nearby. At the defense table, Dale was dressed in dress slacks and a button-down shirt, with his frail mother and loyal brother Gregory sitting behind him. Dale was projecting his status of presumed innocence while the jury could have no doubt that Sam was considered not only guilty but dangerous.

But Mr. Everett's questioning gave Sam a chance to dispel what he considered a false image of the defendant. Dale's lawyer repeatedly poked at Sam's plea deal—which had dropped many of the charges against him, but did not excuse him from the death penalty—insisting that Sam was simply putting on a show for the benefit only of himself. "You don't really care what this jury does, do you, you've got your deal," Mr. Everett declared.

"It does matter to me what this jury does," Sam responded, quietly but firmly.

Mr. Everett wisely left that line of questioning and moved on to other areas. But Arizona is a pioneer in what is called "jury reform," and jurors are allowed to ask questions of their own. At the end of cross-examination, they made it clear they wanted to know more about Sam's feelings in regard to the current trial. Why was he testifying?

Sam looked down and remained quiet. At last he spoke. "There were eight murders. That's eight human beings whose lives were taken. I know Dale. If he got out, it might be a year but he'd start doing it again. I want some measure of justice for the victims in regards to both myself and Dale."

---

*Sam's testimony as well as comments made by Maria Schaffer confirm the strain in their relationship.

Sam's testimony filled in many of the details of the Serial Shooter, how it had looked from the other side of the crime spree. He said it was Jeff Hausner who originated the term "random recreational violence." He said Jeff first used it when the trio had set a Dumpster on fire at Jeff's own apartment complex. They liked fire. In April of 2006, shortly after Sam had met Dale for the first time, the younger Hausner suggested he knew of some dried-out palm trees that were just begging to be burned. After leaving the scene of that post-midnight escapade, the Camry was stopped by Chandler police. "We were still very close to the burning palm trees," Sam testified. "Maybe a half mile, you could see the flames and the fire trucks while the officer talked to us." Nevertheless, Dale used his charm to explain to the officer why he had three firearms in the car. He left the incident with nothing but a speeding ticket.*

Sammy and Jeff, both physically big men, got into bar fights eagerly. Soon, diminutive Dale took to driving the two hulks out at night, looking for someone to engage in violence. That's how Timothy Davenport got stabbed. Sam remembered that the Hausner brothers had intended for Sam to assault the man they saw walking across a church parking lot on May 17, 2006. "But I was too drunk," he testified. "I said I just didn't feel up to beating somebody in my condition. So they [Dale and Jeff] said, 'Well, if you're going to be a pussy about it,' and Jeff took his knife out and he was the one to get out of the car."

By that time, the middle of May, Sam was spending more and more time drunk. His descent into frequent drunkenness had begun well before, mentioned by Ron Horton and others who knew him in 2005. But his most urgent reason yet for blotting out consciousness had occurred on May 2, 2006. On that day, Sam had quarreled with Celeste Vance, and Dale had picked him up to take him back to Mesa for the night, away from the emotional heat of Jeff's apartment. But instead of driving straight

---

*The ticket was introduced at trial, and the ticketing officer testified. Dale testified that they had received the ticket and that guns were in the car, and that he'd shown them to the officer, but denied setting the palm trees on fire.

back to Mesa via the freeway, Dale had dropped off in one of the downtown Phoenix exits. He then began a slow crawl down Van Buren. At Forty-fourth Street, he turned north.

"Lean back," he directed his passenger.

Sam did so without questioning, flicking the catch lever to slightly release his seat.

Dale, operating the control buttons from the driver's seat, lowered Sam's window. "Watch this," Dale said, swinging the shotgun up from near his leg. He extended it one-handed across Sam's lap, placing its nose on the sill, and fired out the open window.

"As horrible as it sounds now, we laughed." Sam finished the story of how seventeen-year-old Sierra Leone refugee Kibili Tambadu got shot. "He didn't seem all that hurt."

Leaving the teenager bleeding and screaming at the side of the road, Dale made a quick getaway by entering the 202 freeway. He got off again at Scottsdale Road and circled back westbound on Thomas Road.

"We were gonna get some booze," Sam testified, his head bent down, "then we saw a small dark figure walking. So he hands me the gun and says 'your turn, dude.'"

Sam confirmed he was only a pace or two away from Claudia Gutierrez-Cruz when he pulled the trigger. The Camry was in the curb lane. The car never stopped, just slowed down as it passed the "small dark figure." At first, Sam testified, they both thought he had missed. Dale was angry about that. But they circled back for a closer look and discovered her collapsed on a grass berm behind the interior edge of the sidewalk. Dale hooted in happy approbation when he saw her there. They drove off.

Two days later, Dale arrived at his brother's apartment and spirited Sam away from all the people who shared that place. Outside, he excitedly showed Sam a newspaper clipping. The newspaper article described the incident on Thomas Road and revealed not only that the victim was a female, not only that she had died, but also that she was the first homicide of the year in Scottsdale.

"Man, I'm jealous," Dale exclaimed. "You got first homicide of the year!"

As he later told Scottsdale detective Pete Salazar, Sam kept as drunk as possible after that first killing. It didn't seem funny, after all. And from the witness stand two-and-a-half years later, he told Dale's jury that he was ashamed of "the piece of shit that I turned into."

———————

Sam testified that as he got drawn into the inner world of the two Hausner brothers, he became curious about the inside jokes between the two. One such joke had the brothers calling each other "you Bill Clinton–lookin' motherfucker." This, Sam said, is how he learned the story of the man killed while defending a stray dog at Twentieth Street and Monroe, a man who turned out to be Nathaniel Shoffner. Other times the trio would drive past a horse in a field, and the brothers would "hypothetically" and gleefully discuss what caliber weapon would be needed to kill it. Perhaps a .22? When Sam begged to be let in on the joke, the stories of Sara Moon and Apache and the other horses shot at Tolsun Farms came out.

But there was a new dynamic taking place. Jeff had made arrangements with the homeowners association at his apartment complex to start providing janitorial services. He started needing a regular night's sleep and "RVing" was increasingly left to Dale and Sam alone. The loyalty between Sam and Dale began to increase while the loyalty of either of them to Jeff waned.

Dale even became angry at Jeff for some reason, Sam testified, and began stealing from him every time he came over. The 12-gauge shotgun, which Dale said had been given to him by their father, Eugene, was at Jeff's. Sam told the court that Dale snuck it out of his brother's apartment when Jeff wasn't looking.

The unemployed electrician also told the court that it was this 12-gauge that had been used to shoot James Hodge on May 30, 2006. The shooting of that troubled Viet Nam vet, according to Sam, had occurred as he and Dale exited the complex after a visit with Jeff. They saw Hodge standing there and Dale passed him. Then he did a U-turn, came parallel to the white-haired man smoking on the grass, swung up the 12-gauge and shot through the driver's side window. Dale had been so thrilled with his stunt that he immediately pulled back into the complex to check out the damage. But Sam and Dale had been almost instantly caught in the headlights of the first arriving police cruiser.

"It was the first thing he could think of," Sam explained, "to flag 'em down."

It was a day or two later that Jeff learned of the attack, from the horrified homeowners association board he now worked for. Jeff, apparently, realized the deadly assault must have been the handiwork of his baby brother. Sam reported a spirited confrontation between the brothers after that. Jeff was "not happy" that Dale had nearly killed a man virtually in Jeff's own backyard, just three or four buildings over from his own home.

As Jeff became more distant from the crime spree, he'd occasionally encourage Sam to "tell my psycho brother to cut it out."

But Dale did not cut it out, according to Sam. Shortly after the confrontation with Jeff, Dale and Sam set two Wal-Marts on fire and shot Paul Patrick to finish off the night. Soon a still photo would be released to the media, a shot that showed the distinctive skull tattoo on Sam's arm, as well as his face. People at the bars Sam frequented began to make jokes about him looking like the photo on the news. He always denied it but grew more and more nervous. Within two or three weeks he had also quarreled to the last of his endurance with Celeste Vance and no longer wanted to live in her apartment. It was Dale who came to his rescue. "Come out to Mesa with me," Dale told the man who would later give this sworn testimony against him, "no one knows you out here. Don't tell my parents where you are. Don't even tell Jeff. Let's just let the 'heat' die down."

So Sam fell completely into Dale's world and became utterly dependent on him; for rides, for companionship, for cash, for drugs and alcohol, for food, and most of all, for shelter.

Were you afraid of Dale? the jury wanted to know.

"I wasn't physically afraid of him, no. Mostly I was afraid of losing my place to stay. But I did sometimes wonder if he'd try something while I was asleep."

The two were constantly together now. Phone records show frequent calls and texts between the pair, often when they were known to be close by each other. For instance, while Sam walked to the Dumpster with their trash or over to Circle K for cigarettes, Dale would begin texting or calling. Prosecutors later alleged that Dale couldn't stand to have Sam out of sight.

One night when they texted each other was July 21, 2006. Dale had taken Sam to Wal-Mart and dropped him off for a session of shoplifting. But Sam had gotten sloppy. He was "too drunk," he recalls, to remove the security device from a stud finder. He was caught with it, as well as with stolen wiper blades and bottles of vodka. He spent a few hours in custody for shoplifting. While Sam was in custody, he and Dale texted. Upon release, Sam arranged to meet Dale at the far end of the parking lot, so the Wal-Mart security officers would not see that he had had a shoplifting partner. They went back to 550 East McKellips, where Dale played bartender and served up several drinks to Sam. Dale got angrier and angrier about the arrest as the night wore on. "Someone's gonna pay for this," he told his friend. *Here we go,* thought Sam. The pair loaded up the shotgun and took the Camry out into the predawn streets. Raul Garcia was shot, Dale at the trigger, around four thirty in the morning.

Dale went to work as a City of Phoenix employee an hour later.

During the summer of 2006, while Phoenix was terrorized by the shadowy Serial Shooter, and national newscasters were shaking their heads at the phenomenon in the desert town, Dale's friendship with Sam was on the rise. Dale was a rocket of energy and ideas, while Sam had the muscle and know-how. When Dale wanted his shotgun altered, it was Sam with his toolbox who expertly sawed off the gun's stock, shortening its length and increasing its maneuverability. The shorter shotgun was also easier to conceal. Sometimes, Sam later testified, they had taken turns sliding the gun down a pant leg and limping out to the Camry, in order to keep the weapon out of sight as they passed from Dale's apartment to the parking lot.

Dale, Sam remembers, took him on a tour of the scenes of his past crimes. There was the bus bench where someone had got shot through the neck. There was the Westside sidewalk where a young man had been lured in with an offer of money and then shot twice. Jeff did that one. Dale was always annoyed with Jeff for shooting twice. He worried that it increased their chances of getting caught. Half a block away from that site, Dale showed him the Burger King where the painted clown window had been blasted. He took him to the spot at Twentieth Street and Monroe where the "Bill Clinton–lookin' motherfucker" joke had originated—and where a man had died while a dog had been saved.

Then there was the glorious little neighborhood downtown just off Van Buren where three men had been shot in one night. That same night, there was another stretch on Van Buren where Dale had gotten a woman. And a park near his parents' place where he'd gotten a woman's dog. Dale referred to the people he attacked as "human garbage" and the shootings were his "way of taking out the trash."

Sam seemed cooperative but sad as he recalled this "victory tour" in court. Later, the jury asked him, "Do you consider yourself a tough guy or do you consider yourself a follower?"

Sam buried his face in his chest. His eyes were downcast for a very long time. He seemed to be experiencing some internal struggle as he carefully considered the question. At long last, he lifted his head. "I tried to think of myself as a tough guy for years and tried to be that." He paused again. "But I'm a follower." Then he gave his longest speech yet. "I got used to being around violence. If you didn't participate, you'd be dealt with. I had to prove myself. That's how I felt with the Hausner brothers. It kept escalating." His head dropped again. "I don't know what the hell was wrong with me."

Sam testified that on July 8 the pair had been cruising city streets in the early morning hours. They spotted the blond woman in the pink top walking along almost at the beginning of her journey. She was still on Indian School Road. They kept an eye on her and circled around. She turned north on Forty-fourth Street, a major artery of several lanes and streetlights. Dale dropped off Forty-fourth into the small residential streets feeding off it. Hidden down a dark tree-lined block, they watched Ashley Armenta cross Devonshire as she headed north. Emerging from the darkness, Dale killed the headlights. He pulled the Camry up to the corner of Devonshire and Forty-fourth and came to a complete stop. "There," Sam recalled him saying, "now you have no excuse not to miss."

Sam remembered Ashley looking back at them, as she herself testified. He fired after she looked away. In spite of Dale's pressure, Sam said he aimed high again.

Ashley's injuries did turn out to be minimal compared to others'. Detective Clark Schwartzkopf examined her scalp and found a wound unlike the others. It was similar to a check mark, rather than the round pellet marks speckling her scalp, back and neck. Investigators had scoured the scene of the crime at Devonshire Street and discovered a valuable piece of evidence, the shot cup. This is the cup-shaped bit of metal in which the pellets of lead are packed inside the cartridge that forms a shotgun shell. The pellets explode out of the cup and the cup falls away. It is the same object that was discovered inside Claudia Gutierrez-Cruz's body because she had been shot at such close range. Schwartzkopf lifted a broken shot cup found at the scene of Ashley's crime to the unique wound in her head. He found the bit of metal a perfect match. He believed the shot cup had hit her in the head and the impact with her skull caused it to split in two. The two sections of the shot cup were found far apart from each other, generally at separate right angles to where Ashley had been standing when Sam fired.

On Sunday, July 30, Robin Blasnek had been stalked for many blocks as well. Dale was gleeful, Sam testified, at finding the target, but frustrated that he kept having to turn away because of other vehicles. One of these would have been Frank Bonfiglio, who later told police he remembered driving past the girl and worrying about her being out on the street. It was Frank who heard the shot a moment after he had arrived home and opened a beer in his backyard. Robin was shot just a block away from his house.

Robin was also only a block away from her destination. "She appeared to be turning into the cul-de-sac," Sam testified. It would have been their last chance to get her. Dale eagerly seized the moment and fired through the driver's side window from the opposite lane. The Camry was pointed north and Robin had been heading south. She was just turning westward. The orientation of her wounds reflects this relative positioning.

Sam remembered the following Tuesday night, when he had met up with Ron Horton. He had no suspicion whatsoever that his old friend had set him up, or that he was surrounded by undercover officers in the bar and on the street. After Ron went home from their last stop, at the casino, he remembered it being a bit difficult to find Dale in the parking lot. He did not know that he was striding right past undercover officers as he and Dale texted each other, trying to locate one another in the huge sea of parked cars. But they were very much aware of a casino security guard who was wheeling around an aisle or two over when they did catch up at the Camry. They studiously waited till the golf cart had sped out of sight before they retrieved their precious black bag from the trunk of the car. They did not realize other eyes were watching them as they placed it in the cab of the vehicle.

Sam remembered the night being difficult for two reasons. First, it was the height of the monsoon season and the night was wet and drizzly. Prey on the ground seemed sparse. Second, witnesses, that is, other vehicles on the road, seemed as if by alchemy to appear repeatedly on mostly deserted streets. He and Dale trolled for hours with no action.

Detective Bryan Benson, the undercover officer who had donned his Kevlar vest and screamed at pedestrians to get off the streets, had already testified about a moment when the Camry seemed out of reach. They had asked the air unit to buzz close by instead. Sam had not heard this testimony. He was under the "exclusion rule" whereby witnesses are not to be exposed to the testimony of other witnesses lest they be influenced.

Nonetheless, Sam himself mentioned a moment well past midnight of that night, two days after Robin's murder. After hours of fruitless "hunting," they at last found themselves without another car in sight. Though they could not quite see the details until they drew closer, there was a figure in the darkness nearby.

It was two kids on a bike.

Dale was eager, Sam testified, to finally have something to show for the night's wanderings. He handed the shotgun to Sam and urged him to fire.

"I picked up the gun," Sam testified, "and put it on the windowsill. But I thought, 'I . . . can . . . not . . . shoot . . . two kids . . . on a bike.'"

Sam shook his head in shock and disgust as he said this on the stand. He gathered himself for a moment, then continued the story.

"I didn't say that out loud. I tried to think what to do. And I looked up and I could see these lights in the air. I didn't admit what I really thought, but I brought up to him that there was a helicopter. In fact," said Sam, knitting his brows, seemingly still unaware of the extent of the juggernaut on him that night, "every time I looked up that night, I saw lights circling. I used that as an excuse."

Dale told him he was just paranoid, but drove off anyway. The shotgun was never fired that night.

The kids on the bike never knew.

Two weeks after Sam's testimony, it was Dale's turn to take the stand. He had glared fiercely at Sam for the first few hours that his former roommate had spoken in the courtroom. But as the days wore on, Dale had become more relaxed and opted instead to mostly avoid looking at Sam but still react to his testimony as he had to other witnesses', by shaking his head, nodding or mouthing words.

Now the witness stand and the microphone were all his, and he took full advantage of them. Most of the other 150 witnesses who had climbed into that chair had been nervous and sat straight and tense, often pausing after questions and asking permission to point at exhibits or for guidance in their responses.

Not Dale.

Dale climbed into the raised witness box and took charge of the space. He swiveled so his chest faced the jury to his right while he leaned toward his left arm, which he placed expansively on the counter rail in front of him. This posture enveloped the attorney questioning him while orienting his attention toward the twenty people—eight would be randomly dismissed as alternates at the end of the trial—who would decide his fate. Only a thinness in his voice betrayed his nervousness.

He first wanted to tell the jury of his many educational accomplishments, starting with his GED. He especially wanted to call attention to his many "credits" of Christian theology earned. He did not mention they were mail order courses taken from jail while awaiting trial as a suspected serial killer.

He wanted these jurors to know him thoroughly, he said, including that he was a terrible liar. He chuckled at himself as he told the jury that people could always tell when he was lying, so what was the point? He went so far as to volunteer that if jurors thought he *appeared* to be lying, it wasn't so, it just had to do with a speech impediment he'd had therapy for as a kid—but the judge and the prosecutor cut him off simultaneously. The prosecutor didn't even have to finish his objection; the Honorable Roland Steinle told Dale he could not make such statements.

Lead defense attorney Ken Everett swept his client away from the faux pas as fast as he could. As soon as he had followed all the legal protocols, he asked Dale straight on, "Are you the Serial Shooter?"

"No!" Dale responded gladly and solidly.

Under friendly questioning from his lawyer, Dale swiveled easily from side to side in the chair and was soon jumping up to illustrate a story in mime or demonstrate an action. One of the first things he did was act out the holding of a shotgun.

He wanted to explain that the stock hits your chest as you aim and fire. His .410 New England shotgun, he explained, had had a defect in a plastic component at the end of the stock. It pinched his chest, he testified, holding his arms up in the shooting position, and had left little marks.

He found it interfered with his very active love life.

"Wouldn't look too good," he said confidently, "if I went to a girl's house and took my shirt off to mess around and I had to say, 'Baby, I swear, these aren't hickey marks!'" It was for this reason, he explained, that he had asked Sam Dieteman to saw off the stock of the firearm, shortening it by about 25 percent. It had had nothing to do with concealment or with the need to maneuver a bulky weapon while driving.

It was true that Dale had an impressive romantic portfolio: several intelligent, capable women would parade through the trial, all uncomfortable, all admitting to having had relationships with Dale, all of the relationships overlapping with one another without their knowledge.

But first, Dale wanted to tell the court about *Sam's* love life. That first morning of his testimony, February 2, 2009, Dale jumped at the chance to spell out Sam's social shortcomings. Mr. Everett asked his client about exhibit number 299, the note in Dale's handwriting that read, "He who asks about the $5 bill is a homicidal maniac, thief, arsonist, destroyer of property, drug taking God among mortals."

Dale swiveled in his chair and thrust his chest forward. As soon as Mr. Everett mentioned the exhibit, Dale said, "I wrote the note. Sam was having a hard time meeting people to date." Then Dale glanced conspiratorially at the judge and said rapidly, "I don't know if the court will let me say this," but without waiting for a ruling, he added, "but Sam's a bisexual. He was gonna go be sitting at a bar, a gay bar. Sam was going to pin a five-dollar bill to his sleeve. The first person who asked about it, like, 'Hey, what's this?' he was gonna open up his shirt," here Dale crossed his arms across his chest and hunched over, then sprang up, standing, throwing his arms open, "and this would be printed on it. Then he would go 'Ha, ha, got you.' I wrote it out on a sheet of paper for him and counted up the words and said it would cost like two hundred dollars to get that printed up on a shirt." The judge reminded Dale to sit down, and he complied, sniffing. "Frankly, it's not a very good pickup line, either."

Dale repeated as many times as he could that Sam was bisexual, and that Dale found it distasteful. The night they had been tailed? He had dropped Sam off at the Star Dust Inn because he knew Sam had a date with his "boyfriend," Ron Horton. Not only was Ron Sam's lover, according to Dale, he was also his drug dealer. Dale did not go inside the Star Dust Inn, he testified, because of how distasteful the whole thing was to him. He dropped in as many potentially offensive remarks about homosexuality as he could until he was admonished by Judge Roland Steinle.

There is no evidence whatsoever to support Dale's accusations about Ron Horton. On cross-examination, prosecutor Vince Imbordino taxed him with it.

"You just said that, Mr. Hausner, because you know Ron Horton is dead and can't defend himself, didn't you?"

Dale did not agree. But his opening up the topic of sexual attraction would snap back on him like a steel trap.

"In fact, Mr. Hausner, it's you who are the bisexual, isn't it?" Mr. Imbordino continued. Dale flushed red and denied it vigorously. But by throwing accusations out at Sam and Ron, Dale himself had opened up a line of attack from the soft-spoken prosecutor.

It also opened up the way for the witness that Dale seemed to fear the most.

But that would come later. After Dale's own six days on the stand were completed.

Mr. Imbordino had also been very interested in Dale's account of the "homicidal maniac" note. Until this point—two-and-a-half years since his arrest—Dale had denied knowledge of the note. The state had gone to a certain amount of trouble and expense to have a handwriting expert establish just who had written it. Mr. Imbordino introduced into evidence Dale's 2006 comments to newspaper reporter Katie McDevitt when she had read him the contents of it: "'Oh my God,' Hausner said with a surprised laugh. 'That's the worst thing I've heard all day. I'm absolutely speechless.'"

Not waiting for the prosecutor to finish, Dale announced, "I lied to her. I lied to a reporter. Absolutely I lied to a reporter."

"And why did you do that, Mr. Hausner?"

"Because I didn't want Sam the Liar to know what I was going to say at trial beforehand so he could make up a story and tell more lies here in court."

The topic of lies was another unfortunate one for Dale. Both under friendly questioning from Ken Everett and cross-examination by Vince Imbordino, Dale repeatedly admitted lying: to his employer, to his girlfriends, to the press and to the police. He said he had lied to police on the night of his arrest, August 4, 2006, for many reasons. One of those reasons was fear. Detective Darren Udd, Dale claimed, had threatened to kill or arrest his two-and-a-half-year-old daughter Mandy.

"I thought they would arrest her and bring her down there and chain her up for fifteen hours without food like they did me. She has to eat every three hours. His face was all scrunched up and vicious when he said it. I thought he was going to kill her."

Imbordino played the tape of the interview with Detectives Udd and Salazar on August 4. Udd's words were, "I won't call you a good father because we found all those meth pipes at your place, but I do think you love her, I will give you that. You need to come clean for your daughter's sake."

On the tape, Dale does not appear to be frightened, but on the stand he confirmed that he believed that to be a threat to the toddler's life, and a reason to lie to those who menaced her.

The topic of Dale's admitted lies and his reasons for them played out for many hours in front of the jury.

As a witness, Dale had a lot to say. And he said it very fast. So fast, in fact, that Judge Steinle asked him to slow down for the sake of the stenographer trying to keep up with him.

After announcing his Christian credentials, explaining away the "homicidal maniac" note, and insulting his enemies, Sam and Ron, Dale's next most urgent piece of business was to get introduced into evidence what he clearly considered the most important evidence in the trial: his day planners.

No day planners had been seized at his apartment. Why detectives and criminalists failed to find them on the night of the takedown August 4, 2006, remains a mystery.

For the duration of his testimony, Dale referred to the day planners frequently, often skipping a beat and tilting his chin down before he uttered the words, as if to make sure everyone recognized their importance. He said he particularly used the day planners to record his dates and trysts with the various women he was seeing. He did not want to get tripped up in his romances by talking about a concert or restaurant with woman A, when he had actually gone with woman B.

On the dates of nearly every crime he was charged with, Dale had a corresponding entry in his day planner. Most of these related to his girlfriends, especially overnight stays—which was serendipitous record-keeping, as it was usually the after-midnight and predawn hours Dale needed to account for. He had elaborate memories for most of these dates, including tales of his own sexual prowess.

He had written a cryptic phrase on one date and had drawn a smiley face next to his notation. Prosecutor Imbordino asked him what it meant. Flicking an eye toward the judge, Dale again gave the disclaimer that he wasn't certain he'd be allowed to tell it in open court, but without taking a breath he went on to say that the girlfriend in question found it difficult to reach a sexual climax. The smiley face was there because he thought it was "funny" that success had been achieved twice that night. Although Dale had claimed the information would be "embarrassing" to the girlfriend, he seemed not only eager to tell the story but proud of it.

But Prosecutor Imbordino didn't miss a beat, either. He picked up three years' worth of day planners and said, "I'm looking all through here—it was just the once?"

Dale flushed deep red and nearly shouted, "No!"

Dale had more scuffles with the state's lead attorney. The evidence of the .22-caliber shells found inside Dale's Camry matching to varying degrees with many of the crime scenes seemed ominous, but Dale told the prosecutor he had nothing to do with the shells.

"They were planted in my car," Dale said. "I did not shoot those bullets and I have never shot from inside my car." Gunshot residue had, indeed, been confirmed by lab tests to be present inside the Camry, but Dale had already explained that he felt it had gotten there when he went sport shooting in the desert and left the windows of the Camry down. The telltale lead, antimony and barium, he theorized, had drifted into the sedan's interior innocently while he did test fires and practice shots at inert desert targets just fifteen feet away from where he had parked.

"Go ahead and tell us who you think planted them, Mr. Hausner," the prosecutor urged.

"Sam Dieteman."

"So you're telling me that Sam Dieteman—living from couch to couch in 2005—borrowed a twenty-two-caliber weapon of which there is no record and no one has ever seen him with, committed these crimes in a vehicle no one has ever known him to have, then carried these shells around from place to place, sometimes sleeping in alleys, hanging on to them for months and months in the hopes that one day he might meet you and plant them on you?"

"Yes," Dale said firmly.

The state of Arizona had called nearly 140 witnesses in thirteen weeks of testimony spread out over four months. The defense called only ten witnesses over just nine days—six of those days were devoted to Dale's own testimony. Dale had defiantly declared, "I like women and I like a lot of 'em" during the tussle with Vince Imbordino over his sexual orientation. But when the defense rested on February 10, 2009, not a single girlfriend had appeared to defend him.

It was now the state's turn for rebuttal, and the parade of women began. Mandy's mother came back to court and said her sexual relationship with Dale had ended by a date well before he had started entering her name in his day planners for alibis. The prosecutor took her through date by date—no overnights with Dale, she said. Occasionally she confirmed a family outing, usually centered on Amanda, but those evenings either ended well before 10 p.m. or had even occurred on different dates entirely.

Dr. Marianne Lescher, who seemed to have braced herself for the ordeal of exposing her private life, answered as succinctly and professionally as possible and her story was much the same. Dressed fashionably in a black skirt and deep turquoise jacket, she took her place in the witness box. She said she was at a "low point" and "vulnerable" when she first met Dale. She was separated from her husband of twenty years. She had been at the airport, outbound, struggling with luggage. He had ridden up on a cart and begun helping her, unbidden. She was grateful. They had exchanged numbers. But by the time she had spent a week away, she had forgotten the incident. But she had been pleasantly surprised when, upon her return to Phoenix, she was met at the gate by this much younger man. Despite the gap in ages and so much else, the Ph.D. and the janitor began dating.

But if Dale had his day planners, Dr. Lescher had an extremely active professional life, marked by the elementary school year and the semesters at ASU as well as conferences and speaking engagements. She knew where she had been on most calendar dates. She testified that she had *not* been with Dale on the nights he had marked. These included the nights that Tony Mendez, Reggie Remillard and Nathaniel Shoffner had been shot. She knew nothing about Dale's whereabouts at the time these innocent citizens were murdered.

She *had* seen him on the night the horse Apache was wounded and the dog Whiskey was killed. They both remembered that night because he had brought over an engagement ring. Dale had said, "I know you're going to say no, but I have to ask anyway," and had then proposed to her. But just as he had predicted, she declined. She had then sent him home. He was nowhere near her at midnight when the Zolcharniks ran outside to the sound of shots fired and found their beautiful Akita with her foot blasted off.

Michelle Botteri, a young woman with highlighted shoulder-length hair, had a quiet demeanor when she took her turn. She was the daughter of a history teacher and was pursuing the same career path herself. Michelle and Dale had met through mutual friends. She, too, had dated Dale during the crime spree, including an exchange of presents during the Christmas season of 2005, which would have been within days of the rampage that overtook three men, one woman, four dogs, a building and a car.

The litany was familiar by now. No, she had not been with Dale at the times he claimed. In fact, even if they did have a date planned and possibly written down somewhere, that was no guarantee it had actually occurred. "He canceled a lot," she said. Another thing she was certain of was that she had never spent an entire night with him. He'd always been gone well before midnight.

Dale had claimed Michelle as his alibi on the night Elizabeth

Clark* had been shot. Elizabeth had been out riding her bike June 11, 2006, fairly close to Jeff Hausner's neighborhood on the Westside. According to Sam's testimony, Dale had been alone when he shot her, and then later that night had bragged to Sam about it. But Dale testified he could not have been out committing attempted murder because he'd had a date with Michelle that night—he had eaten a homemade meal at her place. He remembered it vividly because he had had an allergic reaction to a gravy she had prepared. Michelle remembered the allergic reaction, too. But she said it had taken place in April, not June. The night Elizabeth Clark was shot, Michelle had not only not cooked, she had gone to the Red Lobster with her sister. She had not been with Dale at all. Like the other women, she provided him with no alibis.

There was one woman called to the stand who was not involved in alibis in the first place. By all accounts, she had not laid eyes on Dale in years, certainly not during the Year of the Serial Shooter. But she saw him on February 10, 2009, in an Arizona courtroom. It was less than two hours after Dale's own testimony had wrapped up and his defense had rested. Prosecutors could not wait to put her on the stand to rebut the things that Dale had said.

She entered the courtroom dressed all in black, with long dark hair falling protectively across her lowered face. She was beautiful with big dark eyes and high cheekbones. She was sniffling and shaking before the questioning even began. She spoke so softly the judge admonished not only her but the lawyers responsible for bringing her here—she must speak up.

The defendant was visibly upset by her entrance. His head went down and he never met her eyes. Her testimony had started outside the presence of the jury, to clear up what the scope of her remarks would be. Before the jury would return and see her for the first time, Dale had heard enough.

Three months earlier in the trial, Dale's place at the defense table had been vacant for one day. Jurors were not told why. But the date of his absence had been November 12, 2008. Dale had

---

*Elizabeth Clark survived her injuries, which had not been life-threatening. But she lost touch with law enforcement and could not be found after 2007. She did not surface for the trial.

asked the court to be excused so he could spend the day in his cell contemplating the death of his two little boys in Texas, exactly fourteen years earlier.

Dale would soon ask to be excused again. And the jurors would not be told the reason this time, either. There was nothing special about the date of that February day, but the woman who had just taken the stand seemed to unsettle Dale very much.

She was Karen, Dale's ex-wife who had eventually taken out a restraining order against him, and the one who had been at the wheel the night the young couple's car had plunged into a Texas creek and Dale's two little boys had drowned.

Knowing each other since they were kids, and having spent the worst night of their lives together, Karen seemed to touch Dale's inner world too closely. The tension between the flushing, fidgeting defendant and the shaking, sniffling woman filled up the courtroom. Even Dale's mother, who had sat through hours upon hours of horrific testimony, left the room, taking her oldest son, Gregory, with her.

The prosecutor began by leading Karen through some key points of evidence.

The .22-caliber weapon used in the series of crimes Cliff Jewell connected had never been found. But ATF paperwork established that Dale had owned several .22s, some of which had been purchased in Texas, during Dale's time there with Karen. He had testified at first that the guns were gifts from Karen and he had left them with her in Texas. Later he remembered he had actually sold the guns to a neighbor in Texas—a private sale, requiring no paperwork—and hadn't wanted to tell her he had not hung on to her gifts for their sentimental value.

One of the first things Karen was asked by Prosecutor Imbordino was whether she had purchased a .22 in Texas. Karen said she knew nothing about firearms and had never purchased any for any reason, anywhere, ever.

Because it went to Dale's truthfulness on the stand and not for any other reason, Imbordino asked about Dale's potential bisexuality. Had he ever told her he was attracted to men?

"Yes," she said in her small whisper, "we were arguing once and he told me he thought he was gay and gave that as the reason he and I were having problems. 'That's absurd,' I told him, 'you're not gay.' But he insisted and told me about two different guys he had feelings for. I know he went on some dates with men."

Then Imbordino asked her more directly about Dale's truthfulness. "He testified here that he's not a very good liar. Do you have an opinion about that?"

She stared at the prosecutor full face and considered the question. Then she slowly said, pausing between each sentence, "He's manipulative. He's cunning. He's a chameleon. He shows you whatever he wants you to see. He is the most dangerous person I could think of, to be as good a liar as he is."

Dale was bawling now, tears streaming down his face, his always busy fingers now with a real job to do, flicking the streams off his cheeks. Judge Roland Steinle announced a short break. Dale did not return from the break, nor did he reappear in the courtroom for the next two days.

———————

When the wiretap recordings of August 3, 2006, had been played in court, jurors and other spectators had looked aghast at the hilarity evident in Sam and Dale's voices when discussing the most appalling topics.

Sam's voice is even and nearly colorless as he is heard to read from a newspaper article about Robin Blasnek, killed just three nights earlier. The article, as read aloud by Sam, stated that police didn't know why she was killed.

Dale's voice breaks in. "Because she was a fucking whore, that's why."

At trial, Dale explained he didn't think he had said that. He thought what he was saying was, "Do you want some fucking more?" because he had been serving drinks to Sam and might have been a bit impatient about it.

Pretty much everything else he said on the tapes, he testified, was merely his "dark humor." Jokes. "Doesn't sound funny now," he testified, "but I thought I was alone and it was private between me and Sam."

Sam's voice on the wiretaps is perfectly consistent with his manner at trial. His voice is always heard in the same register, varying just a few notes in the same moderate range.

But Dale's voice on the secret wiretap veers and shrieks and hoots. He imitates Robin Blasnek "crying" after being mortally shot. "Boo hoo!" his voice shrills out from the tape.

He mocks her again, telling Sam her name is really "Blastneck" and yelps happily at his joke.

Throughout the trial, Dale's mother had shown no reaction to any of the testimony or the autopsy photos or even the photos of victims in dire pain in their hospital beds, wounds displayed, tubes and wires tangling their heads, chests and limbs. But the sound of her little granddaughter's voice coming out of the courtroom speakers in the midst of the recorded ghoulish banter found Mrs. Hausner sobbing and shedding tears for the first time anyone had seen at trial.

"Say, 'Good night, Sam,'" Dale's urgings rang out from the many speakers set up for the benefit of jurors and spectators.

"Good night, Sam," a sweet little female voice complies.

"Say, 'Don't kill anybody!'"

The words are unpracticed to the child and her diction is slower, but she's still eager to participate in the game.

The ribbing continues as Sam tells her to qualify the command with "not in the morning—it's too early in the morning."

By now, the baby's comprehension of the words is faltering. But she immediately responds with babbled syllables that sound like an attempt to repeat what she has heard.

Dale is giggling on the tape, proud of her efforts, delighted at the exchange.

In the courtroom, Rosemarie Hausner, Dale's mother, bent forward, her head in her hands, sobbing into her lap. Nearby, her other son, Gregory, also wept, also for the first time that courtroom observers had noticed.

Later, Linda Swaney, Mandy's mother, testified that she would continue to allow Rosemarie Hausner to visit Dale's only surviving child—by then a kindergartner—but she was otherwise attempting to cut off Dale's contact, his parental rights, and his very name from the child heard on the tape.

When it was his own turn on the stand, Dale stated that nothing on the tape was what it sounded like. It was all just misinterpreted, and in any case, he said, it ought to be balanced out by his later saying evening prayers with Mandy that same night.

———————————

Sam was recalled as a rebuttal witness. He said everything heard on the tape was exactly what it sounded like, the two men reveling in their crimes. In fact, he said, investigators had chosen the right night to listen in, precisely because they happened to be doing so.

Sam was also asked on rebuttal if he knew Ron Horton to be bisexual. He appeared surprised by the question and said, "Not to my knowledge."

He was asked if he himself were bisexual. This seemed to surprise him less. He shook his head and just said, "No."

Despite his bartending license, Sam said that Dale (unlike himself) almost never drank. Both men, however, readily admitted to using meth. Methamphetamine paraphernalia was found throughout Dale's apartment and car.

Sam also said that it was Dale who kept him supplied with methamphetamine, and that Dale purchased it from someone he knew through work. Sam had waited in the car or had not been present when the meth deals were made. He said he was "usually" drunk when they went out trawling the streets for victims and occasionally may have been high on meth as well.

———————————

The last bit of new evidence introduced in the trial came from rebuttal witness Detective Jason Buscher. Buscher had pored over reams of telephone records and plotted out the location of Dale's cell phone at critical times. Dale had testified, for instance, that he had not been present at the stabbing of Timothy Davenport in a church parking lot on May 17, 2006, a crime for which Jeff Hausner would soon also face trial and which was very similar to the stabbing of Ray McQueen, to which Jeff had already pleaded guilty. But transmissions from Dale's cell phone had bounced off a transmitting tower very near the crime scene, around the same time that the crime had occurred. Dale then testified that he had left his phone in his brother's car. This would be the first and only time Dale suggested his brother's (Celeste's) Oldsmobile had been used when he and Sam and Jeff supposedly went out for their frequent and innocent dinners at IHOP or Denny's, rather than his own Camry. He said that after he got home from a routine dinner with Jeff and Sam that night, he had used the pay phone at his apartment complex in Mesa. He called both Jeff and his own phone—the pay phone call to his own cell phone would explain why it was bouncing off the tower near the crime scene—to ask for one of the men to bring it back to him. His testimony gave the impression that it was possible that Jeff and Sam—without Dale's knowledge or participation—had stabbed the man in the church parking lot while

Dale himself was miles away, even though his phone was clearly with the other men near the church parking lot.

But after Dale's testimony, Detective Buscher subpoenaed phone records for the pay phones at the Windscape Apartments. Not only had these phones not been used to make any calls in the midnight hour to Dale's cell, or to Jeff's or Sam's—but neither of the pay phones had been used at all between mid-evening on the 17th to 9 a.m. on the 18th.

Some of the cell tower evidence was inconclusive,* but sometimes the records placed Dale's phone, and whoever was holding it, very near a crime scene around a damning time. For example, the night Dale claimed to have had the allergic reaction at Michelle's house, cell phone records show Dale's phone in use at 11 p.m., minutes after Elizabeth Clark was shot, just a half mile away from the crime scene. Yet Michelle's house was more than ten miles away from where that cell phone was active.

The defense presented the theory that the women would rather see Dale go to Death Row than provide him with the alibis they "knew to be true," because of their hurt feelings from finding out about one another, coupled with their embarrassment at his arrest. At the defense table, Dale nodded his head vigorously, ratifying this explanation for the discrepancy between his day planners and the women's testimony.

The evidence phase of the trial was over. Thirteen weeks of prosecution against nine days of defense. One hundred and forty witnesses against ten.

It was time for the lawyers to hand the case to the inscrutable people in the jury box.

---

*Sometimes the phone had not been used at all during the time windows in question.

Chapter Thirty-one

Justice

The trial of accused Serial Shooter Dale Hausner had begun on September 3, 2008, with jury selection. The defense had tried to get a change of venue due to pretrial publicity, but it was denied. It couldn't have helped that Dale himself had held his own press conference the first business day after his arrest.

During later hearings to suppress that press conference, Dale testified he'd felt forced at gunpoint by jail officers to enter the room where the reporters and their microphones were waiting. He also explained away a release form he had signed, saying he thought he was signing for a blanket.

But Sheriff's Deputy Lindsay Smith testified that she brought the form to Sam Dieteman first. He had understood it and declined to sign it or to meet with the media. When she brought the same form to Dale, however, she said "his eyes lit up, he was excited." She felt certain that he had understood the form, including the part that cautions, "Statements you make to the press can be used against you in court." Deputy Smith also testified that none of the officers in the jail had a firearm, including the ones who escorted Dale to his press conference. Only nonlethal weapons are used for jail security because of the fear that guns could end up in the hands of inmates.

After his incarceration, Dale had also regularly made statements to the media over the next two years, writing letters and even making calls to TV stations and newspapers. In one infamous call, he rang the *East Valley Tribune* and asked for a reduced subscription rate, considering how many headlines he created for their profit. He had called himself "Dale the Innocent" while insisting he deserved a "sweetheart deal," the newspaper reported. The newspaper had accepted Dale's collect call—all inmates at the Maricopa County Jail must call collect—but had declined the request for a discount.

Soon after his arrest, Dale had entered into a professional agreement with publicist David Han Schmidt, who then fielded calls from the press on behalf of Dale and the rest of the Hausner family. But Schmidt had troubles of his own. The self-proclaimed "Sultan of Sleaze" had often been involved in brokering sex tapes involving the likes of Paris Hilton and Britney Spears, and exactly a year after Dale's arrest, the forty-seven-year-old Schmidt was himself arrested in a sting by federal agents. This time, a movie star had called the feds on him. In the summer of 2007, Schmidt found himself under house arrest in his Phoenix home and preparing to plead guilty to an extortion plot against Tom Cruise regarding stolen photos of his wedding to Katie Holmes. Some weeks after Schmidt's arrest, well before Dale would go to trial, his beleaguered publicity manager committed suicide. Dale was back on his own in handling reporters.

Dale did try to cultivate relationships with the press, writing letters and making calls and, during court appearances, smiling pointedly at reporters and making gestures to them. In a piece of video that earned itself a lot of play, during the last week of his trial he turned to the pool television camera set up at the back of the courtroom and winked. He sent a Christmas card to *Arizona Republic* reporter Michael Kiefer. He mailed a Bible to *East Valley Tribune* reporter Katie McDevitt, who declined to sign for it. McDevitt was the same reporter whom he later testified he had deliberately lied to. She was the one he had told he had no knowledge of the "homicidal maniac" note and found it "the worst thing," but he later boldly testified that he himself had written it—to help Sam's love life.

While his change-of-venue request had been denied, there was no avoiding the fact that the Serial Shooter and Dale Hausner had been big news in Phoenix. Jury selection began on September 3, but it took four weeks and a pool of six hundred citizens to get a jury seated. Because the trial was expected to last for six months or more, Judge Roland Steinle put twenty people in the jury box: eight would be alternates. He expected to lose quite a few jurors over the course of such a long trial. He figured there would be illnesses, family emergencies and financial hardships.

The trial did last six months. During that time, the jury was not allowed to discuss the case, not with their friends and loved ones, not even with each other. The strain must have been terrible.

On February 24, 2009, prosecutor Laura Reckart, a very slender woman with softly feathered blond locks, turned the rostrum to meet the ten men and ten women of the jury full face. She thanked them for their service, then quoted forcefully and dramatically from the wiretaps:

"'I love shooting people in the back, it's so much fun.' With those words, ladies and gentlemen, the case of the Serial Shooter that had been plaguing and terrorizing this valley turned from a 'whodunit' to a 'hedidit.'" She turned to the defense table and pointed at Dale Hausner.

She led the jury on a tour of the dozens of crimes and over a thousand pieces of evidence and gave them the context she had been prohibited by court rules from giving them earlier. She showed them the newspaper clippings of the June 8 Wal-Mart arsons. "How would he know to keep these clippings in his Serial Shooter scrapbook?" she asked. "These articles do not attribute the fires to the Serial Shooter." She paused. "*He* knew. He wanted, he *needed* to keep them . . . as testament to his crimes."

The prosecutor asked the jury to consider Dale's "whole lifestyle." His cable TV show, his press conference, his brief turn at stand-up comedy, his radio show, his attempts to become a professional sports photographer, his posing with famous boxers, even his appearance in a TV commercial for Phillips and Associates law firm.* "It all points to his desire for celebrity. He kept the *America's Most Wanted* video and he kept the clippings of all these crimes, proudly. The motive for the Serial Shooter

---

*For a civil lawsuit involving a traffic accident. Dale reported he received a cash settlement due to the firm's efforts.

crimes? Fame. Notoriety. Renown." Again she quoted from the wiretaps, "He wanted to be a 'legend,' a 'pioneer.'"

She lifted the marked-up map that had been retrieved from the Dumpster by undercover agent Travis Bird. She pointed to the blue-penciled line across the stretch of Van Buren where so many had felt the agony of hot lead. "There's a line across here instead of dots because there were too many here. This was his favorite hunting ground." Then she displayed the map of Dale's wanderings on the night of August 2, 2006. She pointed to the spot where the Camry had made an awkward detour to the back-side of police headquarters, 620. "He was mocking police," she said and again reminded the jury of his voice on the wiretap tapes, chiding police over their failure to capture the Serial Shooter.

Reckart took pains to separate out Sam's crimes from those she alleged were committed by Dale. On the wiretaps, which she urged the jury to replay during their deliberations, Sam and Dale are talking about media accounts of the Serial Shooter murders, which reach back to 2005, and Sam is heard to comment, "Mine was May of *this* year." She displayed an unhappy photo of Sam, his mug shot from August 4, 2006, with his eyes downcast. "He has never retracted his confession. He stood up like a man. He took responsibility for his actions, unlike some people in this courtroom. And he still faces the death penalty."

The detailed prosecutor, whose pointed style and unfailing organization had impressed spectators for the last six months, then highlighted the defendant's treasured day planners. "He's such a ladies' man he had to document his affairs in order to keep them straight," she declared contemptuously, claiming that these were really just "pathetic post-crime attempts at alibis." But Dale couldn't control what the women themselves would say, and, Reckart said triumphantly, when the girlfriends testified "his alibis turned into ali-Lies."

Throughout a daylong closing argument, Reckart frequently repeated the refrain that the defendant, as the Serial Shooter, had conspired to "kill, maim, terrify, and destroy." She explained the several-month gap in crimes from New Year's to Spring 2006 on the December 29, 2005, rampage—Dale had bragged about the shooting of the vehicle at ABC Bartending School to John Kane, she said, but his new pal had not reacted the way he had hoped. Instead of laughing, as Sam Dieteman later had, John Kane had been shocked and had scolded him. This made the defendant decide to lie low, she said, wondering to himself if he had made things too easy on police.

She returned to the theme of Dale Hausner's admitted lying—to his employer, to his girlfriends, to the press and to police. She added that he had now lied to this jury. Referring to the night he claimed to have left his cell phone in his brother Jeff's car and was not near it when it was bouncing off cell towers near the stabbing of Timothy Davenport, she reminded the jury that Dale had testified he made two phone calls from the pay phone at his apartment complex in an attempt to retrieve the cell, thereby placing himself twenty-five to thirty miles away from the crime scene. "He didn't count on the records for those pay phones still being available after all this time," she said.

Then prosecutor Laura Reckart wheeled around in her black skirt and high-heeled pumps and glared at the defendant. "Gotcha! Dale Shawn Hausner, your fun is over." Exhausted from the five-hour speech, she sat down.

Previously in the trial, Dale had complained about Reckart in a letter to the judge, saying she made "inappropriate facial gestures" at him during testimony. The judge had used Dale's letter to admonish the entire courtroom crew about facial gestures revealing private opinions during the evidence phase of the trial, but to the defendant's consternation, to admonish most especially Dale himself. Now that it was final argument, Ms. Reckart could use dramatic gestures and statements freely and he just had to sit there and take it.

On Wednesday, it was Dale's defense attorney Ken Everett's turn. The public defender had spent thirty years in this line of work, and he knew he wasn't popular in this case. A tall man with a booming voice, Everett had nevertheless fought vigorously for his client, sitting implacably for months while Dale often whispered in his ear and passed him notes. His attention to the proceedings never wavered even during long stretches of arcane testimony, when he would suddenly erupt in a sharp objection over some subtle point. When his client or his witness made some misstep, he assiduously took the blame onto himself.

As Reckart had done, he also began by thanking the jury. He

urged them to consider that they were the finders of fact, not prosecutors Laura Reckart or Vince Imbordino, or even himself.

He took them back in time to the day Phoenix awoke to the news that the Serial Shooter had been arrested. He said being called the Serial Shooter was like being called a "communist" in the fifties or even like being called a witch.

He brought up the Arthur Miller play *The Crucible*, wherein witnesses falsely accuse innocent people in colonial Salem of being witches, to tragic and spiteful results. "What happens," Mr. Everett asked, "when one is branded a witch?" He begged the jury to go through each piece of evidence in a "*Crucible*-like way." He said if they would do that, they would find the evidence against his client suffered from serious gaps.

He claimed the prosecution had asked them to pay attention to facts that "fit" their theory and not to those facts that didn't. He told the jurors that Sam Dieteman, "an admitted killer," was "the lynchpin" of the state's case. By contrast, he said, "my client has never admitted any crimes."

Dale appeared relaxed and confident and in good spirits as his lawyer spoke. He leaned sideways in his chair, his arm over its back. He had chatted cheerfully with others near his table before the proceedings for the day began. Not allowed by law to speak to spectators on the other side of the courtroom railing, he had managed a jaunty wink at his brother Randy. His mother and brother Gregory were also there to support him. While Mr. Everett spoke, Dale resumed his habit of emphasizing the lawyer's remarks by nodding or shaking his head at key statements.

The lawyer told the jury that the state had tried to cram illfitting evidence into a case against Dale Hausner like forcing a square peg into a round hole, "cutting it and sanding it down to fit." His voice boomed ominously as he declared that the array of girlfriends had testified against Dale, not for him, because "as soon as they found out he was a potential '*serial killer*,' they wanted nothing to do with him." Behind him, Dale's chin bobbed in energetic endorsement. Indeed, this point regarding the girlfriends must have been a sore disappointment to the attorney who, as late as February 2009, had been hoping that Dr. Lescher would be a witness for the defense. Judge Steinle had given Everett one last weekend to produce her. However, on the following Monday, Dale himself had been sworn in instead. Dr. Lescher only showed up later, when it was the prosecutors who led her into the courtroom and put her on the stand.

Ken Everett spent the rest of the morning attacking Sam Dieteman as a "lying snitch" who would say anything to "save his own life." "After he confessed to killing Claudia," Everett said, "he knew his life was over—so nothing he said afterward can be believed." He told the jury that while Sam lived on the Westside, the crimes occurred on the Westside. When Sam moved to Mesa, the Serial Shooter crimes moved to the Eastside. He mocked, in a singsongy tone, what he portrayed as Sam's self-serving statements: "I tried to miss!"

After lunch, the tall lawyer turned his attack on John Kane, Dale's friend from ABC Bartending school, portraying him as another dealmaker and snitch, and suggesting that Kane was the more likely culprit in the shooting of Annette Prince's car.

Everett then told the jurors that the wiretap evidence was nothing more than the banter of two "immature" men, akin to what might be heard in a frat house. He said the joke was really on Dale, because only Sam knew that his own kidding was about crimes he had actually committed.

The attorney pleaded for consideration of Dale's own position when he had testified in his own defense. He hadn't *wanted* to reveal insulting intimate information about any of his lovers; it was the prosecutor who had forced him to do so. Dale, Mr. Everett said, was merely a "bachelor guy" keeping typical notes in a "bachelor journal." Mr. Everett then returned to the subject of the girlfriends and launched some salvos of his own. Dr. Lescher, he claimed, had had to distance herself from Dale because she had hundreds of schoolchildren under her stewardship. Her refusal to give him an alibi had to do with her not wanting to admit to a "lurid affair" with a "little janitor punk." Mandy's mother, Linda Swaney, he said, had a motive to lie because she "hates" Dale and wants to keep their daughter away from him forever. He beseeched the jurors to view the girlfriends through the "prism effect" of *The Crucible* and the need of the women to distance themselves from someone accused of being the Serial Shooter.

Everett asked the jurors to consider each crime individually and not join the state in a housecleaning of difficult crimes that he claimed were not really connected. In late afternoon, he finished. He knew the trial would end tomorrow with the lead prosecutor's rebuttal speech. Everett's voice softened as he said his last words. "My fear," he said quietly to the jury, "is that Mr. Imbordino's speech will be the last thing ringing in your ears. If you remember one thing I've said, please remember this—*you* are the crucible, you are the finder of fact, the state has the burden of proof, not Dale."

———————————

The burden of proof *does* rest on the state, so the prosecution was given the last word. Vince Imbordino, a thin man with a gray beard and a voice so soft he'd often been admonished during the last six months to speak up, would deliver the rebuttal argument. He had one morning to do it. Judge Steinle, a stern administrator who had kept the long trial on track by setting strict schedules, had promised the case would go to the jury by noon on Thursday, February 26, 2009. He had already delivered jury instructions after the last witness of the case had been dismissed late Monday afternoon, before the closing speeches had even begun.

During that last week of trial, shooting victim Paul Patrick, who had attended nearly every day, had erupted in several violent coughing fits from the gallery. Sometimes the bailiff even crossed over from her desk near the judge to bring him cups of water from the pitchers provided to the officers of the court. Sometimes the coughing would not abate, and Paul would wheel his electric scooter out through the double doors to recover in the hallway. On Wednesday, during Mr. Everett's speech, the coughing was compounded by an appearance of damp discomfort, possibly signaling a fever. But Paul stayed all day, toughing out his obvious physical distress. He had accepted well-wishing during that day with a casually tossed off bit of wit and had waved off further concerned inquiry.

On Thursday morning, however, courtroom regulars noticed that Paul and his mother were not in attendance, and no one had an answer as to why. Paul had missed fewer than a handful of times during the six months: once because his scooter had broken down, once for doctor's appointments, and perhaps one or two other times for similar reasons. Paul considered it his responsibility to keep a human face in front of the jurors, a reminder that the case was about real people who were suffering, not about files and reports and crime labs.

His absence on the very last day of the trial seemed rather a shame. His mother, who had always ridden in with him on a scooter of her own, was also missing that Thursday morning as prosecutor Vince Imbordino took his place at the rostrum facing the jury box.

Imbordino gently swayed toward the defense table, where Dale Hausner was sitting. "Look at the man," he said to the jury in a low voice. "His attorney called him a punk. I don't disagree." He spoke slowly and left long silences hanging. "You wouldn't notice him if you passed him on the street. Anytime you talk to relatives of murder victims, they want to know, 'why?' There's not always a reason. People who know murderers try to paint a picture of a very ordinary man—except that he killed a lot of people. Ladies and gentlemen, evil doesn't have a face. Evil is unspectacular."

The lanky prosecutor paused and seemed caught up in private thoughts. When he spoke again, it was in an even softer voice. "I grew up on a ranch in Texas. I wasn't much of a cowboy, but I was around a lot of cowboys. I was around a lot of horses." The prosecutor dropped his head and shuffled his notes at the rostrum. All eyes were riveted on him. When his head finally pulled up, he whispered, "If you ever had a horse nuzzle your ear—you couldn't shoot one. Ever had a puppy lick your face? You couldn't kill one."

The prosecutor's voice grew stronger as he told the jury there was "no reason" and "no explanation" for the crimes. The defendant, he said, had no quarrel with any of the people he shot, no quarrel with any of the animals. He had simply gone driving around "our valley, your valley, his valley—shooting." He told the jury that since Dale Hausner had been arrested he could no longer "sneak around in the city in the dead of night with a gun. I guess the gun made him feel like a powerful man."

At the defense table, gone was the expansive and relaxed posture the defendant had exhibited the day before during the hours his own attorney had been speaking to the jurors. Now Dale's high-backed swivel chair was jiggling so rapidly and vigorously, several spectators stared.

From underneath the rostrum, Mr. Imbordino extracted a coil

of white rope. He beseeched the jurors not to follow Mr. Everett's plan of isolating the evidence in each crime. He reminded them of the complex web of matching .22-caliber forensics between Dale's Camry and various crime scenes. Imbordino's long fingers pulled apart strands of the rope. He told the jury the strands must be woven together to make the rope strong.

The prosecutor led the jurors on another journey through all the evidence, emphasizing the ties between the crimes and reminding them of the fact that Sam Dieteman still faced the death penalty. He told them the day planners did not mean anything because "Dale lied so many times you can't keep count—we don't know when these things were written down nor for what purpose."

He returned to the theme of Dale's trappings of ordinary life and quoted from horror novelist Dean Koontz, "Many human beings have no need for supernatural mentors to commit their acts of savagery; they are devils in their own right, their horns having grown inward to facilitate their disguise."

Imbordino had one more quotation to urge upon the jury before he was done. This one, he said, was from Confucius. "The small man thinks that small acts of goodness are of no benefit and does not perform them and that small deeds of evil do no harm and does not refrain; hence its wickedness becomes so great it cannot be conceived, guilt so great it cannot be pardoned."

He turned toward the defendant, full face. "A very ordinary coward of a man who committed an extraordinary series of crimes. There will be no more headlines or broadcasts about serial shootings to give him some thrill." Mr. Imbordino stood staring at Dale Hausner for some moments. "One of the saddest things is," he said in a faltering undertone, "if Shep were here—" His voice broke. He gathered himself. "If Shep were here," he repeated, "he'd probably lick his face. If Sara Moon were here, she'd nuzzle his neck."

The prosecutor pivoted on his heels and abruptly sat down. Some jurors were crying.

It was noon on Thursday, February 26, 2009 when the prosecutor finished his speech. Judge Steinle issued some last instructions, the bailiff pulled numbers out of a hat and eight random alternates were dismissed, and the remaining twelve—six men and six women—filed out of the room. Everyone else dispersed to await the verdict. There were eighty-seven charges, after all, and everyone expected the jury to need some time to deliberate. Many observers, walking down the courthouse halls, remarked that it was a pity Paul Patrick and his mother had missed this last important speech and the big moment when the final twelve jurors were selected and took over the fate of Dale Hausner.

It wasn't until the next day that most found out why. On Thursday morning, while preparing to leave for trial, Mrs. Patrick had become alarmed when she couldn't raise Paul via phone. After 9 a.m., apartment managers had used their master key to enter his room and had found him collapsed. He was taken by ambulance to a neuro center, and it was discovered that Paul had suffered a massive stroke on the very day the case that meant so much to him was going to the jury. Once again, doctors told Mrs. Patrick that her son was unlikely to survive more than a few hours. "I just wasn't ready to let go of him yet," she said in her gentle voice. She authorized some desperate surgery: the right half of Paul's skull was removed and placed in a freezer. If he survived, which was a very long shot, the skull could be thawed and reattached. Without the removal, the bleeding into his brain from the stroke would've killed him within minutes. Inside the skull, the excess blood would've had nowhere to go— the swelling would've crushed his brain. While the jury deliberated, Paul lay in a hospital bed in the ICU with a ventilator and feeding tube, his left arm and leg paralyzed, bulky stitches and staples bisecting his crown and dipping down by his right ear, stitches that made a seam to connect nothing but a thin layer of skin to protect his brain.

February turned into March while the jury continued deliberating, and Mrs. Patrick hosted an assortment of well-wishers at Paul's bedside in the ICU: Paul's family members, his friends, his pastor. But he also had collected a fan club during the last six months—reporters came to his bedside and suppressed tears, Prosecutor Vince Imbordino came by and kissed the top of Mrs. Patrick's head, the victim advocates from the court system arrived and provided hugs, Detectives Clark Schwartzkopf and Cliff Jewell came in with their support. The misery of Paul's condition was overwhelming to all who saw him. As the days drew out and Paul lay helpless and suffering, Mrs. Patrick began to talk about perhaps God needing to call Paul home. His condition slipped further. Colleen, the sister who had provoked the startling reaction from Paul during his 2006 coma, once again got on a plane to say her final good-byes. As Paul had said after the first coma, if Colleen's coming, it must be bad. It was.

Doctors were operating under a severe handicap—they desperately wanted to track the condition of Paul's vascular system with their wonder tool, the MRI. But Paul still had eighty metal pellets in his body: putting him inside a giant magnet was out of the question. They did their best with what tools were left to them.

By the weekend of March 7, the jury had been deliberating for more than a week. They had sent no notes and asked no questions. On that Sunday night, Paul slipped even further away. In the middle of the night, neurosurgeons did more emergency surgery. On Monday, Paul's chances were grim. Mrs. Patrick and Colleen and Ruth (the sister who had been sharing a home with Paul the night he was shot) hovered in his room and prepared themselves for the worst, which it seemed likely would occur that very night.

The jury was still out that second Monday after getting the case. They had no idea what was happening to the man they had seen in the gallery throughout the last six months. They had gotten to know him first early in the trial when he had taken the stand and described the ordeal of being shot out of the blue on a summer night. He had returned to the stand on February 10, 2009—a chair which Dale himself had occupied earlier that morning—to testify about Dale's behavior during the trial. He and Rebecca Estrada, David Estrada's bereaved mother, and victim advocates sitting near them had all seen Dale's eyes sweep the gallery behind him and return to focus on Paul and Rebecca. Then he had smiled. He had then, they all said, put his hand to his cheek as if resting his head but his elbow was in midair. His middle finger extended upward across his face while all his other fingers bent down. Paul and Rebecca and the victim advocates believed it had been an intentional gesture. Paul had hobbled across the courtroom, making a brave decision to leave his scooter behind in the gallery, and had climbed solemnly into the witness stand to tell about being flipped off in court by the man believed responsible for his broken body.

Now Paul's only mode of travel was a gurney with orderlies pushing it, and he had a machine breathing for him, but the jury didn't know about any of that. And on Monday March 9, 2009, while they sifted through boxes of photos and bullets and wiretaps and debated what it all meant, Paul was on a terrible descent. The stoic Mrs. Patrick was tearful and exhausted. It seemed Paul Patrick, who considered it his "beautiful duty" to attend the trial on behalf of all the victims, living and dead, would not live to hear the verdict.

When Cliff Jewell heard about the turn for the worse, he made a phone call. It seemed nothing else would help Paul now, so he figured that a little superstition couldn't hurt. Police chores include their share of ghoulish paperwork, and Cliff Jewell had a certain track record with that. He thought he could call that track record into play now. "I phoned the hospital and introduced myself and left my number. I told Paul's team that I was the detective to call when he passed away because I needed to fill out a certain form for the medical examiner. I would take care of it as soon as they called me upon his demise," said Cliff. He could tell the medical team recoiled from his cynicism. But he felt he had a good reason, one which he could not share with the hospital. "Every single time I've called a hospital prematurely about that form," he explained, "the victim recovered. Every single time."

That night, Mrs. Patrick and Colleen made plans to stay in the ICU room until the very end. They would not go home and miss Paul's final passing.

But Paul, whose courage and spirit had inspired everyone who attended that fourth-floor courtroom for six months, was not ready to give up. Rather than dying as expected, he rallied. He rallied so much that visitors who arrived on Tuesday, bracing themselves for the sight of an empty bed, instead were treated to the sight of Paul breathing on his own. It was a stunning turnaround.

The twelve jurors knew nothing of the drama that was threatening to convert one of their assault cases into a murder case before they were even done. They knew nothing of the agony of those waiting for them to reach a decision. Frustrations on the outside began to mount.

On Friday, more than two weeks after Vince Imbordino's emotional last speech, the jury finally returned to the courtroom to announce their verdicts. All the players gathered. Mrs. Hausner arrived and took her place on the hard bench. She was followed shortly by her sons Randy and Gregory, who sat on either side of her. At last, Dale himself was brought in. Wearing a gray dress shirt and dark blue tie with bright turquoise accents, in less than an hour, would he walk out through the front of this courtroom as a free man? Or would he disappear through the back passages, never to wear street clothes again in his life?

All rose when the jury came in. They took their places in the jury box with somber faces. The forewoman handed a thick stack of papers to the bailiff. A man's life was in those forms. The bailiff crossed the room and handed them to the clerk. The clerk set the stack down and lifted the top one off. In a clear and firm tone, she said, "Not guilty" for count one. She picked up the next form and said the words "not guilty" for count two. She picked up the third form and read "not guilty" for count three. She picked up the fourth and read "not guilty" for count four.

Across the aisle from the Hausner family, Rebecca Estrada leaned forward with a stricken and panicked look on her face. Her son David's case would be count five.

The clerk picked up the fifth form and read out "guilty." Mrs. Estrada turned to her companions in wonderment, as if looking for confirmation or explanation, but the clerk was already on to the next form, which also pertained to David. The clerk repeated, for count six, "guilty." There was no mistaking now. Mrs. Estrada's shoulders crumpled first, then she threw her head back to the ceiling and muffled the sobs racking her body.

Neither the Hausner family, nor Dale himself, had reacted to the first four verdicts. They remained still when the "guilty"s started coming in. They would hear that word a total of eighty times. It took twenty minutes to read through all the papers on the clerk's desk.

The jury had had an awful responsibility having a man's life in their hands. What they had decided after an exhaustive examination of more than a thousand pieces of evidence and six months of testimony was that this was a power that Dale himself enjoyed very much.

The seven counts Dale was not convicted on were:

Counts 1 and 2, murder in the first degree, drive-by shooting: Tony Mendez

Counts 3 and 4, murder in the first degree, drive-by shooting: Reggie Remillard

Count 10, cruelty to animals: Little Man, the miniature horse

Count 13, conspiracy to commit cruelty to animals: the unharmed stray dog at the scene of the Nathaniel Shoffner murder

Count 18, aggravated assault: Marcia Wilson

Marcia Wilson had been standing near her shepherd dog, Cherokee, when the Toyota Camry had slowed down and the driver had fired. Prosecutors had indicted Dale for aggravated assault against Marcia as well as for cruelty to animals. Marcia was unharmed, but Dale was found guilty of killing her dog, count 19. The stray dog that Nathaniel Shoffner had stepped forward to protect had been photographed at the scene but never taken into custody. Still, Dale was found guilty of killing Nathaniel himself, count 14.

When Sam Dieteman testified against Dale, he had told the jury that what he and Dale had done together was unforgivable. "If I were on my own jury," he said, "I would give me the death penalty." He wanted to do "some good" now.

He had accomplished his goal. Dale was convicted.

Eighty times over.

Back at the ICU, nurses had watched Mrs. Patrick and her daughter Colleen leave Paul's bedside. The caretakers knew what the family had been waiting for and they had come to know why their patient was in this condition and how much the trial had meant to him. He mostly was unconscious but sometimes floated back up, depending on what level of sedation was flowing through his IV. Since his turnaround on Monday night, Paul had even spoken a few sentences, his mouth operating only from the right side, his comprehension limited to short intervals. Colleen and Mrs. Patrick rushed back from court to tell Paul, whatever level of consciousness he was experiencing that day, that

his own counts, 52, 53, and 54, had been a clean sweep and that
Dale Hausner would never prowl the streets again.

But when they arrived, they found that Paul already knew.
When the ladies had rushed off to court, the nurses had discovered the verdicts being carried live on television. They turned
the TV on in Paul's room. Against all odds, Paul saw the eighty
guilty verdicts for himself.

Afterword

When we lived through the Year of the Serial Shooter, the only person involved with whom I had any previous personal experience was Phoenix mayor Phil Gordon. His impassioned speeches at victims' funerals, where he declared he was not just a mayor, but a father, too, and his public pronouncements, where he declared the city was "not just hunted, but on the offensive, we are hunting them," punctuated that awful time. He spoke in a familiar voice, from a long career in public service, but with a previously unheard fury.

The trial itself was a like a circuit board laid bare, exposing the many ways these crimes interconnected us all. It's impossible to drive around this expansive county without seeing a spot where someone died, or someone else left a blood trail or undercover teams tracked a silver Camry or dogs rushed a fence for the last time. The bus bench where Officer Darren Burch placed a rubber shoe against Reggie Remillard's spurting carotid is on my daily route. Officer Burch, by the way, was also followed out to the hallway after his testimony and embraced by Reggie's grieving sisters. I not only frequently pass both of the hospitals that received most of the gunshot victims, but I have been treated at them myself. I walk my dogs in the park where Frederick Sena staggered, bleeding, into the VA hospital. I know that everyone in that courtroom experiences the same sense of unhappy recognition as they go about their lives, driving by death scenes, walking into once burned stores, noting a familiar bullet strike in a brick wall. With the tally of victims in excess of forty, if you were not directly affected by one of the crimes, you knew someone who was. I looked up in surprise one day to see one of my own former coworkers from KPHO take the stand. He had been one of the first on the scene when Kibili Tambadu, the refugee from Sierra Leone, was shot.

And one day, a veterinarian took the stand. A veterinarian I had met only once, but whom I recognized instantly. She came from one of those emergency animal clinics that had seen so many of the shot-up dogs. During the writing of this story, I had rushed in the early morning to her clinic myself, with my own beloved dog in my arms. My companion of thirteen years could not be saved, and this woman on the stand had been the one to push eternal sleep into the veins of her little paw.

The previous day, I had received a shock that made my knees buckle and my regular veterinarian reach out to catch me. I had taken the little beast in for coughing. When the veterinarian summoned me to the X-ray display, I pointed to a bright spot on the screen and asked, "Is that her microchip?"

"No," he said, "that's a bullet."

As I swayed, he assured me that the bullet must have been there for some time and he was more concerned about another condition. We left with a prescription for her and a confusing whirlpool of thoughts for me. Here I was, writing about bullets in other people's pets, and it turned out there was one in my own. I decided that the next day I would call Cliff Jewell, the pet detective, and ask him what to do.

But in the dawn hours my black-eyed friend, true to her own stubborn soul to the last, showed me she would not let me have my way. I rushed her to the emergency clinic, my regular vet was roused by phone from his bed, and that awful decision was made. Afterward, I surrounded her with blankets and toys and took her to a place that would transform her into star stuff.

When I received her back, I looked at the container of remains, both shaken and puzzled. I had to ask for the bullet. Alas, I got my first lesson in forensics: lead is soft, apparently, and melts easily.

A few days later I did meet with Jewell, and I told him about the shocking X-ray. His back straightened, his eyes narrowed, and he immediately asked me for the bullet. I was sorry to tell him I could never provide it to him. He asked me as many questions as he could. But I will never know if my own little darling shared something deeply frightening and painful with the other victims in that courtroom, and if she might have had her own name written in the huge black binders started on December 29 by Cliff Jewell.

It is probably more likely that she was shot by someone else, perhaps long ago. But I learned the stealthy nature of a bullet and the overwhelming sense of shock it brings, the confusion and bewilderment. Even in my small experience, so paltry and out of league compared to that club to which Paul Patrick, Daryl Davies, Rebecca Estrada and so many others in the courtroom belonged, I felt the rage and deafening stupefaction of the presence of a lead projectile. I can never write the words that will ease their pain, soothe their hearts or make their lives whole again. I hope in some tiny way to have made their stories count, to make them visible to those who would wish them well.

On that private day of loss for me, I did become one of those who saw firsthand how Cliff Jewell worked, how he alerted like a pointer, how he carried files in his head, how he never, ever, failed to chase a lead.

I hope no community will ever again need to shut down two serial killers in the space of one year, the way Phoenix did in 2006. We all owe much to Cliff Jewell, Ron Rock, Pete Salazar, Hugh Lockerby, Don Bellendier, Don Byers, Ron Horton, Darren Udd, Darrell Smith, Bryan Benson, Matt Shay, Darren Burch, Jason Buscher, Don Sherrard, Travis Bird, Kevin Shuster, James Hartman, Clark Schwartzkopf, Mike Blair, Maria Vida and the hundreds of other men and women who sacrificed, made hard decisions and walked into harm's way.

Killers are out there. There will be new cases. Murder is as ancient as man himself. The old poem *Beowulf* recounts for us the fear we have felt of the dark for thousands of years:

> *But the evil one ambushed old and young*
> *death-shadow dark, and dogged them still,*
> *lured, or lurked in the livelong night.*

The venerable rhymes tell the tale of a single hero who sought out "the ghastly gore spattered track left by the monster" and saved his people. However, the Year of the Serial Shooter brought us one single thing to remember and learn and keep hold of, and that is that while there were three killers waiting in the dark, there was not just one hero—there were hundreds. Murder may be ancient and enduring, but its opposite number, generosity and courage and love, is everywhere among us, vastly among us, astonishingly deep and wide among us.

As both an observer of the trial and a Phoenician who lived through the terror, I am struck not just by the havoc caused by three men, but by the much greater quantity of good that leaps forth from the human heart. Hundreds of professionals worked on these cases individually, before they were linked, and together, after they were. But ordinary citizens also put themselves through scenes of horror to offer succor and assistance. I think of neighbors mobilizing to transport and pay for medical care for Cherokee, the Australian shepherd. I think of Issac Crudup resolutely guarding the bullet that killed his dog against the day some officer might take an interest in it. I think of TV crews and neighbors and retired missionaries clustered around a donkey with a fever and a hanging head. I think of Daniel Green, a mechanic just driving home, who stopped to comfort and assist a young girl with her entrails protruding. I think of Saul Guerrero rushing into the unknown with a .45 in one hand and a first aid kit in the other. I think of a father rushing out of his house to provide the last loving arms for another man's daughter as Robin Blasnek's lead-pierced heart began to fail. I think of Nathaniel Shoffner, losing his life in defense of a stray dog.

When I started delving into this huge case, I made many public records requests for police documents spanning across a fifty-mile or more spread of jurisdictions from Glendale and Avondale on the west side of the Valley of the Sun over to Scottsdale and Mesa on the east side. From this massive and diverse pile of documents, many names came wafting up like steam. These were people who took a direct part in the dragnet that closed in around the Serial Shooter, from citizens who ran across traffic to phone 911; to dazed and bloody-faced victims who coughed out valuable details; to paramedics who came riding in on shrieking trucks with life-saving equipment; to patrol officers, both on and off duty, who took charge of a scene of mayhem and chaos; to men and women of science of who turned their years and years of education to the study of a bullet fragment or the suffering victim through whom it had passed. There were office workers who pored through files and forklift drivers who hoisted Dumpsters. There were detectives who climbed into trash and patrol officers who crawled in the dark. I wish I could tell the story of each person who contributed to the rescue of all of us who were targets that year. But even a book is not long enough to list all these names, much less give meaning to their contributions. So I have picked some of the stories and names that floated most insistently to the top, in hopes of capturing the overall flavor and texture of that terrible year and the investigation that brought it to an end.

There was one man whose footprints I found everywhere I went. Detective Cliff Jewell was not someone I had ever heard of before I started this research. But I soon came to recognize his quiet manner, which masked a deadly efficiency. I realized that Phoenix owed more to this detective than to any other player. The characterization of Cliff Jewell in this book is completely from my own research and observations, including not just the many documents—which record forever his quiet little touches such as bringing an Egg McMuffin to keep a suspect talking or phoning Charisse Kane at 7 a.m. to pursue one more possible piece of damning forensic evidence—but also his testimony from the witness stand. On that stand, Detective Jewell could recall every detail of every case that he had pursued and discarded (as well as those that did end up being charged to the three suspects, of course), severely constricting the defense's ability to suggest competing theories of the crime spree. From the moment he entered the case on December 29, 2005, he quietly went about his work, sometimes in the face of severe skepticism and exclusion. This is clear from the public record. In my interviews with him, he was always generous in his praise of his colleagues and associates. All of the law enforcement I interviewed—those who went on the record and those who didn't—praised one another generously. None of them, least of all Cliff Jewell, ever asked for any credit. Indeed, I suspect he may be embarrassed by the characterization of him when he reads this book. I can only refer him, and others, to the words of that famous fictional gumshoe, Sergeant Joe Friday. These are "just the facts, ma'am." They are the facts as I see them. Unlike Mayor Gordon, Cliff Jewell was not someone with whom I'd ever had any acquaintance at all. I got to know his saga in the mounds and mounds of public records that I plunged into like a snowdrift. I had no reason, other than the story I discovered there, to portray him as I have.

Later, after all the events portrayed in this book had occurred and been written up, it became my privilege to witness a powerful moment between Cliff Jewell and a man hanging on to life by sheer willpower. That story begins a week after Dale was convicted of eighty crimes:

I drove out to the hospital for my almost daily visit to Paul Patrick. It was a sad duty and my heart sank every time I looked at the swollen and broken body in the bed. Mrs. Patrick had often expressed to me her doubts about having authorized the extraordinary measures to prevent Paul's death. Catastrophic illness, especially involving the brain, does not present a static picture. Some days are better than others, and in Paul's case, sometimes the change was from minute to minute. Although I had heard Mrs. Patrick describe some moments of apparent consciousness from Paul, to this point I had never witnessed it myself. And neither could she be sure that he retained information or comprehension from one day to the next. He spent most hours completely unconscious, the ventilator chugging loudly and various tubes performing other metabolic functions. When he did emerge briefly from his deep sleep, brain deficits were evident. Wondering how much of the essence of Paul's spirit and personality and intellect could ever be revived, I privately shared her doubts. I could hardly bear the thought of Paul's sparkling mind forever reduced to an organ barely capable of regulating lungs and blood pressure, no longer expressive or comprehending.

On St. Patrick's Day, I had first heard Paul say lucid words myself. When I arrived in the ICU that day, all the nurses dressed in green, he was alone in his room. Normally I left if there was no family member present, but this time his eyes happened to be open and looking right at me. In case he recognized me, I did not want to just walk away, so I stepped across the threshold toward him. Finding a green and glittery novelty leprechaun hat in his room, I put it on my head and gently pranced around to place myself in Paul's line of sight. Until then, I hadn't seen much sign of volition from him. But with my silly holiday antics, Paul's extremely swollen face rippled into a lopsided smile. I heard hoarse whispering. But I leaned forward, not confident whether I was hearing actual words. Almost certain I was mistaken, I thought I'd give it a try anyway. I asked Paul, "What?" Eyes sunken deeply in the edema of a seriously distorted head blinked up at me. A tube was draining blood directly out of the top, on the left side, where he still had skull. The left side of the mouth remained dead but the right half moved and the hoarse whisper repeated itself: "Faith and begorrah!"

I was delighted, yet over the next several days, I never saw Paul quite so conscious or focused again. The fears returned to plague me. He had been living without half his skull for three weeks by that time. The swelling on his brain emerged in an awful balloon of shaved skin across where the skull had been sawed away. What kind of life would this be?

On Friday night at the end of that week, Mrs. Patrick called me, dejected and weary, to inform me that Paul had been transferred to a different facility. Her suffering was palpable, and I knew I had to make the drive the next day for her sake. Other than the incident on St. Patrick's Day, I hadn't had any evidence that Paul would know I was there—or that he would ever "know" much of anything ever again. As I plodded through the hospital corridors that Saturday, I wondered how much more his mother, a gentle senior citizen, could take. When I arrived that day, one week after the guilty verdicts, I glanced through the open door of his new room and saw right away that she was not present at this hour, but what really made me hesitate was the sight of the person in the bed. It did not look like the swollen, insensible and nearly dead being I had been visiting for weeks. It looked like . . . Paul Patrick.

He looked back at me with cognition and the quickening that signifies a living human spirit.

He smiled.

I was stunned. I stopped in the doorway and wasn't sure how to proceed. "Paul?" I said. I announced my name and asked if I should come in. He smiled, his right cheek wrinkling with pulled muscles, his left cheek stock-still, but both eyes focused and comprehending, and nodded "yes" vigorously.

I entered the room and walked all the way around to the far side of the bed. His eyes followed me. So much of the swelling was gone, his features were recognizable again, and the look of imminent demise had vanished.

"Paul," I said, incredulous, unable to filter my emotions, "You . . . were . . . dead!?"

A very hoarse whisper from deep in his throat answered me, "I'm too mean to die!"

We talked a little more. Paul blurted out the isolated phrase "broken units," several times and I realized he was remembering a conversation we had had months ago. After Sam had testified, admitting to being the one to pull the trigger on Paul on June 8, 2006, I had asked Paul for his reaction. "Flush 'im," he had said from his scooter in front of the court room, "he's a broken unit." I had laughed at the term "broken unit" and joked that I'd steal it from him and use it in the book. Now, on his first day back to full consciousness, Paul was remembering that and wanted to make sure that I did use it. (Here it is, Paul!)

He showed off the reduction in swelling of his face and head. But I still hadn't absorbed the dramatic turnaround. I had seen him twenty-four hours before. When I had spoken to Mrs. Patrick the night before, she had not mentioned any such turnaround. It must have happened sometime today. I stared unabashedly and repeated my earlier words. This time Paul gestured down and away with his chin, as if expressing some strong emotion, and said in that very hoarse whisper, a sound coming from a throat thick with weeks of disuse and sore from tubes having been forced in and out repeatedly, "I got things to do."

I knew what he meant. "Dale?" I said.

A darkness overtook his face as he nodded yes.

"I gotta do it for Becky."

I choked up even more. Becky was Rebecca Estrada, the mother of young David who had been murdered before he'd had a chance to really grow up. She and Paul Patrick shared a bond none of us on the outside could ever truly understand; what they'd had to go through to develop that bond was unspeakable. Paul had made a promise to her before the trial started that he would be there every day, always providing a human face to the long list of the Serial Shooter's victims. Dale had been convicted by this point, but he had not yet been sentenced. Paul's promise to his friend in tragedy was now motivating him to live.

Before I left, realizing each word he forced out of his abraded throat must exhaust him, Paul told me to "give Becky a big hug and kiss" from him. I promised to do so. I left his room and stood out of sight in the corridor and sobbed. The date was Saturday, March 21, 2009.

On Thursday, March 26, the survivors of those who died at the hands of the Serial Shooter took the rostrum and told the jury of their grief. Adriana Gutierrez-Cruz, the sister of hard-working Claudia, said she had been so distraught she had not wanted to tell her parents what had happened. She had wanted to tell them the fable that Claudia had merely left Arizona and had not left a phone number. At the end of her statement, gulping and crying, she addressed her dead sister directly. "Forgive me," she said, "for not protecting you."

When it was Rebecca Estrada's turn, she told stories of the joy David had brought her "since the day he was born." She told how as a second grader she had brought him home a baby sister. Holding the infant, he had speculated what he would name a boy baby. "What's wrong with 'David?'" he had asked her. She had teased him about naming his children David Number 1, David Number 2 and so on, like George Foreman. "The point of the story," she told the six men and six women in the jury box, "is that David will never have a wife, there will never be a David Number 1 or David Number 2."

Dale himself had taken the stand that day. Against the advice of his lawyers, he had waived mitigation—the legal term for presenting a case to persuade jurors to be lenient. But he had reserved the right to make a statement to the people who held his life in their hands. He tried to be charming and brave, but his tone seemed barely to mask an attitude of belligerence. "You believed Sam and not me," he said to the jurors. "I accept that." He told them some good had come out of the case. "Sam Dieteman is off the streets, and he will never go out shooting innocent people again, and that's a very good thing," he said. He also told how the jail had been out of Bibles when he'd requested one. When he persisted in putting in a requisition for one, "Praise God, we got a shipment of seven hundred of them. If only ten percent of those are used by inmates," he continued, "that would be seventy people I have made a difference in their lives."

Dale never admitted to being the Serial Shooter, often referring to "the crimes you convicted me of." Several times, when
he was proclaiming his innocence outright, Judge Steinle intervened and told him the time for such statements had passed.

Dale said he was sorry for getting involved with Sam Dieteman and that now the name "Hausner" would go down in history
with "a black cloud" like that of "Manson." Although his words
technically apologized for this connection to the infamous California murderer, many in the courtroom felt the way he said it
telegraphed that he was pleased by it. He told of his strong family support throughout his life and how his big brother Randy
had tutored him as a small child. In the benches, Randy's face
turned red and tears sparkled at his eyes. Dale talked about his
brother Gregory's service in the Navy. Sitting on the same bench
as Randy, Gregory broke down, his head lowered into his hands
almost in his lap. Between them, the mother of the brothers,
Rosemarie Hausner, remained stoic.

Dale told the jury that he knew they would be contemplating
the death penalty or life in prison for him. He said what they
didn't know was that he had already died, the day his two toddler sons had drowned in a Texas creek. He told the jury he believed in an eye for an eye and urged them to teach a lesson to
those "liberal bleeding heart countries where they don't have the
death penalty." He said he wanted to "take it like a man—give
me death."

On Friday, after deliberating less than two hours, they did.
Dale S. Hausner received six death sentences. As armed deputies led him out of the courtroom when the proceedings were
concluded, he passed closely by the jury box. It was still full of
the twelve people who had condemned him to be executed.
"Thank you!" he said to them and smiled big. None of them
responded. "Thank you!" he said louder, his face craning toward
them as his steps took him farther. Each of the twelve kept their
faces averted. Dale abandoned his effort to engage them and
disappeared into the chambers behind the last wall.

No matter what he had done, it is still a very serious thing to
calmly and politely order the termination of a human life. I felt
empty and agitated.

I could think of only one place I wanted to be.

I drove out to the hospital.

Gathered in Paul's room were his mother and the girlfriend he had met some months earlier in the same public housing complex. Paul's girlfriend had suffered some serious brain trauma herself and was afraid to leave the apartment building for fear of being unable to find her way back. Before his stroke, Paul had been gently encouraging her to venture out, always assuring her that, though he couldn't *walk* beside her, he and his scooter would lead her back. Now that he was stranded in a hospital bed, she had vowed to help him recover from brain deficits as she herself once had.

They were all discussing the death sentences when I entered the room. Mrs. Patrick gave the opinion that she didn't believe in capital punishment. They asked me what I thought. I said, "They did the most they can do, but it is not enough." She asked me what I thought should happen, then. I was standing by Paul's bed. The swelling had receded even further. Now the right half of his head was actually concave. He reached up to scratch it and my stomach lurched as the soft brain tissue underneath visibly yielded to the slight pressure.

"I want you to have your life back," I said directly to Paul.

He looked up at me, flat on his back, now his permanent position. "How do we do that?" he responded. We all fell silent.

On the following Monday, Dale would be sentenced for the non-capital cases. During Dale's speech to the jury, he had gestured from right to left with his hands as he said he was very glad that "Paul Patrick did not get moved from the attempted murder pile to the murder pile." It was the first time the jury had been alerted to some change in the fortunes of the man whom they had not seen at his usual spot in the gallery since February 26. After giving Dale his six death sentences Friday morning, March 27, 2009, the jury had finally been excused from almost seven months of service. Judge Steinle alone would decide the sentences for the other crimes, the ones against property, animals, and against the men and women, who, like Paul Patrick, had managed to survive. In the hospital room, we all talked about the upcoming Monday proceedings, which would be very personal to Paul. Monday would be the last time any of us gathered in that courtroom for this case. Although I was glad I had come to Paul's room after the death sentences had been handed out, my sense of agitation had not dissipated. Paul was tired. I bid them farewell.

But in the parking lot, as I slid behind the wheel of my car, I saw a familiar tall blond figure approach me. I felt a little lift in my spirits as Cliff Jewell asked me to help him find Paul's new room, since the patient had recently been moved yet again. I was glad to perform some service, no matter how small, to the people who mattered. Paul was clearly delighted at the sight of the detective. Jewell told him that he'd come straight from a three-hour debriefing session with the jurors. The twelve, he said, had been greatly alarmed at Dale's comments from the stand the day before regarding whether Paul should be "moved into the murder pile." They were deeply concerned about him and wanted to hear what had happened.

The shooting victim had had yet another surgery that week: he showed the detective thick bandaging on his right hand, the good one, reaching all the way up his forearm. The hand had been severely injured by his fall when he suffered the stroke. One month after the injury, doctors were just now deeming it appropriate to repair it—they had been preoccupied with the colossal task of keeping him alive. For four weeks the hand had dangled swollen, bloody and discolored near the bed rails.

Paul and the detective continued to chat and trade masculine barbs. Paul pointed at his missing skull and said, "I went to pieces." The detective asked about the particulars of the transfer from the other hospital, and it came out that Paul's skull was in a freezer at the other facility, miles away. "I hope they don't put it with the lunches!" Paul quipped.

When I had been in the room earlier in the afternoon, before encountering Cliff Jewell in the parking lot, the family had been talking about their preparations for Monday, when it would be their chance to give a victim impact statement. They had bemoaned not having the personal strength to read it themselves, nor the energy to navigate the bureaucracy to see to it that Paul's own choice, Cliff Jewell, would be the one to read their statement to the court. Now Jewell was standing right in front of them.

Paul paused with his jokes about his defenseless head. He must have been seriously fatigued at this point. He was able to put more words together in a row than he had a few days earlier, but the hoarseness was as pronounced as ever, reminding me not only of the weeks on a ventilator but also of the many procedures involving throat tubes he still underwent regularly. Paul shot a look at his mother. She took her cue and began to talk about the victim impact statement written by the Patrick family. Paul interrupted her as soon as the most complicated words had been said. He raised his good arm, bandaged, awkward and un-bending, to point at Jewell. "You," he croaked out. "You, my friend, would you read for me? My friend?"

I knew Cliff Jewell well enough by now to notice the bright-ening in his eyes, the sudden tautness in his face and the tighten-ing of his voice. "It would be my honor," he managed to say.

Author's Note

A Special Word to Everyone
Who was Directly Involved in this Case

It has not been my intention to slight anyone who contributed to this investigation. I hope that no one will feel that I have. As someone who, like everyone else in Phoenix, was afraid to go outside during 2006, I am deeply grateful to each of you and in great awe of many of you. I have written this book in order to let the rest of the country know what a magnificent and unprecedented job you all did and to give Phoenicians a glimpse of what you went through. I hope each of you feels that you can hand this book to your relatives and friends and say, "My name may not be in here, but this is my story." Thank you, each and all, very, very much.

Appendix One

TALLY OF VICTIMS ATTRIBUTED TO THE SERIAL SHOOTER

Humans: 29 (6 female*, 23 male)
    8 murders
    18 injured by firearm
    2 injured by knife
    1 uninjured (shot missed)

Horses: 5
    3 dead
    2 injured (1 horse, 1 burro)

Dogs: 8
    5 dead
    2 injured
    1 uninjured (human victim intervened)

---

*Intended victim of car shooting was a female, which would make a total of 7 female victims

Property Damage: 4 buildings, 1 vehicle
2 buildings shot at
2 buildings burned
1 car shot at

CHRONOLOGICAL LIST OF 47 VICTIMS/TARGETS*

Tony Mendez, May 17, 2005, .22-caliber, deceased

Reginald Remillard, May 24, 2005, .22-caliber, deceased

Burger King, June 29, 2005, .22-caliber, clown window shot (not charged)

David Estrada, June 29, 2005, .22-caliber, deceased

Sara Moon, bay quarter horse, June 29, 2005, .22-caliber, deceased

Apache, painted quarter horse, July 20, 2005, .22-caliber, survived

Whiskey, Akita dog, July 20, 2005, .22-caliber, deceased

Little Man, mini-horse, July 25, 2005, .22-caliber, deceased

Unnamed quarter horse, July 25, 2005, unknown small-caliber, deceased (not charged)

Buddy, burro, July 25, 2005, unknown small-caliber, survived (not charged)

Shep, Anatolian shepherd dog, November 11, 2005, .22-caliber, deceased

Irving, mixed breed dog, November 11, 2005, .22-caliber, survived

Nathaniel Shoffner, November 11, 2005, shotgun, deceased

Stray dog at Twentieth Street and Monroe, November 11, 2005, uninjured (count 13: conspiracy to commit cruelty to animals)

---

*Caliber is listed where known. Some bullets are still inside their victims and therefore cannot be sized. For shotgun victims, caliber can only be determined in some victims if evidence is developed such as recovery of the shot cup or confession by the perpetrator/accomplice.

ABC Bartending School, December 29, 2005, .22-caliber, car windshield shot out

Chiropractor's office, December 29, 2005, .22-caliber, window damage (not charged)

Cherokee, Australian shepherd dog, December 29, 2005, shotgun, deceased

Jose Ortiz, December 29, 2005, .22-caliber, deceased

Marco Carillo, December 29, 2005, .22-caliber, deceased

Timmy Tordai, December 29, 2005, .22-caliber, survived

Clarissa Rowley, December 29, 2005, shotgun, survived

Peyton, Transylvanian hound dog, December 29, 2005, .22-caliber, deceased

Martin, black dog, December 29, 2005, .22-caliber, survived

Peanut, shepherd mix dog, December 29, 2005, .22-caliber, deceased

Tim Boviall, March 2006, unknown caliber, survived (not charged)

Ray McQueen, April 14, 2006, stabbing, survived (charged to Jeff Hausner)

Kibili Tambadu, May 2, 2006, .410 shotgun, survived

Claudia Gutierrez-Cruz, May 2, 2006, .410 shotgun, deceased

Timothy Davenport, May 17, 2006, stabbing, survived

James Hodge, May 30, 2006, 12-gauge shotgun, survived

Miguel Rodriguez, May 31, 2006 (past midnight, after Hodge shooting), shotgun, survived

Daryl Davies, May 31, 2006 (past midnight, after Hodge shooting), shotgun, survived

Wal-Mart (Camelback), June 8, 2006, arson, multimillion-dollar property damage

Wal-Mart (Northern), June 8, 2006, arson, multimillion-dollar property damage

Paul Patrick, June 8, 2006, 12-gauge, shotgun, survived

Elizabeth Clark, June 11, 2006, .410 shotgun, survived

Frederick Sena, June 20, 2006, .410 shotgun, survived (but died 3 weeks later of unrelated liver failure)

Tony Long, June 20, 2006, .410 shotgun, survived

Dianna Bein, July 1, 2006, .410 shotgun, survived

Jeremy Ortiz, July 1, 2006, .410 shotgun, survived

Joseph Roberts, July 3, 2006, .410 shotgun, survived

David Perez, July 7, 2006, shotgun, survived

Ashley Armenta, July 8, 2006, .410 shotgun, survived

Garry Begay, July 8, 2006, .410 shotgun, survived

Michael Cordrey, July 11, 2006, 12-gauge shotgun, not injured

Raul Garcia Lopez, July 22, 2006 .410 shotgun, survived

Robin Blasnek, July 30, 2006, .410 shotgun, deceased

Appendix Two

LETTER TO COURT FROM DAVID ESTRADA'S AUNT

   I. Thank you to all the police officers, detectives, district attorneys, medical personnel, friends and clergy for their efforts to solve David's murder or to comfort our family.

  II. Particular gratitude to Detective Rock of the Tolleson Police and Detective Jewell of the Phoenix Police for solving David's murder.

 III. Thank you to the jury for enduring the long, stunningly depressing volume of evidence and for coming to the appropriate conclusions.

  IV. Deep gratitude to Judge Steinle for deliberate efforts to present case in most fair manner.

   V. To Hausner

   1. You are a despicable coward, trolling the streets for victims you knew couldn't defend themselves nor suspect you were about to murder them.

2. You are a snake that laid in wait, coiled in the darkness, lapping the air with its forked tongue to savagely destroy your prey.

3. I never dreamed a subculture could exist that creates a weasel so subversive and uncivil as you. That there are more like you in your own family is disgusting. What kind of environment could have created such monsters? What kind of upbringing relieves you of accepting responsibility for your actions and leaves you with no conscience whatsoever?

4. What kind of arrogance do you have that derives sadistic pleasure from taking life? How dare you think you are superior to your victims knowing they would be helpless against you?

5. Surely you are a General in the Devil's army creating pain and chaos from your very existence. Thank God this jury could see through your pathetic lies.

6. While your victims or their next of kin deal with each stage of grief for what you have done, you must be dealt the vengeance we have in our souls. I only regret you have but one physical life to pay for all those you have taken. I can accept that life isn't fair, but your measly one life in exchange for all these others is grossly inequitable.

7. Before you die maybe you can find the guts to admit to **all** the crimes you have committed, not just the ones for which you have been found guilty (because it is obvious you spent a great deal of time satisfying your sadistic need to kill). Countless other families wonder who and why their loved ones were harmed. Only you can answer their need to know.

8. Perhaps my family will find peace knowing our vow to never rest until David's killer was found has been kept. We have already gone through the denial, depression, bargaining and anger stages of grief because of your actions. Perhaps some of our family will find acceptance for David's

murder. I will remain at the anger stage. I will never forgive you for what you have done. You have no right to David's life and I beg this jury to sentence you to death. I only hope those that participated in this despicable activity with you will also be held accountable.

Acknowledgments

It was an honor to be the chronicler of these stories and to be allowed into some private and painful places. I thank everyone, but I must especially single out Paul Patrick, Mary Patrick, Rebecca Estrada, Becky Lewis, and Marci Matt. You touched me deeply and inspired me. I would also like to give a special word to Judge Roland Steinle, whom I came to admire very much.

Every writer approaches the acknowledgments section with trepidation because writing a book is such a comprehensive undertaking it requires the cooperation and support of a huge array of people. It feels impossible to come up with both the right words and all the right names. To all those who should be included here—please forgive me for making an incomplete list and coming up with inadequate thanks. In no particular order I wish to heap thanks upon:

My editor, Shannon Jamieson Vazquez, for her dedication and passion, and for caring about what happened to us in Arizona that terrible year.

My agent, Amy Moore-Benson, best business partner ever. Every writer should be so lucky.

Pyrographx for a wonderful cover design.

Copyeditor Rick Willett for an eagle eye in an arduous job.

Those who shared their stories, looked up documents,

explained a procedure or put their finger in a knot enabling me to tie it, and all the other countless tasks this project required: extra-special commendation to Tolleson PD Records and to Avondale PD Records and to Karen Sunderland of Scottsdale PD.

J. W. Brown, a top-notch media specialist, on both sides of the fence. Elizabeth Hill, the princess of Public Records, who has a wonderful way with logjams.

Dan Barr of Brown & Bain, my Virgil guiding me through the nine rings of Arizona media law.

I have been fortunate to have superb friends come to my assistance in every way imaginable: To Larry for longstanding support, and Brigid for much appreciated applause. To Howie and Gabe for shelter in a storm and so many other things. Tom P., from a very affectionate and grateful Wanda. Mark, for so very, very much on a very long journey, and to Jeff for his friendship and support. Linda W., who has an amazingly open heart that kept me from circling all the way down the drain. To Kim H. and her circle of secret angels who made some very important things happen for me. Jill Suzanne, my darling, you are spectacular. And to Joan and Bob, I was so very lucky to have a place at the table, so very lucky. Erik, Ted and Connie—I can't thank you enough.

For inspiration and golden rays of sweetness: Sherry, you changed everything with one phone call. Bill, dear pal, I wish I wrote half as well as you. Shanna and Chris, I blow you a kiss. Jason and Mark, you amaze me daily. To Patti—my own private Lucy, what a gift you are, a thousand million thanks wouldn't cover it. Z and Zola, you rock! Chris and Christy, your support and camaraderie have meant the world to me. Bob O., the best thing that ever came out of New York is you! Nedda, thanks for your welcoming heart and wonderful food. Maggie, a comrade down in the foxhole with lots of incoming, sharing the Kevlar.

Cathy and Gary, you are the best people in the world and I wish I could think of the exact right thing to say. Spencer, thank you. Shauna Nelson, you put me back on the grid and did so much more. Alex, Molly and Rachael, for great support and generosity and knowing some things none of us wishes we did. To George K., for the soup and George G. for the lawn! To Chuck Coughlin, for many of years of generosity and friendship. To Ken Okel, for calling me "B.L." when I sure didn't deserve it. Patrick and Patricia H., for all you've done and shared. To my cousin Tammy, for being kind and sweet. To Mary Link, you may have forgotten, but I haven't. To Terry Ashjian, I haven't forgotten that, either, and thank you for your kind efforts in my behalf.

Thanks to Vicki Gans and Gary Finlinson. And to linguistics pros Richard A. Rhodes, Paula M. Flora, and Chris Kennedy of Cal Berkeley and the U of Chicago.

To Kathy Cano Murillo, for some well-timed phone calls. Robert and Abby and Pamela, thank you for the wonderful evenings. Christy S., for deft and artful hands! Kristy K., what a lifeline you are—I can't say it better than that! An absolute lifeline. Maureen, you are a generous writer and friend who provided me invaluable material. To Karen Abbot, Maggie Dana and Tom Schreck, I thank you so much for your support and input and guidance.

To Mike B., for tremendous support and thoughtfulness and joy.

To Mike Watkiss, I am afraid your secret is not safe with me—I will be telling people *everywhere* what a lovely fellow you are. To certain members of the transportation industry, it was a beautiful thing and so very appreciated. I just wish you could have seen it. Michael Kiefer and Nick Martin, thanks for being there in the trenches and tossing me a rope when I needed it over a very long and complex trial. To Julio Jimenez, thanks for the wonderful shots and your great professionalism. To Richard deUriarte and the folks at MAG, six hundred miles of thanks!

And to Buddy the burro, I just have to say, thanks for being you! I started this grueling project by reaching out for the one happy ending, and you gave me a great kick start!

Dan Hayes at MSK, you will never know how important you were and how much I appreciate it. To Ted and Hrayr, for saving my life and giving me a chance to live again, which sounds like the same thing but how can you say it enough? I can't say it enough. I could never say it enough.

To HCK, I miss you and respect you more intensely with each passing year—thank you for the legacy that made any of this possible. To my Keva, thanks for the neverending faith and enthusiasm—one and five, all the way! To my certain ones, forever and for always, Tiny Is My Is.